BRITISH BIRDS

Lifestyles and Habitats

IAN PRESTT

British Birds

Lifestyles and Habitats

B. T. BATSFORD LTD.
LONDON

To my wife

ISBN 0 7134 1864 8

Phototypeset in Linotron 202 by
Graphicraft Typesetters Hong Kong
Printed and bound in Great Britain
at The Pitman Press, Bath

Drawings by Rob Hume

for the publishers
B. T. Batsford Ltd.
4 Fitzhardinge Street
London W1H OAH

Contents

Foreword

There are probably more bird lovers for each head of population in Britain today than in any other country. The vast majority are not experts, nor do they wish to devote a great deal of time or effort to studying birds. Watching birds simply forms a part of their leisure activity and adds to their enjoyment of their surroundings.

Numerous excellent field guides are now available, listing and describing the birds present in different geographical regions. But one of the attractions of birdwatching is that it has far more to offer than identification, although this is an essential beginning and 'ticking' the first sighting of a new species has its own excitement.

There is the sheer beauty of birds – their exciting colours, grace and skill of flight, their attractive songs and thrilling calls; they can be persuaded to overcome their natural timidity and feed close at hand in our gardens; their behaviour and habits are readily observed, so we can learn about their lives and feel closer to nature; and they make excellent subjects for photography, painting and sketching. Above all this – or perhaps it is an amalgamation of all of them – for many people birds seem to have a magic all of their own and lend atmosphere to beautiful surroundings.

This book attempts to add to the enjoyment of bird lovers by exploring the countryside of Britain and considering the birds to be found. It examines the backcloth – the habitat – in which the different species live; it reveals the variations present within apparently similar habitats which enable the different species to co-exist; it considers the way of life of the birds and endeavours to explain why they are there and how they benefit from and exploit their own special surroundings. The thrill of seeing a new bird is enhanced by an understanding of why it is where it is and future sightings are enriched by an insight into its behaviour and activity.

The book assumes no previous knowledge of ornithology and deliberately restricts its contents to a consideration of the commoner birds present in the better known and more readily accessible parts of Britain. The only essential equipment is a pair of binoculars, a field guide and suitable clothing, although in the final chapter more information is given about both equipment and birdwatching societies in case the reader should be inspired to develop his interest further.

The measurements given in this book after the first mention of each species are taken from the tip of the beak to the tip of the tail with the bird placed flat on its back. Because beginners often find it hard to visualize the size of a bird when given in centimetres, it might be helpful to have as a handy refere.ce six birds familiar to most people from which practical comparisons can be drawn. These are: Blue Tit (11.5cm); Robin (14cm); Blackbird (25cm); Wood Pigeon (41cm); Mallard Duck (57cm); Golden Eagle (76–89cm).

Acknowledgement

An important part of my job is to promote as wide an interest as possible in wild birds. After discussions with friends and colleagues I concluded there was still a need for a popular book giving more information than a field guide, less than is to be found in a handbook and relating birds in a simple way to one another and to their habitat. This book is an attempt to meet this need and I would like to thank friends and the publishers for advice and encouragement given.

Although I have seen all the birds included in the book and studied many of them, I make little claim to any originality in the information included. Like many authors before me, I have drawn extensively on the fund of knowledge accumulated by generations of amateur and professional ornithologists. For the basic data on plumage, food and breeding I have relied on the five volumes of the classic work *The Handbook of British Birds* by Witherby, Jourdain, Ticehurst and Tucker and the first two volumes that have now been published of the new *Handbook of Birds of Europe, the Middle East and North Africa* by Cramp and Simmons *et al*. Information on population size and breeding distribution has been obtained from the excellent *Atlas of Breeding Birds in Britain and Ireland* prepared by the British Trust for Ornithology and the Irish Wildbird Conservancy. I have also referred to specialist works on groups and families of birds although there is only limited opportunity in a popular work of this kind to do justice to the subtle ecological factors such studies have revealed.

Preliminary versions and the final manuscript were all typed by Mrs Petal Biegel and I wish to express my appreciation to her not only for the typing but for the help given over the form of presentation of the material. I would also like to thank Mr Rob Hume for his delightful sketches.

·1·
Birds and Their Habitats

ADAPTATIONS OF BIRDS

At first glance the novice birdwatcher may conclude that he is faced with a bewildering choice of birds. The most superficial examination reveals, however, that most fall into fairly distinct groups, each containing birds of generally similar appearance. They may, for example, have a long, slender bill and long legs, characteristics associated with wading and mud-probing; or by contrast have extremely short legs and a short, broad bill, but possess long, narrow wings indicating a life primarily spent on the wing capturing flying insects.

The different characteristics of each group represent adaptations evolved over many thousands of years and relate to particular modes of life. By specializing in this way, each has been able to exploit more effectively a particular ecological niche and thus assure for itself a higher chance of survival by reducing competition with other species. This concept of the evolution of the specialized form, producing as it does a wide variety of different plants and animals, is now well understood and widely accepted although when first advanced by Charles Darwin, Alfred Russell Wallace and others during the first half of the nineteenth century, it met with scepticism and disbelief.

The more extreme the adaptations, the greater the dependence of a species on a particular habitat. Thus it becomes possible to anticipate the surroundings in which birds of a particular appearance are most likely to be found. We would look for wading birds on sandy coasts, muddy estuaries or marshes inland; while those that take flying insects will be found wherever sufficient numbers of insects have congregated – perhaps under trees in an orchard or over the pond in a farmyard.

Habitats are rarely unchanging and most undergo regular seasonal variations – the marsh freezes over, the sheltered wood becomes open and exposed as the trees shed their leaves. The adaptations of animals cater for these differences. Ground dwelling animals with limited mobility must survive in the face of the changes. For some the alteration of lifestyle is not great – the weasel in northern regions, for instance, undergoes a change of coat from russet to white and then continues to live much as before. For others the change required is more extreme. Snakes, because they are cold blooded and cannot remain active at low temperatures, hibernate throughout the winter months. Birds by contrast, because of their tremendous mobility, are able to circumvent such changes in habitat conditions by moving elsewhere. So when the cold weather returns to Britain at the end of the summer and insect life diminishes, most of our insectivorous birds travel south to warmer climates. At the same time the vast Arctic tundras begin to freeze over again at the end of the short northern summer and the birds occupying them fly south to pass the winter in similar habitat round the coast of Britain.

This enables many species of birds to pass the greater part of their lives within a particular type of habitat, undertaking often long and regular seasonal movements between widely separated geographical areas to countries where such a habitat is to be found. Hence the bird life of a particular area differs markedly at different times of the year. The same estuary which in December and January contains many thousands of birds may be almost deserted in May and June except for a few scattered breeding pairs of waterfowl. Such changes can only add to the enjoyment of birdwatching and the attraction of particular places and there is always the thrill of anticipation that something totally unexpected may have happened since a previous visit – whether this was earlier in the year or even the day before. It is a common experience for birdwatchers to walk over an area one day and find disappointingly little, only to retrace their steps the following morning and discover that a group of migrants has arrived overnight.

THE DEVELOPMENT OF
THE BRITISH COUNTRYSIDE

Most of the land surface of Britain has been greatly modified by Man's activities. Only the very remote and highest peaks and the loneliest and most inaccessible seashores can be said to remain in something approaching a natural state. Much of the countryside in the southern half of Britain is intensively managed for food production; but even the less populated upland regions of the west and north, often described as semi-natural, bear little resemblance to the great woodlands that formed their natural cover prior to Man's arrival.

The development of the countryside as we know it today can be traced from the end of the last Ice Age, some 10,000 years ago, when Britain was still connected by a land bridge to the rest of Europe. As the great ice sheets that covered most of what is now Britain retreated northwards in the face of an improving climate, vast areas of open, treeless tundra were left behind – boggy hollows associated with grasses, sedges and dwarf shrubs. With the continuing improvement of the climate in the south the tundra was invaded by trees, at first principally birch and pine but soon to be followed and replaced by oak with varying amounts of other species including lime, elm, ash and eventually beech. Alder woods would predominate, as they do today, on many of the wetter lower slopes with willows in the still wetter hollows. Long before primitive man exerted any influence on these forests, the broadleaf woodlands had advanced well up into Scotland with the result that, apart from remnant areas of pine and birch in the extreme northern parts of Scotland, the summits of the highest mountains above the tree-line and flooded fens and marshes unsuitable for trees, most of Britain was dominated by a covering of oak and associated broadleaf woodland.

It was into these broadleaf woods that Stone Age Man advanced and began to exert his influence. At first, living as a fisherman and hunter of the forest animals, his impact was not great. By 3500 BC, however, elementary farming techniques developed on the continent began to spread to Britain and the simple hunting tribes were gradually displaced by more organized communities. Open fields for grazing crops were now required in preference to woodland and tree clearing began. A thousand or so years later metal working techniques were discovered. The use of timber as fuel for metal smelting and other developing industries, building and increasing intensification of agriculture, particularly the extension of sheep pasturage on higher ground, eventually produced the treeless landscapes of the present with Britain one of the least wooded countries in Europe.

It is important when considering our heritage of wildlife to appreciate this historical background. Although the countryside today bears little resemblance to the great forests out of which it was hewn, the natural habitat of very many of our surviving resident animals was one of woodland.

Man's attention, while at first directed towards the forests, was later to turn to marshlands occupying the central lowlands and flat land adjacent to the coasts. Soon most of these, including the great East Anglian fens, were also to be transformed into farmland. Fortunately many large inland lakes and parts of the coast, particularly the more inhospitable rocky stretches and the lower muddier reaches of estuaries, proved less attractive for exploitation and in consequence valuable examples of these have survived. They are of particular importance for nesting seabirds and wintering wildfowl and waders, and Britain harbours significant proportions of the European populations of these birds.

While Man's impact on the British landscape has been profound and extensive, and in the main detrimental to its wildlife, some of the changes he has brought about have produced habitats in their own right. While these artificial habitats are dependent on a particular type of regular management, be it draining, ploughing or burning, they have been in existence for a sufficient length of time to support their own unique associations of plants and animals. Indeed the changes brought about by Man in Britain to the natural habitats have been so extensive that these now form a vital element of our countryside.

MAJOR HABITAT TYPES

The most outstanding example of such a semi-natural habitat is to be found in the vast areas of rolling moorland in the upland regions of Britain. These great expanses of heather or grass-covered hills, often devoid of trees apart from those surviving in steep sided valleys or maintained as shelter belts, provide the home for our upland birds. They include largely resident species such as the Golden Eagle and Raven, which previously occupied the great forests, together with breeding waders such as Curlew, Golden Plover and Dunlin, which pass the remainder of the year elsewhere. Intensive grazing, coupled with controlled burning, ensures that invasion by trees and the re-establishment of the natural forest cover does not occur. Along with the summits of the higher mountains (the montane zone) which rise above the natural limit at which trees can grow – a height of about 600 metres over most of Britain – these moorlands form the Upland Habitat and support a unique and important element of our birdlife.

A second major habitat is formed by the huge mosaic of fields, hedges, ditches and copses, managed and maintained by contemporary agricultural Man. The birds present are indicative of the natural habitat which the area now most resembles. Hedges, scrub and copses carry typical woodland birds such as finches and thrushes while the open fields have partridges and skylark, more naturally associated with open plains. Where wetter areas remain, we find snipe, duck and the Moorhen and other waterbirds.

Integrated with farmland are most of the surviving examples of a third habitat type – Woodland. While many of our larger broadleaf woodlands may at first glance appear natural, the evidence suggests most have been extensively managed, often for specific purposes. The New Forest in Hampshire is associated with shipbuilding and hunting, the great beechwoods of Gloucestershire and the Forest of Dean with sport and local industries. Despite this artificial aspect many, particularly those covering large areas, provide habitat conditions closely resembling those of their natural precursors. In areas of rich soil and mild climate these woodlands contain the highest numbers of different species of resident breeding birds of any habitat.

Another element of the Woodland Habitat is provided by the more recent and obviously artificial forests formed by plantations of (often) alien conifers. These are usually less rich in birds. However, under conditions of rich soil and climate, stands of different age groups separated by rides and unplanted valleys can also support an interesting and varied birdlife.

Also to a considerable extent associated with farmland, we find another of the major habitats – the Freshwater Habitat. This includes ditches, ponds and streams which often form an integral part of farming activities, as well as the larger rivers, meres and lakes. Again Man's influence affects much of it, as testified by the all too numerous canalized stretches of river with their steep, straight, treeless banks and dreary concrete-sided water storage reservoirs. These are but a poor visual substitute for a twisting torrent, with its alternating pools and rapids, or the gently shelving, reed-fringed shore of a tarn. Fortunately for the birdwatcher, despite their unattractive appearance, many of these provide sites for a large number and variety of waterbirds which helps to compensate for their disappointing aesthetic quality. In more sensitively treated artificial sites, such as carefully landscaped disused sand and gravel workings or well planned reservoirs with shallow bays and islands, the result can be both visually attractive and rich in birdlife. In the eastern part of Cambridgeshire, for instance, excavation of numerous sand and gravel pits has provided breeding sites for previously absent species such as the Great Crested Grebe, Little Grebe, Little Ringed Plover, and Common Tern, in addition to several species of duck.

Notably in England, but also in parts of South Wales and central Scotland, great chunks of land have been swallowed up to make our sprawling towns and cities. At first glance the opportunities for birds, particularly in the concrete canyons of city centres, seem pretty remote. It is true that compared to the countryside they represent a greatly impoverished habitat. Nevertheless some birds, if only the indomitable House Sparrow and feral pigeon, manage to live in the most unlikely parts of urban centres. As one moves towards the suburbs, the situation improves with the appearance of parks, gardens and reservoirs. Rarely do these possess distinct groups of birds, but rather contain a depleted representation of those present in more natural habitats in the countryside. Our gardens, particularly if they contain thick hedges and trees, carry the commoner species associated with woodland, – the Blackbird, Song Thrush and Robin. Two species, the Swift and House Martin, are notable in that they have adopted buildings as their main nesting sites. This habit is now so widespread in Britain that it is the exception to find them nesting on cliffs which represent the natural situation. One of the outstanding merits of the suburban area, especially for the beginner or less mobile bird lover, is that it can provide excellent opportunities to watch and enjoy the commoner birds close to as they come to our bird tables or join us during spells of gardening.

This leaves one major habitat – the Coast. It is a habitat of great importance to wild birds because of its extent and variety and its perpetuation of some of the finest examples of near natural conditions. Despite its popularity with holiday makers, there are still hundreds of miles of remote coast, ranging from intertidal mudflats and salt-marshes, through offshore islands, to some of the highest and finest seabird cliffs in the world. Not only are many of these sites of great international importance for the conservation of birds, but they provide some of the most spectacular gatherings of birds to be found anywhere in the world. The noise, smell and visual excitement of a large seabird colony, once experienced, is impossible to forget.

SUB-DIVISIONS OF MAJOR HABITATS

Having identified the major habitats in Britain and before going on to to describe each in detail, it is worth considering briefly the numerous sub-divisions contained within each. The variations provided by small, but often highly significant, differences of such components as the underlying rock, the soil, topography, temperature, humidity, aspect and vegetation are enormous. Rather in the way a modern city offers a choice of different dwellings such as high rise flats, hotels, houses, offices and factories, so each habitat will contain a range of differing sub-habitats.

On a mountain cliff, the Golden Eagle and Raven nest on the larger ledges towards the top, the Jackdaw and Rock Dove find refuge in fissures lower down on the rock face, the Whinchat occupies scrub growing out of the scree near the base, while close by the Wren hides amongst rock-covered boulders at the cliff foot where it grades into the moorland. Similarly, within a wood, the Rook and Heron nest in the very top of the larger trees, the Mistle Thrush and Jay are hidden amongst the branches nearer the middle of the tree, while Great Spotted Woodpecker and Great Tit occupy holes in the trunk and the Woodcock tucks its nest into the vegetation at the foot of the tree.

Similar progressions exist in all habitats. Sometimes the change is gradual: the Coot, because it builds a nest firmly anchored in branches or reeds, is restricted to the shallows near the lake edge, whereas the floating nest of the Great Crested Grebe can be sited further out in deeper water. In other habitats the change may be more sudden – a sink hole into the underlying rock far out on an otherwise uniform stretch of moorland can contain a pair of Ring Ousels, or a small area of wet bog on a dry fell top may harbour a pair of nesting Dunlin. The exploitation by birds of such apparently small differences within a habitat is truly remarkable and explains why, within a short distance, one can pass from an area of little interest to another full of activity.

It should be appreciated that although different habitats with their characteristic bird species can be described, they represent artificial sub-divisions of the countryside categorized for Man's convenience. In reality nature is rarely precise and usually one habitat merges gradually with another or may even encompass parts of another – woodland may enclose a lake, for example. Nor do birds always conform to expectations. Some species are sufficiently adaptable to survive in what in many ways appear to be differing habitats. The Kestrel, now a familiar sight as it hovers over motorway verges, seems equally at home on sea cliffs, moorland or in city centres. In extreme conditions individuals may be driven away from their more usual locality. During spells of prolonged frost, Snipe have been recorded in suburban gardens and during migration many species are blown off course and turn up in the most unexpected places. It is unwise, therefore, to be too dogmatic about which birds one will encounter in any particular area. In the following chapters each major habitat is discussed in turn with the commoner species typically associated with it. Briefer mention is made of the less common species that may be present. Nature is rarely completely predictable, however, and one should always be ready for the exceptional or unexpected.

·2·

The Upland Habitat

The uplands of Britain, which cover a total area of 6.6 million hectares, are situated in the north and west. The main areas are: the Scottish Highlands (comprising the north-west Highlands and the Grampians); the Southern Uplands of Scotland; the English Lake District; the Pennines; the Welsh Cambrian Mountains (including Snowdonia in the north); and the Black Mountains of South Wales. Smaller areas include the Cheviots on the Scottish-English border; the North York Moors; and Exmoor and Dartmoor in south-west England.

To most species of wild bird the uplands represent a bleak and inhospitable environment. The soil is usually poor and deficient in minerals, vegetation is sparse, providing little cover or food and the climate is harsh. This explains the relative dearth of species and the small numbers of those that are present. The northerly latitude and height (over 900 metres) of many of the Highland mountains means that in most winters they suffer prolonged snow and severe frost. The low temperatures and snow often persist well into the summer, producing conditions beyond the endurance of most birds. The more southerly latitude of the remaining uplands renders them less prone to such severe winter conditions, but because of their westerly location they are subject to a heavy, even distribution of rainfall associated with high humidity and cloud which also results in conditions unattractive to many birds.

Upland habitat varies considerably through such factors as topography, nature of the substrate, aspect and land-use. One of the most striking contrasts is that between the steep, craggy, almost bare summits of some mountains and the smooth, vegetated slopes of others. In the Highlands, the Lake District and North Wales the two forms occur together, rugged peaks forming a backcloth to the lower rounded hills. This contrasts with the rolling contours of the Pennines and other moors, formed almost exclusively from well weathered, soft, carboniferous rock. The basic form is punctuated haphazardly by natural features such as corries hollowed out by accumulations of ice, and screes of loose rock and gulleys cut by streams, as well as by man-made features such as cliffs and caves produced by quarrying and mining.

The vegetational cover of British uplands is remarkably consistent in form and composition. It changes with altitude and three broad zones can be distinguished. First come the lower, better drained slopes, often carrying remnants of oak or birch woodland. These are superseded at higher altitudes by rough grassland or heather moor with dwarf shrubs, the determining factor being past management – heather and shrubs benefiting from the absence of frequent burning and heavy grazing. Above these, at elevations over 750 metres, lies the exposed 'alpine' or 'montane' zone of mosses, lichens and sparse grassland among rock debris. Within each zone there are many variations arising from local geographical conditions and past management practices.

The flatter profile of the lower hills results in accumulation of peaty soils. In hollows, where drainage is impeded, these can become deep and waterlogged leading to the formation of blanket bog typified by sedges, cotton grass and heathland shrubs in conjunction with poor grassland. Variation is produced by lakes, streams and springs with their associated sphagnum moss. In limestone areas the soil is usually better and flora and invertebrate fauna richer and more varied. Limestone rocks are widespread in the British uplands, but only infrequently are they extensive in area. Where present they provide valuable feeding sites for many birds.

THE LOWER SLOPES

The main valleys and better drained lower slopes are usually farmed and contain cultivated fields and fertile meadows, blending with rough grazing land at the valley head and higher levels on the valley sides. The bird life of the lower valley is much the same as that found throughout the lowlands. The proportion of one species to another may differ, but the familiar Robin, Blackbird and Song Thrush are present in the hedgerows and Rooks and Starlings are invariably found in the fields. The outstanding difference is the importance of these areas, particularly the rough grass fields, as feeding sites for many of the wading birds breeding on the moor tops – species such as Curlew and Golden Plover. In favoured spots during spring and early summer these may be seen in considerable numbers. A further difference is the presence of large birds of prey. For most of these it is often only a brief visit during a hunting foray, the exception being the Buzzard which is resident and, in central Wales, the Red Kite.

The **Buzzard** formerly bred in every county. Like so many of our birds of prey it suffered intensive persecution from game interests in the mid-nineteenth century. At the turn of the century, when numbers were at their lowest, it was confined to the remote mountain regions of western Britain. The only lowland population to escape destruction was in the New Forest in Hampshire. Greater tolerance and better legislation have enabled the Buzzard to regain some of its former range and it is now present throughout much of Scotland, Wales, north-west and south-west England, but is still only found in small numbers in the very north of Ireland. It occurs at high altitudes in mountains and on moorland crags, but numbers are smaller there than in lightly wooded valleys with well hedged meadows. The densest populations are in parts of Wales and Devon where it tolerates high rainfall and humidity. The British population is now thought to number almost 10,000 pairs.

The large size (51–57cm, the females being larger) and majestic soaring flight draw attention to it. Individuals will circle for long periods with large, rounded wings outspread, the feathers at the tip separated and upturned and the tail fully fanned. Several will soar in unison in a thermal and rise until out of sight. The rather uniform brown back contrasts with the varied mottled and streaked underparts. Confusion is possible with the Golden Eagle in Scotland and the Lake District where both are present. The even greater size of the Golden Eagle (75–88cm), its uniformly dark plumage, boldy projecting head and more ample tail help to separate them.

Prey for the Buzzard consists primarily of mammals and carrion and before myxomatosis rabbits formed the principal item for many populations. Rabbits and leverets are still important, but moles, voles, lizards, beetles, worms and a variety of birds may all be included. In spring and autumn when adders lie out sunning, they too will form a common prey species. The Buzzard's catholic diet and versatility at finding and capturing it must account for much of its success. Prey is usually located by the Buzzard circling at height and then hanging or hovering clumsily before planing down or stooping swiftly on half-closed wings to pounce. It will also perch on trees, hedges and posts from which it drops onto prey.

Early in the breeding season pairs circle together over their territories, occasionally diving at each other and dropping steeply on half-closed wings. Their rather plaintive, but far-carrying mewing call 'peeioo peeioo' is uttered both in flight and when perched. Nests are built in bushes, trees or on cliff or quarry ledges and are large, often up to one metre in diameter. The typical clutch of three eggs is laid in late April or early May and incubated by both birds for about five weeks. Young remain in the nest for seven or eight weeks, tended at first by the female which later assists the male with the hunting.

But for the extensive persecution to which the **Red Kite**, like the Buzzard, was subjected during the nineteenth century, it would still be present in England and Scotland. In historical times it was common to the extent of being accepted as a scavenger in city centres. By the start of the present century, its numbers may have fallen to as few as three pairs and for the next fifty years probably remained below fifteen breeding pairs. Since then the numbers slowly increased and there are now probably as many as forty pairs, about half of which successfully fledge young.

There can be no mistaking the Red Kite because of its large size (60–66cm), long, deeply forked, chestnut tail and long, angled wings. They hunt by sailing in wide circles at high altitudes over the moorland plateaux, before dropping onto prey on the ground. Food includes carrion, especially mutton, small mammals and birds. In its selection of prey and hunting techniques it is closest to the Buzzard, but the two will co-exist within the same general habitat. The nest sites are in woods in the valleys and on hillsides adjacent to the upland hunting areas. Relict mature oakwoods are regularly used, but they have also been recorded from a wide range of broadleaf trees and also in conifers. The nest is large, usually in a main fork, and the typical clutch in Wales, laid in April, is two eggs. Incubation, mainly by the female, lasts just under five weeks, the young then remaining in the nest for seven weeks. For the first fortnight hunting is by the male alone, but thereafter both sexes take part.

Breeding success is low and the Red Kite is vulnerable to several factors during the season. Human disturbance and a growth in tourism presents an increasing problem and extensive periods of bad weather make hunting difficult. Egg collecting is still a hazard and nest wardens have to be employed each year. Probably the most serious damage is caused by the traditional use of strychnine against moles by hill farmers and other poisons deliberately laid against crows and foxes which also kill kites. Perhaps the most eagerly awaited event is the establishment of a breeding population outside Wales.

A bird which frequently comes into conflict with the Buzzard is the **Carrion/Hooded Crow**. Like the Buzzard, it is a highly adaptable and versatile species. Despite its unpopularity with gamekeepers and many farmers, it still breeds in all parts of the British Isles and is the second most widespread British bird, exceeded only by the Skylark. It is difficult to conclude which is its most favoured habitat, because of the continuing and often harsh persecution to which it is subjected in many areas. In spite of attempts at control, its distribution extends from the uplands down to sea level and it is found on bleak fells, in woods, on farmland and even in city centres. The highest concentrations are usually on the lower slopes and in the partially wooded valleys in the vicinity of sheep farms. The total breeding population of the British Isles is about a million pairs.

The Hooded Crow, with its grey mantle and underparts, is unmistakable and the all-black Carrion Crow is only likely to be confused with the Rook. The grey face and more slender bill of the latter provide good distinguishing features. At one time the Hooded and Carrion Crow were considered to be separate species, but as they freely interbreed and produce fertile offspring they are now recognized as geographical races of one species. The two colour forms are thought to have evolved during the last Ice Age when different parts of the European crow population became separated. Although apart for a sufficiently long period to allow the development of a distinct plumage variety, the period was too short for them to form distinct species. In the British Isles, the Hooded race predominates throughout Ireland, the Isle of Man and north-west Scotland.

A large (47cm), bold bird, it subsists throughout much of the year on soil invertebrates supplemented with carrion. During the breeding season its diet extends to include the eggs and young of other birds such as ground nesting waders and gamebirds but it will also take hedgerow species and the eggs of duck, the Grey Heron and other waterbirds. It can appear clumsy in flight and only infrequently soars and glides when flying high, prey usually being detected from a look-out position such as a tree, post, wall or boulder. A pair will often attack in unison which helps them circumvent the persistent mobbing to which they are subjected by their larger victims such as Curlew, Lapwing or Oyster-catcher. They are also opportunist feeders and frequent rubbish tips and farmland in winter when cattle fodder is being distributed.

Breeding pairs are strongly territorial throughout most of the year and inter-territorial skirmishes are common. Where present in large numbers, non-breeding birds will form flocks and in times of hard weather and food shortage territorial birds will join communal feeding flocks. They have long been regarded by shepherds and hill farmers as serious predators of young or sick lambs. A recent study in Scotland, however, clearly demonstrated that it is exceptional for them to kill even weak lambs and that they feed on mutton carrion. In contrast to the Rook they are solitary nesters. Typically the large nest is built in a mature tree in a small wood or hedgerow or at the base of a crevice or on a ledge in a cliff or quarry face. In most years a new nest will be built, although earlier nests often survive for several seasons and are used by Kestrel and Merlin falcons. The nest is deep and well lined with sheep wool; the blue-green eggs are usually laid in April in an average clutch of four. The female incubates them for just under three weeks and the young remain in the nest for about five weeks, thereafter staying together as a family party for several weeks before the juveniles disperse. In certain parts of the North Wales uplands there is another, all black, but smaller, crow – the Chough. It is however more commonly associated with sea cliffs and is considered in the chapter on Coasts.

THE MOORLAND FRINGE

Between the upper meadows of the valley sides and the open moor beyond lies an intermediate zone – the moorland edge. Where well developed and particularly if remnants of woodland have survived, this provides a distinct sub-division of the habitat. The scattered trees, scrub, gorse and other shrubs offer comparative shelter in contrast to the more open land on either side. Two species in particular prefer the opportunities afforded by this niche – the Black Grouse, a large resident gamebird and the Whinchat, a much smaller bird, a summer migrant arriving in Britain from tropical Africa during the first weeks in April.

The large size (c. 50cm) of the male **Black Grouse**, usually referred to as the **Blackcock**, is a valuable distinguishing character. This, with its glossy blue-black plumage, red eye wattles and lyre-shaped tail, distinguishes it from all other birds. Identification of the female, the Greyhen, is less easy because of possible confusion with the female Capercaillie and Red Grouse. As with the male, the white wing bars and forked tail serve as distinguishing features, but neither is always easy to see.

A vegetarian, feeding extensively on the shoots and leaves of heather, sedges and grasses, with a greater emphasis in winter on berries and the buds of larch and birch, it will perch in trees while feeding and roosting. Today it is widely distributed throughout Scotland, the northern Pennines and Wales with smaller numbers in the Peak District and on Exmoor. For reasons not fully understood, it has declined since the nineteenth century, when it was still present in many parts of England. During the last fifty years, however, there has been a marked recovery. This, it is suggested, is associated with increased afforestation of moorland, but it seems probable that other factors have been involved and numerous reintroductions of birds to different areas have confused the picture. The total breeding population is now thought to be between 10,000 and 50,000 pairs.

Although frequently found in small flocks during winter, the sexes tend to remain separate. The courtship display of the males provides the highlight of the breeding season. This is performed at dawn and dusk from March to April on traditional areas in the heather or grass known as leks. Several males will gather in the presence of docile females, rival males facing each other with puffed bodies, down curved wings and erect tails. Birds dart at each other in mock combat making a musical 'roo roo roo' for most of the time, but occasionally there is actual physical contact. Mating frequently follows a lek, but the full purpose of such gatherings is not understood as it is not always the most aggressive males which mate most frequently with the females. The typical clutch is six to ten yellowish-white eggs laid in May in the nest scrape hidden in thick ground vegetation. Incubation is by the female and lasts twenty-four days, and she then tends the young, which leave the nest immediately, for two or three weeks. Males are polygamous.

The **Whinchat** can easily be overlooked because of its small size (12.5cm) and generally brown-streaked appearance. It often draws attention to itself by its habit of perching on the top of bushes, tall plants and posts, while at the same time uttering a sharp 'tic-tic' alarm note. Its identity can be confirmed by its black cheeks, noticeable eye stripe and white sides to the tail. Its short-tailed appearance and rather upright stance are characteristic, but care must be taken to avoid confusion with the Stonechat. The latter is more typically associated with coasts and is considered under that habitat, but is not uncommon in some years along moorland fringes.

When feeding, the Whinchat drops from its perch into the rough grass and heather amongst the gorse and bracken and hops with flicking wings and tail in search of insects, before flying to another observation post. By early June breeding has usually started and incubation of the six eggs and feeding the young in the nest each lasts about two weeks. Incubation is by the female, then both birds feed the young in the nest, bringing food in the bill. The nests, which are well hidden in grass tussocks, are difficult to find and breeding is more usually confirmed by finding a party of three or four young on the wing still being fed by the parents.

Until recently the Whinchat was present throughout much of Britain. During the last fifty years its range has contracted until now it is more usually associated with upland areas where it can be found at elevations up to 500 metres. The reasons for its decline are not known. Loss of habitat has played a part, but this is not the complete answer as Whinchats are now absent from areas in the lowlands where apparently suitable, previously occupied, habitat persists. Small numbers are still recorded in the lowland regions along the coast and in rough meadows, heaths and railway embankments. The total breeding population of the British Isles is between 20,000 and 40,000 pairs.

MOORLAND

Above the valleys and beyond the limited shelter afforded by the more thickly vegetated moorland fringes lie the open moors. In some regions they give the impression of being almost endless and featureless. On the deeper, peaty soils, where they still support a thick continuous cover of vegetation, the bases of the shrubs and tussocks remain cold and wet throughout the hottest day. On the thinner soils, where vegetation is overburnt and overgrazed, extensive areas of exposed ground quickly become baked by wind and sun into a dry hard flaking pan. A very different habitat indeed from that existing before the destruction of the tree cover is produced and one that only a small number of specialized birds can tolerate. For many of these occupation of it is for the summer months only.

Birds associated with the open moorland can conveniently be considered in four groups: small birds, waders, gamebirds and predators. There are three species of small birds. Two, Meadow Pipit and Twite, are resident in the British Isles, but while the former represents our commonest upland bird, the latter is now confined to north-west Scotland and a few southerly outposts, notably the South Pennines. The third, the Wheatear, is a summer migrant and although widely distributed it is only common in favoured localities. Four of the five wading birds – Lapwing, Curlew, Golden Plover and Dunlin – are also widely distributed although the numbers of each differ. By contrast the fifth, the Greenshank, is found only in the Highlands. The Red Grouse alone represents the gamebirds but it is an important one, as much of the management of the lower hills has been directed towards creating grouse moors for sporting estates. Predators include the Short-eared Owl, Merlin and Hen Harrier, all of which hunt and nest on the open moors.

SMALL BIRDS

The commonest and most ubiquitous moorland bird is undoubtedly the **Meadow Pipit**. This small (14.5cm), slim, rather inconspicuous, brown-streaked bird is extremely widespread in Britain. Occupying almost any area of rough ground from sea level to over 1,000 metres, it is least successful in intensively cultivated regions. Its significance to

Meadow Pipit

uplands stems from the fact that it is by far the most numerous small bird breeding at over 500 metres. By virtue of this it plays a vital role in the ecology of moorland. It forms a major part of the prey of the Merlin and Hen Harrier and provides the commonest host for hillside dwelling Cuckoos. In one Pennines study area it was found that one in five Meadow Pipit nests contained eggs or young of the Cuckoo.

In both rough grassland and heather the Meadow Pipit can be extremely difficult to find. Even where vegetation is short and sparse it is easily overlooked and often the only sign of its presence is a faint 'tseep tseep' uttered while on the ground and the notes are quickly lost on the wind. When seen, the slender bill, spotted breast and white outer tail feathers are characteristic. It spends much of its time hidden in the vegetation searching the stems and surface debris for the insects that almost exclusively make up its diet. Confusion is only likely with the closely related Tree Pipit which in appearance it resembles. Habitat, song and behaviour provide the most valuable clues to separating the two which can overlap where scattered woodland, the habitat of the Tree Pipit, extends high up the valley sides.

One of the Meadow Pipit's outstanding adaptations to its open surroundings is its song flight. For this is flies to a height of about thirty metres and then glides down making a thin piping song. The song gradually increases in tempo as the bird nears the ground until, during the final quicker 'parachute' descent back onto the ground, it gives a musical trill. This song is quite distinct from the drawn out, hovering, aerial song of the Skylark. The typical clutch of four or five eggs is laid towards the end of April in a nest well hidden deep in the heart of a tussock. Even though nest surroundings may be exposed, it is remarkable how sheltered the selected nest sites can be. Incubation takes about two weeks and the young are then fed in the nest on beakfuls of insects brought by the parents.

There are possibly over three million pairs of Meadow Pipits in Britain. Most appear to be resident, although the more northerly birds and those nesting at high altitudes move south, often in small flocks, to pass the winter on coastlands and lowland pastures. The highest nesting densities, in places exceeding well over seventy pairs per square kilometre, have been found on sand dunes and saltmarshes, although densities only slightly below this are known from certain areas in the Pennines. On impoverished and degraded uplands their density may be reduced to fewer than five pairs per square kilometre.

The Skylark, like the Meadow Pipit, is a widely distributed small bird dependent on open habitats. It occurs throughout most upland areas with the Meadow Pipit, but as it is more popularly associated with lowland agricultural regions it is considered in the chapter on farmland.

The **Twite** contrasts in many ways with the Meadow Pipit. Far from being widespread it is largely confined to the north and west of

Scotland. Indeed it could be claimed as a bird of the coast with much of the British population living on cliff tops. Flourishing populations are to be found, however, on moorland in the central and western Highlands and further south in the southern Pennines. In Ireland it is very largely restricted to the north and west coasts.

This unusual distribution is believed to reflect its origins. It is considered to be the only European species having its derivation in Tibetan avifauna and its principal world population is still to be found on the high steppes of central Asia. Descendants from this population are presumed to have spread during the Ice Ages as far as the tundras of central Europe, contracting at a later date when the ice sheets retreated. This left an isolated European breeding population now largely confined to the coast of Norway and parts of Britain and Ireland. Contraction of its range in Britain still continues and it now no longer breeds in previously known sites in Cheshire, Shropshire and Derbyshire and some of the northern English counties. It is thus an interesting example of a once widespread species, now dependent on a relict artificial habitat provided by short, wet, cliff top vegetation and damp moorland.

Its appearance is that of a typical small finch (13.5cm) with rounded head, sharply pointed, thick, yellow bill and slightly forked tail. The main outstanding features relieving its dark brown appearance are the whitish wing-bar and pinkish rump of the males. It seems to prefer open disturbed ground and good views can often be had as it feeds along the sides of rough tracks and sheep walks.

Primarily seed-eating, it is associated with moorland areas in the vicinity of rough pastures supporting common weed species such as daisy, dandelion, sorrel and charlock and in winter will take the seeds of saltmarsh plants. In many hill districts it is popularly known as the 'mountain linnet' and it is not inappropriate to consider it as the counterpart of the Linnet at altitudes over 300 metres. At the boundary the two species do overlap and the Linnet may be advancing against the Twite. In such situations they can be found breeding in close proximity. The total breeding population is thought to be between 20,000 and 40,000 pairs.

Breeding usually starts in late May and some pairs rear two broods in a season. The song, a series of twitterings, is performed in flight as well as from boulders, posts or shrubs and during courtship the male repeatedly depresses its wings to display the pinkish rump. Individual pairs in local populations frequently nest close to one another and the nests are usually built close to the ground in grass tussocks or shrubs. The typical clutch is five or six and the duration of incubation and feeding in the nest just under one month. Twites are gregarious outside the breeding period, often forming considerable flocks, and move down to the lower ground and especially coastal plains to find winter food.

The **Wheatear**, unlike the Twite and Meadow Pipit, is a summer migrant. Although much the same size (15cm) as the Meadow Pipit, it differs from it both in appearance and behaviour. It has a tall upright stance and short-tailed appearance with bright and simple coloration. Both sexes possess prominent black cheeks and a striking white rump which is clearly visible in flight and when perched, males being grey above and females brown. They appear restless as they dart from boulder to boulder or from wall top to tussock, dropping every now and then to the ground to feed. While feeding they bob and bow vigorously amongst the roots and stems to find the beetles, flies, bees, moths and butterflies which form their diet. If overlooked they often attract attention to themselves by their sharp 'whit-chuck chuck' alarm note.

Wheatear

Their arrival in Britain from tropical Africa occurs from mid-March onwards and the males are usually first. They are able to nest in open and featureless areas of moorland at altitudes exceeding 1000 metres and prefer sites with short vegetation. In areas of rank heather they will select territories such as grazed roadside verges and tracks or near old enclosures, quarries or screes.

In their display males will hop and bow to the female, uttering a soft warbling song. The nest, made of dry grass, is built primarily by the female and is well hidden in a crevice amongst boulders or in a stone wall or down a rabbit burrow. The five or six pale blue eggs are laid in May and incubated for about two weeks by the female. Young remain in the nest for about fifteen days before emerging in their mottled brown plumage. Most of the family parties leave the breeding areas during August, and by September few will remain. In both spring and autumn numbers are temporarily supplemented by the slightly larger Greenland and Iceland birds passing through Britain. The total breeding population of the British Isles is about 80,000 pairs.

Now very much a bird of moorland, with only small numbers elsewhere in isolated localities on sand dunes, cliff tops and offshore islands, the Wheatear was at one time locally extremely common in the south of England on heaths and the chalk Downs. During the last century these were kept free of trees and scrub, in the case of the former by cutting, burning and cattle grazing and in the latter by sheep grazing. In the open conditions then prevailing Wheatears abounded to such an extent that they were trapped in hundreds as table birds. The gradual reduction of heathland through building and afforestation and the replacement of Downland sheep by cultivation, combined as it was with the disappearance of rabbits from myxomatosis, caused the short cropped habitat to become overgrown and accelerated the final demise of these southern populations.

WADERS

Uplands provide an important part of the breeding areas of British waders. Of these the **Lapwing** is the commonest and also the one most frequently encountered on the lower ground, where its breeding densities are generally greater than those found in upland areas. It requires an open habitat with short vegetation and breeds in every county of Britain largely by virtue of its ability to live on farmland. With the continuing drainage of wet and marshy areas, the spreading practice of ploughing and re-seeding old traditional permanent pasture and the general intensification and mechanization of farming, its breeding numbers in lowland areas are declining and it is becoming increasingly dependent on marginal land in hill country.

It hardly seems necessary to have to describe such a distinctive bird. Its large size (30cm), black and white appearance and long thin crest render it quite unmistakable. In flight it is equally distinctive because of unusually rounded black and white wings and a slow flapping beat. Although strictly territorial, several pairs may nest in close proximity and males may begin to take up their territories as early as February. In display they will rise from the ground with slow flaps which quicken as height is gained. Suddenly the flight becomes highly erratic as the birds plunge, twisting and turning quickly from side to side, at times almost turning complete somersaults. This will continue until the closing sequence – a spell of level flight, twisting from side to side, with heavy wing beats producing a loud humming from the flight feathers. Throughout they utter a rather plaintive 'pee-wee weet weet – peeweet'. Several males may perform the flight together, as though they stimulate one another.

The nests are a simple depression in the soil lined with grass and are often on a slight rise or adjoining and partially concealed by a tussock. The male will build the nest by scraping vigorously with its feet and then sink forward onto its breast, turning in circles to create a smooth hollow. Because of the open terrain, exposed nature of the nest and bright colouring of the adults, survival depends on an early departure by the sitting bird and well camouflaged eggs. If surprised, females are adept at distracting enemies with convincing broken wing displays and are aggressive towards cattle which may trample on the nests. They will mob carrion crows and gulls, potential predators of eggs and young. The typical clutch of four eggs hatches in just under a month and the well camouflaged young leave the nest almost immediately, becoming fully fledged in four to five weeks. The total breeding population of the British Isles is about 200,000 pairs.

Sheep pasture, newly ploughed land and sprouting corn provide the principal inland feeding sites. In winter, particularly during cold spells, large numbers will congregate on coastal plains and mudflats. Flocking begins in June and most breeding areas are usually deserted by July when a general southerly movement will begin. Many of those from northern Britain winter in Ireland, while others migrate to the Continent to pass the winter in France or Spain or even further south. Some of the birds breeding in southern England are sedentary. Using the short slender bill, they obtain a wide range of invertebrates living on or just beneath the surface. They are vulnerable to winter frosts and to circumvent these they will make short term, usually westerly and southerly, winter movements when faced with deteriorating weather conditions.

The larger **Curlew** (55cm) is equally distinctive in its upland breeding areas. It is the largest British wader and its size, long slender curving bill, tall slim legs and streaky brown plumage readily confirm its identification. Its flight is fast and direct and effected by slow, steady, strong beats of long narrow wings. It will frequently glide over long distances before landing. The only possible confusion may arise with the slightly smaller but otherwise very similar Whimbrel. This species only quite exceptionally breeds on mainland Britain, however, being confined to Shetland.

In a mild spring the first birds will arrive in the uplands towards the end of February, but late frosts may delay their appearance for several weeks. While they disperse widely and occupy almost all varieties of moorland including heather, grassland and bog, the most favoured sites are hill pastures and rushy fields. These provide particularly good feeding areas for the adults and later for the young. Nesting commonly occurs at altitudes of up to 600 metres. On high ground the number of breeding pairs will be lower and isolated pairs disperse over large tracts of moorland. The number breeding in Britain has increased during the present century, largely as a result of their spread to lowland pasture and heaths and the total breeding population of the British Isles is now between 40,000 and 70,000 pairs. This trend may be reversed, as with the Lapwing, in the face of increased intensification of agriculture and the draining of marshland.

By late March and April breeding activity is clearly in evidence from the attractive territorial flights of the males. In these males will circle the breeding grounds, flying low before suddenly rising almost vertically with a quick, hovering flight and then gliding on slightly upheld wings. After losing height the process is repeated to be followed once again by the glide. This manoeuvre is enacted many times and the bird calls throughout. During the glide the note is a drawn-out, almost moaning 'ooorr-ooorr' which suddenly bursts into a bubbling trill in the rapid rise.

Both parents incubate the typical clutch of four blotched eggs laid in an open scrape. Although well camouflaged, the sitting bird will leave the nest at the approach of danger, usually forewarned by its mate standing on guard nearby which gives a sharp 'curleek curleek' call as it flies off. The young leave the nest within twenty-four hours of hatching and take up to five or six weeks to fledge, during which time they are attended by alert and at times very noisy parents. The Curlews' skill and speed in flight is well demonstrated as they drive away crows and gulls entering the breeding territories. While on the uplands the food of adults and young consists almost entirely of worms, insects, larvae and some seeds and berries. Small young have straight bills, but by the juvenile stage they closely resemble their parents in appearance.

By late July the breeding grounds are deserted and mixed flocks of adults and juveniles have formed on lowland farmland and coasts. Most of the northern British birds move southwards and westwards and some cross to Ireland to winter. Others travel south to France and Spain to be replaced in Britain by continental immigrants.

The **Golden Plover**, unlike the Lapwing and Curlew, is almost exclusively an upland breeder, with most nesting on the flat moor tops at 500–1000 metres. Although wintering in large flocks on lowland farms in the south of Britain, few remain to breed and there are possibly no more than ten pairs in the south-west and only about five hundred pairs in Wales. It is not until the northern Pennines that large numbers are found. The total breeding population of Britain now stands at between 25,000 and 30,000 pairs, but these numbers are almost certainly decreasing, albeit slowly, as they are elsewhere in central and southern Europe. The reasons for this are not fully understood, but recent climatic amelioration, upland afforestation and agricultural improvement are all probably contributory factors.

In appearance it is a typical medium-sized wader (28cm) with a large rounded head, short slender bill and compact body. At close quarters the black and gold spangled upper parts and black cheeks, throat and underparts can be distinguished. During winter (September to April) the black below is replaced by white. The British breeding population comprises a separate form, distinguished from northerly breeding birds by a broader, more distinctive white border to the black underparts. The wings are narrow and pointed and the flight quick with regular beats. On the ground it runs in short bursts, stopping to 'dip' its body as it feeds. During the summer months its food, like other upland waders, consists almost entirely of worms, insects and spiders, supplemented by vegetation and berries. Flat ground with short vegetation offers easier foraging and is particularly valuable for the young and higher nesting densities occur under such conditions.

The first birds will arrive in the vicinity of the breeding sites in late February and form flocks on the lower pastures, frequently pairing before the territory is selected. By March breeding activity is well underway and once again it is the beautiful territorial flight which confirms the presence of breeding birds. During the display the males sail low over the ground with deliberate, flicking wingbeats, at times appearing almost stationary on the wind. Throughout, at regular intervals, they utter a plaintive, drifting whistle 'peee-yur-yur'. Darker birds are more aggressive and more successful in obtaining territories.

Three or four mottled eggs are laid from mid-April in a simple scrape. This will be positioned in areas in short heather or grazed moor grass, not uncommonly in rather exposed or recently burnt areas. Rough hummocky ground is frequently selected and the off-duty bird uses a tussock or boulder as an observation platform. The faint, rather monotonous alarm note 'tee-ee' can be heard over a considerable distance and it can prove surprisingly difficult to spot the calling bird. Both parents share incubation and quickly vacate the nest at the approach of danger but, unlike Lapwings and Curlews, they rarely display aggression towards sheep or crows and gulls. In some particularly rich nesting areas, for example on limestone grassland, they will nest in close proximity to one another and amongst Lapwings.

The eggs hatch after a month and the young leave the nest within a few hours to be tended by both parents. After another month, almost as soon as they can fly, the birds leave the uplands to form flocks. At first these will remain on nearby farmland, but soon move on to join other flocks, not infrequently including Lapwings, further south.

The **Dunlin** is the smallest (18cm) and least numerous of the common upland breeding waders. To every pair of Dunlin there are something like thirty-five pairs of Lapwings, ten pairs of Curlew and five of Golden Plover. This means there are vast tracts of moorland in Britain from which Dunlins are absent. The explanation for this is not so much a lack of habitat, but rather that in Britain the species is at the southern limit of its Palearctic breeding range. As with the Golden Plover, few breed south of the northern Pennines and the small population that became established on Dartmoor just under fifty years ago represents the most southerly breeding Dunlin colony in the world. The total breeding population of the Britain Isles is between 4,000 and 8,000 pairs.

Their diminutive appearance, long, slightly decurved bill, and

Dunlin

distinctive large black patch on the lower breast, confirm their identification when on their breeding grounds. However, they present a more difficult problem of recognition when on the seashore in their grey and white plumage alongside numerous other species of small waders.

Their upland nesting sites will be found on the higher and wetter parts of moorland plateaux, often in the vicinity of a group of small, shallow, tussock-filled, boggy pools. Nests have been found up to 1,000 metres. This breeding habitat is also suitable for the Golden Plover and the two species are not uncommonly found together. The nest is a small cup formed within a tussock and the typical clutch consists of four eggs.

British breeding birds pass the winter in southern England, southern, Europe and parts of North Africa. Their return migration to the breeding grounds takes place during late April and May and as they will engage in nuptial display while still on passage, the numbers recorded at a potential breeding site early in the year can be misleading. In the display flight the males will rise almost vertically into the air and appear to hover while gently rising and falling, uttering their trilling cry throughout. This display is interspersed with low circling flights around the territory and includes gliding on upheld wings. Several pairs may nest in the same locality and then aerial chases can occur. The eggs are laid in mid-May and both parents share the incubation which lasts for about three weeks. The young quickly become active and feed themselves and the fledging period lasts about twenty-five days. Soon after fledging, the birds will leave the high tops so that by July they are once more deserted. In contrast to these upland breeders, small colonies exist on some northern saltmarshes at sea level.

Although uncommon in Britain and restricted in breeding range, the **Greenshank** is sufficiently in evidence in certain upland areas to warrant at least a short mention. Its world breeding range extends through northern Asia and Europe and our small Highland breeding population, limited to about 500 pairs, represents the westernmost outliers. Nests are extremely difficult to locate and the bird's presence

Greenshank

is indicated by single birds or, later, family parties feeding in bogs or at loch or river sides. Feeding sites are, however, frequently separated by many kilometres from the nest. The bird's length is 30cm and the tall stance, generally slim appearance, prominent white rump, dark wings and the green legs from which its name derives, distinguish it from the similar Redshank. In breeding plumage the black centres to the feathers and spotting on the head can give a mottled appearance.

Breeding in the Highlands takes place from sea level to over 600 metres. The more northerly sites tend to be on treeless, boggy moors, while further south they will occupy dry heath with scattered pines where they will perch on trees and stumps. Birds returning from Africa are found as early as late March and the first eggs hatch by the end of May. The males arrive first and take part in elaborate courtship displays, including an undulating song flight, aerial chases and bowing and hopping ground displays. The nest is a shallow scrape made by the female amongst short heather and lichen and is often positioned near a stump or stone. The typical clutch is four and both sexes share incubation. Immediately after hatching the young will leave the nest and, tended by both parents, move to the feeding areas. Food is found by probing and sweeping with the long slender bill in shallow water and consists of insects and aquatic invertebrates. The young fledge at about four weeks.

GAMEBIRDS

Of the three upland gamebirds the **Red Grouse**, which is only found in Britain, occupies the middle ground from 300 to 600 metres, between the Black Grouse of the lower moorland edge and the Ptarmigan of the montane zone at about 750 metres. It is a large (38–41cm), gamebird

Red Grouse

with small head, plump body and short rounded wings and tail. British birds form an all dark geographical race of the Arctic White-winged Willow Grouse, whose range extends across Eurasia and America. In contrast to the Ptarmigan, they remain dark throughout the year, but share the characteristic of feet feathered down to the toes. Males are slightly larger than females, but both have the same red-brown body colouring and whitish feathered legs. Feeding primarily on heather shoots, supplemented by berries, grasses, rushes, seed and grit, they are only present in significant numbers on heather dominated uplands. The total breeding population is now possibly less than half a million pairs, but it is still present throughout Scotland, northern England, Wales and Ireland, and in small numbers on Dartmoor and Exmoor.

Like many northern species such as lemmings, the numbers of Red Grouse fluctuate fairly regularly over a period of years. This natural cycle is less obvious in Britain, where numbers in local populations can be greatly influenced by heather management. With a growing interest in grouse shooting in the nineteenth century, more and more of the uplands became subjected to controlled burning regimes to provide grouse moors. Practical experience, reinforced more recently by research, has shown that excellent conditions are provided by a mosaic of strips of burnt heather alternating with unburnt stretches. The older, deeper, unburnt heather offers cover and nest sites and the three to four year old heather provides the nutritious young green shoots so important as food. The highest numbers of grouse are to be found on well managed heather moors on lime-rich soils.

The Red Grouse is sedentary and strictly territorial and the numbers of pairs in an area are finally determined by the number of territory-holding males. Individuals failing to establish territories in the autumn are forced to move to the less suitable peripheral areas where food and cover are poorer. Many will perish from disease and starvation or through predation by Golden Eagles and Peregrine Falcons, which direct their attention to these disadvantaged birds.

During February and March territory-holding males display, fanning their tails over their backs and springing from the ground calling 'go-back back back'. Nests are built by the females which hollow out a clump of heather and then line the cup with grass. During April and May the six to eleven eggs, heavily mottled with dark chocolate colour, are laid and incubated for twenty-one to twenty-six days by the female which sits very tight.

Incubation lasts just over three weeks, during which time both birds remain quiet and unobtrusive. The young leave the nest immediately after hatching to be tended by both parents and can flutter over short distances within two weeks. Should a family be disturbed at this stage, the sudden scattering of the young and the injury feigning of the adults can prove highly effective in confusing enemies. During autumn and winter family parties will frequently form into flocks.

PREDATORS

The Short-eared Owl, Merlin and Hen Harrier range widely over the moors and to a considerable extent co-exist in the habitat. They differ in their selection of prey and hunting techniques and so remain ecologically distinct. Merlins feed almost exclusively on small birds taken in flight, Short-eared Owls specialize in small mammals, the short-tailed vole predominating in the diet, while the Hen Harrier, the least specialized, takes both birds and mammals and small numbers of reptiles in wide-ranging low level aerial forays.

The **Short-eared Owl** is the most numerous and easily seen of the three upland birds of prey and in contrast to other large British owls regularly hunts in daylight, especially during the early evening. (In spells of hard weather or when feeding young, the smaller and whiter Barn Owl will hunt in daylight). A large (38cm), light brown, heavily streaked bird, paler beneath, it is characterized by long narrow wings and a buoyant flight. For beginners confusion is only likely between it and a female Hen Harrier in flight, but the prominent white rump and longer tail and more hawk-like appearance of the latter readily distinguish the two.

Small mammals tend to be more numerous in deeper patches of old heather and amongst large tussocks in old grazings or along forest and field edges and track verges and it is in such places that the owls are to be found, flying low over the ground with steady beats interspersed with gliding, and sweeping methodically back and forth. At frequent intervals they well perch on posts, walls and boulders and peer intently into the nearby vegetation before catching prey in their talons with a short headlong dive.

The display, principally by the males, generally takes place during March. It is most dramatic and reveals powers of flight not normally associated with owls. A good time to observe it is early on a warm still evening when it may last for fifteen minutes or more as the bird circles over a wide area of moor. Flapping slowly or gliding, it will vary its height and from time to time tumble in mid-air and clap its wings. Every now and then it will rise to a considerable height before falling dramatically, almost to the ground. After a fall it may utter its soft 'boo boo boo' song call.

Short-eared Owl (wing-clapping display)

The nest is a simple scrape in ground vegetation and the incubating female sits tight while the male brings her food. During much of the time the young are in the nest, the male will continue to do the major share of the hunting, providing food for the female to feed to the young. The dull white eggs hatch in about a month, usually early in June, and after a fortnight the young may retreat into temporary dens formed in the vegetation adjoining the nest. They fly when about a month old.

The normal clutch is four to eight, but in vole plague years up to fourteen have been recorded and many pairs rear two broods. In some areas young owls suffer from fox predation, although parent owls will mob human intruders. During winter the moors will be deserted while the birds occupy lowland farmland and coastal regions. The total British breeding population is between 1,000 and 10,000 pairs and is supplemented by continental winter immigrants. Winter daytime roosts containing several birds are not uncommon.

The **Merlin** is much the smallest British raptor, the smaller male (27cm) being no bigger than a Mistle Thrush. In the field, because of its strong flight and long wings and tail it appears larger than it really is. Generally Merlins remain unobtrusive and, particularly during the breeding season, are difficult to find or see except when in pursuit of prey or with newly fledged young in the vicinity of the nest. Males are slate-blue above and have streaked underparts (contrasting with the barring of the similar male Sparrow-Hawk). Females and juveniles are dark brown above with boldly streaked underparts.

Merlin

Outside the breeding season they will occupy lowland farmland, choosing coastal plains adjoining saltmarsh where they will harry flocks of finches, bunting, larks and pipits. In winter the British population is supplemented by continental immigrants. Their hunting technique is distinct from that of the high circling and hovering of the Kestrel or the short, surprise dash from cover of the Sparrow Hawk or the high stoop of the Peregrine. Merlins favour open ground and a hard, swift, direct pursuit, usually close to the ground. The selected prey is closely followed with every climb, dive, twist and turn being matched, until the victim is finally snatched while still in full flight. The rapidity and spectacular nature of the chase makes it difficult to follow. The Merlin's aerial skills no doubt account for the continuing popularity of this species with falconers.

In early spring pairs will return to traditional nesting territories on the fells. Open heather is preferred and the nest, a mere scrape in the peat, is hidden in deep, leggy heather. The site is often on the sloping side of a valley or near the summit of a lower fell ridge. On occasions old crow nests in hawthorn bushes or trees are used with equal success. The display is unspectacular, males making short flights between prominent boulders within the territory occasionally calling 'quek-ek-ek'. At times the pair will circle overhead and they can be aggressive in defence of their territory, boldly attacking, often as a pair, birds up to the size of Buzzards, Ravens and even Golden Eagles. The four to six boldly marked, rich, red eggs are laid in early May and hatch after thirty days. Females sit tight, often not leaving until an intruder is only a few paces away. Throughout the month the young are in the nest the male does most of the hunting. Prey is brought to a nearby plucking site for collection by the female which then feeds the young.

The British Merlin population has declined in recent years, although precise information is lacking, and is now thought to be under 1,000 pairs. Up to twenty-five years ago breeding pairs were extensively persecuted on grouse moors and during the autumn passage they proved particularly vulnerable to cage traps baited with live sparrows, commonly used by lowland keepers. Following stiffer legislation and a more enlightened attitude, persecution has lessened and loss of their moorland habitat to afforestation, overgrazing and excessive burning is now the principal factor controlling their numbers and distribution.

The re-establishment of the **Hen Harrier** as a breeding bird on the mainland of Britain during the 1950s is a conservation success. Two hundred years ago it was widespread in Britain; then fierce persecution by game preservers, coupled with the loss of lowland heaths and marginal land to more intensive agriculture, brought about its demise. Significant numbers of breeding birds remained only in Orkney. Here, in the absence of game interests and through the efforts of a small group of Orcadians, it survived and eventually flourished. A reduction of keepering on the mainland during the war and a more generally tolerant attitude towards birds of prey and better legislation helped its return. The colonizing birds, presumably from Orkney and possibly also Norway, benefited also from large areas of young conifer plantations which provided suitable, safe nesting sites. Breeding has now been confirmed as far south as Wales and the mainland population has probably reached 750 pairs. Regrettably it is still heavily persecuted and this, coupled with the loss of moorland to mature pine plantations which, unlike the younger stages, are unsuitable as breeding or hunting areas, means that its future remains uncertain.

Because of their large size (43–51cm) and characteristic sailing flight, confusion is only likely with the extremely rare Montagu's Harrier and, for the females, with the Marsh Harrier. The distinctive white rump (ring-tail as it is known), of the immature and female Hen Harrier contrasts with the all brown upper parts of the Marsh Harrier, which in any case is not a bird of the moors. The differences between the Hen and Montagu's Harriers are slight and reference should be made to a field guide. A hunting Hen Harrier ranges widely, quartering over open ground at low level. Prey is surprised and pounced on and small birds snatched when flushed out. Harriers rarely engage in aerial pursuit of flying prey. During winter they move south to lowland farmland, heaths, commons and coastal marshes. Communal roosts in boggy or heathy areas are used with up to twenty or more birds arriving independently at dusk to drop into the heather or rushes.

Nests are sited in flat tracts of boggy ground on moorland, in deep heather or in tussocky vegetation in young plantations and forest rides. Colonial nesting can occur with several nests within a limited area. Early in the season the dramatic sky-diving display is started. Both sexes do this, although more commonly it will be the male. The bird rises and falls in a series of undulating switchbacks, rolling or looping at the bottom and top. The purpose is to claim a territory and attract a mate and this display, coupled with the food pass, confirms occupation of a breeding site. Females tend to predominate in breeding areas and males are promiscuous, so observations of display alone do not necessarily indicate nest numbers.

The three to eight pale blue eggs are generally laid during May in a shallow, grass-lined nest and incubated for about thirty days. The male brings food in its talons to the vicinity of the nest, to be joined in mid-air by the female for the food pass. For this she approaches from below and flips over to catch the food as the male drops it or else takes it from the male's claws. Incubation begins with the first or second egg so the young hatch at intervals and in times of food shortage the smaller perish or are killed by the larger ones. Females are vigorous in defence of the nest and young, diving at humans, sheep and other intruders. The young take their first flight after about five weeks.

CLIFFS

The vertical, largely bare rock faces scarring at intervals the rounded moorland landscape and skirting the summits of the higher mountains, provide a vital refuge for three characteristic upland species - the Raven, Peregrine and Golden Eagle. The more remote and inaccessible they are, the greater the value of these places as nesting and roosting sites. Cliffs provide little food, so the birds range out over the nearby moorland to feed. In areas where high cliffs are infrequent, all three species, but most strongly Peregrine and Raven, regularly compete for cliff space to an extent thay they will use the same ledge as a nest site. Interspecific aerial combats are frequent and in different years it is impossible to predict which species will be in occupation of any section of cliff. It is a commonplace on many cliffs to find a Raven nesting within a few hundred metres of a pair of Peregrines. Eagles and Peregrines, however, rarely nest in close proximity. Hunting techniques are different so this interspecific competition for nest sites does not extend to the same extent to the feeding grounds.

Although all black, its larger size (64cm) and heavier bill distinguish the **Raven** from the Carrion Crow. Further aids to its identification include a large, wedge-shaped tail, a deep, far carrying croak 'pruck pruck' and flight aerobatics, involving rolling, dropping and flying upside down. Its history in the British Isles parallels that of the

Raven

Buzzard – initially breeding in every county then, following severe persecution by game interests, being eventually reduced to limited numbers confined to the western uplands. It is still persecuted, but to a lesser degree, by some shepherds, hill farmers and gamekeepers and its eggs still attract collectors. In spite of this, it has recovered some of its former range and, like the Buzzard, is now generally distributed throughout Scotland, Wales, the Lake District, northern Pennines and south-west England. It is omnivorous in its diet and, like the Carrion Crow, sheep carrion, in particular the placenta left by the lambing ewe, insects and soil invertebrates provide the staple diet. It will also take eggs and young of the larger ground nesting waders and gamebirds. In many upland areas its presence is dependent on sheep farming and where this has been replaced by afforestation the Ravens have gone or dropped in number. The present total population for the British Isles is about 5,000 pairs.

Breeding pairs remain together, possibly for life, and are strongly territorial. Where plentiful, immature birds and those not in territories will form flocks and feed communally. Territory-holding birds find food by brief aerial forays or by watching from crag tops, trees and boulders. They do not soar like Buzzards or quarter the ground methodically like harriers and owls, although as part of their display or when in thermals they will sail and circle for protracted spells. During high flights the shorter and more pointed shape of the wings is clearly seen. Nesting starts early in the year and eggs are sometimes laid in February, although most are laid during March. The pair indulge in aerial display flights and together build the nest. Most commonly sited in vertical fissures or on ledges on large, open cliffs, the nests are large, composed of substantial sticks with a deep earth cup lined with moss and hair. Trees, quarries, old mine buildings and chimneys, railway viaducts and sea cliffs are also used. In the uplands most are found between 350 and 450 metres and only rarely do they occur above 600 metres. They are single brooded but will repeat if a first clutch fails at an early stage.

The eggs are blue-green and the clutch varies from two to six. The same section of cliff face and even the same nest may be used for several years in succession by a pair, or they may use several alternate sites in successive seasons in different parts of the territory. Incubation is by the female which is fed by the male, and lasts for three weeks. The young, at first naked and blind, are brooded by the female, but later both parents hunt and bring food in their bills and throat pouches to the nest. The young leave the nest at about six weeks of age and the family remains together for a short period once they are on the wing.

The **Peregrine** is the largest British breeding falcon and the female (48cm) is larger than the male (38cm). Its flight is strong and powerful with typically a series of quick wing beats followed by a glide. The long pointed wings and shortish pointed tail are distinctive as it circles or hangs on motionless wings, often at great heights. When perched, most commonly on rock pinnacles, boulders or ledges, the stance is upright and the blue-grey back and heavily barred underparts distinguish it from all other raptors. Its powers of flight are most dramatically demonstrated in its hunting technique. A Peregrine will tower aloft over flying prey before stooping onto it in mid-air, striking or grabbing with its claws before the victim has time to dive to cover on the ground.

There are few species of bird of any size that have not been recorded as prey. This wide range of prey species is shared by few other birds of prey, and helps to ensure a constant food supply for local populations of Peregrines which as a consequence remain remarkably stable from season to season.

A breeding pair requires an extensive hunting area and high, vertical cliffs for the nest. The major populations have by necessity, therefore, been located in the uplands and on the sea cliffs of Scotland, Wales and southern England. During the last two centuries, the British population has probably not risen much above 1,000 pairs, but through Man's action it has at times been reduced below this. In the nineteenth century, like other birds of prey, it suffered continuous persecution from game interests which resulted in many territories remaining empty. In some places persistent stealing of eggs or young over long periods affected breeding success. A temporary reduction was achieved by deliberate shooting during World War II to lessen their predation on carrier pigeons. After the war a satisfactory recovery from this control was interrupted by a sudden and extensive population crash. This reached a climax in the early 1960s, by which time most of the English, Welsh and southern Scottish populations had been wiped out and a high proportion of the surviving pairs were failing to breed. The cause was confirmed to be certain persistent organochlorine pesticides. Subsequently use of these pesticides was reduced and by 1980 the British population had recovered to about three-quarters of the pre-war level.

In winter some Peregrines, especially northern birds, move to southern coasts and estuaries, while others will remain as pairs or singles in their old territory. By February, preparation for breeding becomes evident, and pairs roost and hunt together and later indulge in aerial and ledge display, including food exchanges. A nest is not built, the eggs being laid in a scrape on a ledge or in an old Raven, Buzzard and occasionally an old Eagle nest. The same site may be used year after year or alternatives selected in different parts of the territory.

The typical clutch is three or four and most are laid in April. Incubation, which lasts a month, is shared, the female undertaking the larger part to enable the male to hunt and bring food. The eggs hatch synchronously, so there is equal opportunity for survival in a brood. The small young are guarded, fed and brooded by the female, which only later helps the male in hunting. It takes five to six weeks before the young are on the wing and then for a short period they remain in the vicinity of the nest before wandering further afield. In contrast to the parents, the young are dark brown above and have streaked buff underparts.

The **Golden Eagle** is usually the dominant bird of cliffs. It is well adapted to survive in harsh montainous conditions, breeding at greater elevations (although rarely at altitudes of over 600 metres) and in more

Golden Eagle

northerly conditions than the Peregrine, Raven or Buzzard. In competition with them for nest sites it is invariably successful. Breeding frequently starts in conditions of snow and ice. With a body length of 76–89cm and wing span of about 1.8 metres it is much the largest bird of prey. In appearance the sexes are alike in their uniform dark brown plumage with the nape and sides of the neck a pale golden buff (from which its name derives). The female is slightly larger than the male and both have the massive curved bill. The broad wings and wide-spread, upturned primaries can lead to confusion with the Buzzard but the head of the Eagle projects further in front of the wings and both wings and tail are larger and even at long range the flight of the Eagle gives an impression of size and power not apparent in the Buzzard.

The total British population probably now lies between 200 and 300 pairs, most of which are in the Highlands. A small number of pairs breed in south-west Scotland and in most years two pairs attempt to breed in the Lake District. Prior to persecution in the eighteenth and nineteenth centuries, the Golden Eagle also bred in Ireland, Wales and elsewhere in England. While it suffered severely on grouse moors, it was tolerated in deer forests and this probably helped its survival. Later it benefited from a more enlightened attitude, hence its modest southerly extension of range, but it is still persecuted and its eggs still collected.

Breeding begins in late March, the first sign often being an 'advertisement' flight by the male soaring over the territory which may cover thousands of hectares. Mutual display flighting follows and the pair soar together in spirals, mewing. Tremendous heights are reached in these flights which are interrupted by successions of headlong dives with half closed wings, ending in an upland sweep. The nest can be on a ledge or in a tree and usually several traditional alternatives within the territory are used in successive seasons. New nests are often small but those in favoured sites can reach a diameter of 1.5 metres by the annual addition of material.

Incubation is by both sexes and lasts six weeks; they are single brooded but will sometimes re-lay if the first clutch is lost. The normal clutch is two, the second egg being laid three or four days after the first, resulting in young of different ages. In times of stress, usually food shortage, only one survives. The nestlings, initially covered in pale grey down, remain in the nest for about ten weeks, but then linger in the vicinity for a further two or three weeks. At first food is brought to the nest by the male, dismembered by the female and fed to the young but later the female will help with the hunting. A variety of food is taken including deer and sheep carrion, large and small mammals and large birds. Open ground is required for hunting and with maximum use of air currents the Golden Eagle can soar for long periods. Live prey, such as mountain hare, is pursued with remarkable agility at low level following a stoop and it can dive expertly onto Ptarmigan and take birds in flight.

Two other species commonly found on cliffs are Jackdaw and Rock Dove. As these tend to occur in greater numbers and are easier to see on sea cliffs, they have been discussed in that section (page 73).

GULLEYS AND RAVINES

At irregular intervals, moorland is dissected by narrow, steep-sided gulleys and ravines cut by streams out of the underlying rock. Their boulder-strewn floors and precipitous unstable flanks are unattractive to sheep and in the absence of grazing they are frequently overgrown with grasses, ferns and trees. Four upland species – Ring Ousel, Grey Wagtail, Dipper and Common Sandpiper – favour these sites. While the Ring Ousel is frequently present in gulleys containing streams, it is not dependent on running water and also occupies dry ravines, clefts in the cliff face and sink holes. The other three are dependent on running water.

The Grey Wagtail, the most adaptable of the three, is found at high altitudes on very small streams while also occurring on reservoirs and canals in lowland areas. The Dipper and Sandpiper require larger streams where they often co-exist and both can be found well down the valley where the streams have broadened into fast flowing, boulder strewn rivers. The Common Sandpiper will also breed on lake shores and in estuaries, but the main populations of both are at altitudes above 300 metres. The feeding techniques of the three differ, the Dipper feeding under water on the stream bed, the Sandpiper probing at the stream sides and the Grey Wagtail taking insects in flight, from streamside vegetation and from the water surface.

In size (24cm) and general appearance, the **Ring Ousel** resembles the common Blackbird, the outstanding difference being the white crescent across the top of the Ring Ousel's breast. The female is browner with a paler crescent and the crescent is entirely lacking in the juveniles. The flight is strong and direct as it travels swiftly along ravines and gulleys, skimming low over the vegetation before perching boldly on a boulder, wall or post. It has a penetrating whistle and a sharp 'clack-clack' alarm note. The diet includes flies, moths, butterflies and other insects and their larvae, worms and later, in season, blackberry and other fruits and berries of rowan, hawthorn, sloe, and ivy. When feeding it works its way methodically through the vegetation, diligently searching the soil, roots and leaves, stabbing at intervals with its short, sharp, yellow bill.

Ring Ousel

It is very much a bird of mountain and moorland. Most nest between 350–650 metres and in some parts of the Highlands they will be found as high as 1,000 metres, although small numbers also nest on sea cliffs at much lower levels. It is migratory, spending the winter in southern Europe and North Africa, and arrives in Britain between mid-March and April. Nesting starts shortly after arrival in the uplands and the first eggs are laid late in April. During display the pair face each other, the male exhibiting the white crescent. The males have a rather quiet but far-carrying song, comprising melodious piping and chuckles, uttered from different song points on boulders and outcrops within the territory. The nest, built by both birds, is made of grass and hidden on a rock ledge or heather slope, with artifical sites in quarries, old mine shafts and buildings not uncommon. The typical clutch is four and many pairs are double brooded, second clutches being laid in June or early July. Incubation and fledging each last about two weeks, the female often starting the second clutch while the male looks after the first brood. The return migration south starts in August and continues to September.

The status of the Ring Ousel in the British Isles has probably not changed very markedly, although there has been a slow, long term decline, most evident in Ireland and Scotland. In some areas this can be attributed to loss of habitat, but the decrease is more widespread than can be fully explained in this way. Greater competition between it and the Blackbird caused by improvement in the climate has been suggested as an alternative explanation. The present total breeding population of the British Isles is between 8,000 and 16,000 pairs.

The **Grey Wagtail** (18cm) is a typical wagtail in appearance, with short legs, short, slim bill, slender body and very long tail. The flight is undulating and the tail bobs up and down almost continuously. Invariably noisy and actively conspicuous, it flies low along the stream or perches on a stone in it. Its grey back and bright lemon underparts and its sharp, distinctive 'tzissick' call distinguish it from the other wagtails. Males have a black throat. Food includes insects, their larvae, water beetles, molluscs and crustaceans.

Pairs are territorial, occupying stretches of a stream or river,

Grey Wagtail

45

frequently with adjoining territories when fights between neighbouring pairs will be common and spectacular. In display the male makes slow flights from perch to perch, flicking its wings and splaying its tail. The first clutch, typically four to six eggs, is laid in late April or early May, to be followed by second and sometimes third clutches. The open nest of moss and grass is sited amongst rocks, on a ledge, in tree roots or the ivy of the trunk and sometimes in the old nest of a Dipper. They are usually at or very close to the water's edge. Both sexes share incubation which lasts for two weeks and then share the feeding of the young for twelve days before fledging, bringing food to the nest in their bills.

In winter some remain in, or close to, their breeding sites; many will move south to lower altitudes in southern Britain, while others migrate to France and Iberia. During periods of severe weather when rivers and lakes freeze over, there is a movement to the coast. The total breeding population of the British Isles is between 25,000 and 50,000 pairs, similar to that of the Common Sandpiper and somewhat greater then that of the Dipper.

The **Dipper**, with its plump rounded appearance, short tail and brilliant white throat and breast contrasting with the dark brown of the remainder of its plumage, is unmistakable. It is confined to streams and is most usually to be seen on a boulder in mid-stream or flying strongly in direct flight low across the water. Its body length is 18cm. The food includes aquatic insects and their larvae, molluscs, crustaceans and small fish. These are obtained by the bird walking, partially sub-

Dipper

merged, in the shallows and rapids or by plunging into pools where, using its wings and feet, it travels along the stream bed. When perched it has a habit of bobbing up and down and the white third eyelid is often evident as it flicks sideways across the eye, presumably clearing it of excess water.

The nest, which is built by both birds during February and March, is domed and formed from moss and grass in a steep bank, rock face, in tree roots or under a bridge, but always with the nest opening near water. The three to six white eggs are laid in March and April and incubated by the female for sixteen days. The young leave the nest after about three and a half weeks and some pairs are double brooded. Each pair will occupy a length of stream which can vary, depending on the quality of the stream, from a half to three kilometres in length. These territories are held throughout the year and in exceptionally severe winters when streams and ditches freeze over there can be high mortality. Territories are common at altitudes up to 600 metres and some go as high as 1,000 metres. Breeding display begins from January onwards and includes wing shivering, bowing and high flights and song. The young have the white breast but otherwise are sooty grey. Roosting outside the breeding season is amongst rocks, on ledges or in crevices under bridges. Apart from minor fluctuations related to bad weather conditions, the British population remains constant and probably now numbers above 30,000 pairs.

Unlike the Dipper, the **Common Sandpiper** is migratory. Although a very small number have recently started to winter in Britain, the main British breeding population arrives from Africa at the end of March and in early April. Small numbers nest on estuaries and lowland lakes, but most will occupy upland areas at altitudes up to 500 metres with some in the Highlands as high as 800 metres. The return movement begins early in July.

A slim wader, (20cm) with long legs and long, fine, straight bill, its brown-grey upper parts are undistinguished, but contrast with the white underparts. It is most readily recognized by its behaviour, in particular persistent tail bobbing and a distinctive flight low over the water, with a series of wing beats interspersed with glides on down-curved stiff wings. When disturbed, it usually utters the shrill 'twee-wee-wee' rippling alarm note. It perches freely on stones, walls, stumps and branches and frequently bobs its head up and down.

The food is principally aquatic invertebrates, including insects, spiders, molluscs and crustaceans which it picks off rocks, shingle and mudbanks. It will wade at the water's edge and in shallow rapids and stalks flies with outstretched neck. More open conditions are preferred and narrow, densely vegetated, steep-sided torrents avoided. Typically a pair will establish a territory along a one to two kilometre stretch of a stream or river, although in many areas where conditions are less favourable, territories of much greater length are taken up. The total breeding population of the British Isles is bigger than that of the Dipper and possibly exceeds 50,000 pairs.

Display begins shortly after arrival in the breeding areas, the males circling in rapid flight and often rising to high altitudes and ground and aerial chases involving both sexes are common. Although the birds are waterside feeders, the nests are not uncommonly located some distance from the water's edge, often in deep vegetation near trees or in bracken and heather. Unlike that of most upland waders, the nest will be hidden deep in the vegetation and both sexes sit tight during incubation which lasts for three to three and a half weeks. The typical clutch is four eggs, laid in May or early June. The young become active soon after hatching and are tended by both parents which display great agitation if the nestlings are endangered. They are able to fly within two or three weeks, but remain as a family for some time after this.

THE MONTANE ZONE

Above the moors and cliffs on the stony slopes and mountain summits lies the exposed montane zone of arctic alpine heath. Frequently swept by icy winds and rain, often buried in the mist, through most of the winter and sometimes well into summer much of it lies blanketed in snow. The vegetation of lichens, dwarf willows, crowberry and short heather is thin and sparse on the stony ground. The Ptarmigan is the only numerous bird to inhabit this zone throughout the year. Most live over 800 metres and some as high as 1,200 metres. There are two other species, the Dotterel and Snow Bunting, both rare, that breed in small numbers in a few areas at similar altitudes. The three species are very different and have no links with each other apart from their toleration of montane conditions.

The **Ptarmigan** (35cm) is grouse-like in appearance and flight. During winter it is almost pure white, and at other times is a mottled brown and black, although the wings and underparts remain white and stand out. It is the only British bird to turn white in winter. Males and females can be separated by their coloration, males being greyer and females more golden. They make the maximum use of the limited food available, including in their diet the leaves, stems, shoots, flowers, seeds and berries of plants. During summer, when feeding takes place primarily in the early morning and late afternoon, heather, blaeberry and crowberry will form the principal food items.

March and April are the months of peak territorial courtship activity. Like the Red Grouse, Ptarmigans are territorial and individuals failing to establish territories are forced to the less suitable peripheral areas where they may form flocks and become vulnerable to predation by foxes and Golden Eagles. Aerial and ground chases are frequent as males prominently display themselves on boulders in

Ptarmigan

different parts of the territory. The nest is a hollow scrape, sparsely lined with grass, in short vegetation or amongst stones often sheltered by a rock. The typical clutch is six to ten, laid in May or early June, with smaller clutches in poor springs. With the male on guard, the

Snow Bunting

49

female sits tight, perfectly camouflaged amongst the rocks and vegetation. The eggs hatch in just under a month, the black striped chicks initially being cared for by the female as the males form temporary flocks during the final stages of incubation. Later they join family parties which will remain together until the autumn. They then disperse to form large winter flocks which can contain over 100 individuals. Ptarmigan are largely restricted to the summits of the west and central Highlands and the total breeding population is probably under 10,000 paris.

Less than 100 pairs of **Dotterel** nest in Britain and most of these are in the Highlands with only small varying numbers of scattered pairs in south-west Scotland, the Lake District and north Wales. A small (22cm) wading bird, with a chestnut lower breast and black belly, they are migratory and arrive on the breeding grounds in early May, where males, less brightly coloured than the females, incubate the eggs. The **Snow Bunting** is even less numerous with under twenty pairs confined to the Highlands. Finch-like in size and shape, the breeding males are unmistakable in their black and white plumage.

UPLAND LAKES

The combination of landform and high precipitation produces a variety of water bodies in the uplands. These range from large deep lakes or lochs in the valleys, through shallow tarns and smaller lakes to small lochans and moor pools, often at considerable altitudes. In addition there are the flows and bogs on the plateaux, many of which contain large numbers of pools of varying depths and sizes, sometimes extending over vast areas. Together these provide an important and special element of the upland habitat, of particular importance as breeding sites for seven aquatic species – the Common Gull, Goosander, Red-breasted Merganser, Red-throated and Black-throated Divers, Greylag goose and Wigeon duck.

With the exception of the Common Gull, all are relatively uncommon in Britain with breeding numbers under 3,000 pairs. Also, for all of them, the major part of their British breeding population is in northern Scotland. The Common Gull is omnivorous, the Greylag and Wigeon vegetarian, while the remaining four live on fish obtained by swimming under water. The fish feeders differ in their requirements and thereby reduce inter-specific competition. Of the similar Goosander and Merganser, the former predominates on rivers and smaller freshwater lakes inland, while many of the latter remain to breed in sea lochs and estuaries although they are also to be found on lochs in remote valleys and on the upper reaches of mountain rivers. Of the two divers, the Red-throated favours nest sites on smaller, shallow pools, while the Black-throated is usually restricted to larger, deeper lakes.

So, although all are dependent on aquatic upland sites, their association with each other and the habitat differs.

In its general appearance, the **Common Gull** is a middle-sized (41cm) grey-backed gull. Distinguishing features are its greenish-yellow legs and bill. Although less strongly associated with marine conditions than most gulls, it breeds in both coastal and upland sites. Its inland sites are on or near water, most at altitudes of about 500 metres, but some as high as 1,000 metres. Nests may be on heather slopes, lake shores or on islands in lakes and rivers and very occasionally in low bushes. Common Gulls rarely nest in large colonies and occasionally a pair may nest alone.

Common Gull

Returning to its breeding sites during February or early March, it lays the first eggs at the end of April. Display includes typical gull behaviour as pairs face each other on the ground and throw their heads back and call. The nest is a simple scrape in sand or shingle or in the heather, built up with grass until often quite substantial. The two to three blotched, olive eggs are well camouflaged and incubated by both sexes for about three and a half weeks. The young, also well camouflaged with black-brown blotches on buff down, are fed by both parents and fledge in about five weeks. Food includes small fish, worms, seeds, crustaceans and molluscs and occasional eggs or young of other species. Food is sought by low flight or walking and searching.

The British breeding population is almost certainly increasing, particularly in Scotland, and is estimated at about 50,000 pairs. It is still absent from most of England and Wales, but is now distributed throughout much of southern Scotland. The largest established English outpost is at Dungeness in Kent where it first bred in 1919 and there are several pairs around the coast of Anglesey in north Wales. Many more winter in Britain than breed here and there are large numbers of immigrants from Scandinavia.

Several other gull species breed in the uplands but have been considered under different habitats. The Black-headed Gull, which has the widest inland breeding distribution of any gull in Britain, is not uncommon up to altitudes of 700 metres on small tarns and large bog pools. There are also colonies, a few extremely large and containing thousands of pairs, of Herring and Lesser Black-backed Gulls in the Pennines and Scottish hills. At one time these were more numerous and would be again were it not for pesecution. These upland sites represent only a small fraction of the total British breeding population, the great majority nesting on the coasts.

The Red-breasted Merganser and Goosander are adapted to swimming under water and are very similar in general appearance. Considerable care is needed, particularly with the females and juveniles, to distinguish them in the field. They belong to a group popularly referred to as sawbills. The name derives from the slender, tapering, rather long bill, which has backward sloping, teeth-like serrations and a hooked tip to facilitate catching and holding live fish. Slender in appearance, they fly like ducks with outstretched neck. They will fly high, but more often remain low over the surface and the wings, which have noticeable white patches, make a hum or whistle. They sit rather low in the water and are sociable.

The male **Red-breasted Merganser** (58cm) has a red bill, bottle-green head, white collar, chestnut breast and black back. The female has a chestnut head and brownish-grey upper parts. Both have a crest that divides into two prominent tufts at the back of the head. During the eclipse moult from May to September the juvenile and male resemble the female. Winter is spent on the sea in flocks along the coast and in estuaries. The greater part of the population remains to nest near the coast, but during April and May considerable numbers fly inland to breed on small lochs, rivers and streams in remote upland glens. Display and sometimes pairing often occurs while they are still on the sea. The male will approach a female with head held up at a steep angle, opening the bill wide to display the red mouth. The head and neck are then held straight out and the wings flapped to display the white markings.

Nests are on the ground in long grass or heather, under gorse or bramble bushes or amongst tree roots and occasionally down rabbit burrows. They are lined with down and the seven to twelve eggs laid towards the end of May and in June. Incubation, which lasts for four-and-a-half weeks, is by the female, the male remaining absent. Where there are several males in close proximity, they will sometimes gather in flocks, but will rejoin the females later to help tend the young. After hatching, the young take to water, often having to travel a considerable distance, and initially are tended by the female alone. Neighbouring broods sometimes unite to form nursery flocks and the young fly after about eight weeks. They are single brooded. Fish makes up over three-quarters of the diet which includes a wide range of marine and freshwater species with crustaceans and worms. They sink quickly but smoothly to swim under water and usually remain submerged for about half a minute.

The British population is increasing steadily and now totals about 2,000 pairs. Most are in west Scotland, but small numbers are distributed widely across northern and south-west Scotland. Breeding started in the Lake District and Wales during the 1950s. In some parts of Scotland the Merganser is still persecuted by fishing interests because it takes young salmon and trout.

While the Red-breasted Merganser has certainly been present in Britain for many centuries, the **Goosander** by contrast is a recent immigrant, breeding for the first time in Britain in Perthshire in 1871. Since then, despite persecution by fishing interests, it has continued to increase and spread and the British population has now probably passed 1,000 pairs. The major part of the population is in Scotland with small numbers in the Lake District and Northumbria. It bred for the first time in Wales in the '60s. The male has a bottle-green head and white breast and sides, the female a chestnut head, grey back and flanks and both have a red bill and a mane-like hanging crest. Body length is 66cm. The juvenile and male in eclipse resemble the female. As with the Red-breasted Merganser, fish forms the major part of the diet and they hunt and catch them using the same technique.

Although less marine than the Red-breasted Merganser, some winter at sea in flocks and in mid-April will move inland to lochs and rivers. These may be adjacent to well wooded areas, have only scattered trees or adjoin open treeless fells. Display includes rapid stretching of the head and neck, bill gaping, wing flapping and rising upright in the water with head tossing. The nest is not infrequently in a tree hole or rabbit burrow or under cover amongst boulders or deep vegetation. (In Sweden and elsewhere they have been successfully attracted to nest-boxes). A paucity of nest material is compensated for by plenty of down. The seven to thirteen eggs are incubated by the female, the male remaining elsewhere, possibly having joined other males in a flock. After about five weeks the eggs hatch and the female leads the young to the feeding area. Fledging takes five weeks.

Divers are highly adapted for swimming under water and rarely come onto land except to breed. Their movement on land is slow and clumsy, and frequently they simply drag themselves over the ground.

They have an almost tailless, bulky body with long, stout neck and pointed bill and tend to remain on open water and avoid danger by diving. They can fly strongly and will go high. Flight is direct with regular rapid beats and they have a hunchbacked appearance because of a slight down curve of the neck and set-back, small, pointed wings. To land they plane down swiftly and come down heavily, breast foremost, making a considerable splash. When fishing, they will sink quickly without splashing and frequently remain submerged for over a minute. A common form of fishing is a series of underwater swims separated by only a short emergence. The food is primarily fish, including a wide range of marine and freshwater species, supplemented by crustaceans.

The **Red-throated Diver** is the commoner of the two in Britain, and has a total breeding population of between 750 and 1,000 pairs. The sexes are alike and in breeding plumage have a uniform grey-brown back, grey head and red throat. It is a more slender and smaller (53–58cm) bird than the Black-throated Diver and has a slightly upturned bill. In winter plumage it is dark grey-brown above with white cheeks, throat and underparts and is difficult to distinguish from the Black-throated Diver. The breeding range of both extends across north and down west Scotland with a marked difference in Shetland and Orkney where the Red-throated is common but the Black-throated absent. Small numbers of Red-throated Divers breed in Ireland, where the Black-throated is also absent. Its population is probably increasing slowly despite low breeding success. Much of the failure is attributed to human disturbance at the nest sites, which causes the birds to fly and leave the eggs unprotected to be predated by gulls and crows.

Winter is spent at sea and a return to the breeding grounds made during April and May. Nest sites are selected on small peat pools and lochans in remote hill and moorland regions. In contrast to the Black-throated Diver, the Red-throated is able to land and take off from surprisingly small, shallow pools and in extensive areas of blanket bog with large numbers of such pools, several pairs will nest in close proximity. Display includes diving chases, swimming one behind the other with arched necks, and two or more birds dashing across the water with the forepart of the body clear of the water and the neck held stiffly and bill inclined upwards. Their extraordinary 'Kwuk-kwuk-kwuk' call and a long drawn moan can be heard during the breeding season.

The nest is typically a hollow, rarely built up, formed in the vegetation close to the edge of a pool. The clutch of two olive-blotched eggs is laid in late May or early June and incubated for about a month by both sexes, the female taking on the larger share. Both parents will then tend and feed the young for about eight weeks. The adults find food by flying, often over considerable distances, to nearby large lakes and sea lochs. The juveniles join the adults on the sea to form winter flocks.

The **Black-throated Diver** (56–68cm) is larger than the Red-throated. In breeding plumage it can be distinguished by its grey head, black throat and the broad white bands on the back. The bill is black. In winter it closely resembles the Red-throated, being grey-brown above and white below and care and experience are needed to distinguish the two with confidence. The sexes are alike and the juveniles' plumage is similar to the adults' winter plumage. The total British breeding population is under 200 pairs and, with the exception of small numbers in south-west Scotland, these are confined to the north and west of Scotland and the Outer Hebrides. Its numbers and distribution have not changed greatly in recent years, although anxiety exists for the future because of reported low breeding success. Recent studies of sample populations have shown successful breeding by less than one-third of the pairs studied. The main loss was through nests being flooded.

Black-throated Diver

Winter is spent at sea, on estuaries or on large lakes near the coast and breeding takes place on the larger and deeper lochs in the hills. Breeding birds will arrive during April and usually there is only one pair on a loch. The most common site selected for the nest is a small island well away from the shore but occasionally a nest is built on the loch's edge. The nest is invariably only a few metres from the water, on a gradually sloping stretch of shore above water level. The risk from flooding is obvious, especially when nests are built beside unsuitable artificial water bodies which have frequent changes in water level.

Breeding starts early and the two dull, olive-green, blotched eggs are laid in late April or early May. Incubation lasts about a month so young may be seen on the water before the end of May. Both birds probably take part in incubation, the off-duty bird retiring to a distant part of the loch. The nest is simply a flattened hollow or slight scrape and after hatching the young will take to the water to be fed and tended for about eight or nine weeks by both parents. Fish make up the greater part of the diet. The birds have a 'kwuk-kwuk-kwuk' and wailing call similar to that of the Red-throated Diver and this is uttered when flying and when on the water.

The origin, present numbers and distribution of the **Greylag Goose** in Britain are difficult to disentangle. It is the only indigenous British goose but there is a lack of historical information, the surviving breeding population is widely scattered and difficult to census and there is uncertainty surrounding numerous attempts at reintroductions. In addition, some pairs are thought to have escaped from wildfowl collections and established themselves in the wild. In winter the British breeding population is supplemented by large numbers of immigrants, mostly from Iceland, with virtually the entire Icelandic breeding population, now comprising over 60,000 individuals, coming to Britain.

The present British breeding population is under 1,000 pairs. Some of these are direct descendants of a much larger British breeding population which at one time bred in many parts of Britain, including England and Ireland. Loss of habitat and persecution reduced their numbers until at most only a few hundred pairs survived in the Highlands and Hebrides. In the 1930s eggs and young taken from the Hebrides were successfully reintroduced in south-west Scotland and further reintroductions elsewhere followed. These, together with fuller protection of the Highland and Hebridean birds, have resulted in a recovery in numbers and distribution.

The Greylag is the largest of the geese to be found in Britain (76–89cm). The head is heavy, the bill orange and the legs pink. It is dark grey above and lighter grey below with a white abdomen and in flight the pale grey forewing and rump are noticeable. In winter they are sociable when feeding, roosting and flighting and they invariably fly in formation.

The wild Highland and Hebridean populations are active on their breeding sites by the end of February and the young hatch by early May. Breeding sites are well vegetated islands in lochs or heather surrounding moorland bogs. Display behaviour will include neck stretching with the head close to the ground and loud 'triumph' calls. They are aggressive to neighbouring pairs and other species in the vicinity. The nest is a hollow in the ground hidden under thick vegetation built up with grass and moss and lined with down. The four to nine creamy white eggs are laid in April and incubated for a month by the female with the male on guard nearby. If approached on the nest the female will sit with neck stretched forward on the ground. Both parents attend the young which are covered in grey-brown down, for about eight weeks. After breeding they assemble as families to moult, at which time they are flightless, and near the end of August will combine to form big flocks. Feral birds breed in a variety of freshwater sites which, in addition to natural lakes, include reservoirs, gravel pits and park lakes. Food includes grass, stubble and root crops such as potatoes and turnips and on water they will dip and up-end to obtain bottom weed.

The greater part of the world's population of the **Wigeon** breed in the north Palearctic. The small British population, numbering less than 500 pairs, represents a recently established south-westerly outpost. Breeding was first confirmed in 1834 in Sutherland, after which numbers slowly increased until now they remain relatively stable. Most of the British breeding birds are scattered through the Highlands. Small numbers breed in south Scotland and the Yorkshire Pennines with further scattered occasional records, possibly including birds that have escaped from wildfowl collections, further south. In winter large numbers of continental birds migrate to Britain and congregate in large flocks along muddy coasts and estuaries and low-lying flooded meadows inland.

A medium-sized duck (46–56cm), the male has a grey back and rufous head with a creamy crown. The female is a uniform rufous brown and in the eclipse moult, between June and September, the male resembles the female. The voice is a very distinct whistle 'whee-oo, whee-oo', and with a little experience is a good aid to the identification of distant birds. The diet is entirely vegetarian, in coastal regions mainly comprising eel-grass (zostera), seaweeds and saltmarsh grasses and seeds, which they uproot as they wade in shallow water. Inland they will graze watermeadows.

Many British Wigeon breed at high altitudes on moorland tarns, lochans, moor pools, in streams and upland rivers. Loch Leven, south of Perth, has the only large breeding colony at low altitude. In display, several males will gather round a female, constantly whistling and raising their crown feathers. Neck stretching with head close to the ground and then raising the wings high over the back follows. Small islands, stream banks and bracken and heather slopes close to water are favoured nest sites. The nest, several of which may be built in a relatively restricted area, is a hollow in the ground concealed in thick vegetation. It is lined with grass and down and the typical clutch is seven or eight cream-coloured eggs. First eggs are laid in early May and incubated by the female for twenty-five days. After hatching, the female takes the young to water where later they are joined by the male. Fledging takes about six weeks, after which the family will begin its southerly move to the wintering areas.

It may seem strange to end a review of the special birds associated with British Uplands by discussing a duck, but it illustrates clearly the importance of this habitat for a wide variety of species including small passerines, waterbirds, gamebirds and large predators. Despite their harshness and the loss of much of their natural cover, the Uplands are still of vital importance for many British bird populations. Most of these are thinly spread with individual breeding pairs requiring large areas for their existence and their future, in the face of increasing use of mountains and moorland for leisure and the continuing changes in upland agriculture and forestry, will depend on understanding and careful land-use planning.

·3·

The Sea Coast

The coastline of the British Isles is over 11,000 kilometres long. Because of its complex geology it is highly varied, ranging from cliffs towering out of the sea to heights of over 300 metres to gently shelving mudflats. Along many stretches it is highly indented with sea lochs, bays and estuaries and there are numerous offshore islands.

The shallow coastal waters above the continental shelves surrounding Britain are rich in nutrients. Many of these, such as nitrate and phosphate, are transported by rivers from inland regions. Once in the sea, tidal currents, storms and temperature differences ensure mixing and circulation with other nutrients to produce an abundant source of food to support the teeming plankton on which marine fish and seabirds ultimately depend. Whilst, therefore, the coast may present a narrow confined habitat when compared to an inland plain or group of mountains, its length, variation and proximity to rich feeding grounds enable it to support a wealth of life unequalled in other habitats.

CLIFFS

Seabirds are highly adapted to marine conditions and many spend much of the year away from land. Specialized for swimming and flying over the sea, they are often ill-suited to terrestrial conditions. They have to come ashore to breed, and steep cliffs, headlands and islands, close to deep water, offer suitable conditions. The advantages they provide include ease of landing and take-off, comparative safety for eggs and young, direct flight to feeding areas and ready access to the sea for newly fledged young.

Cliffs vary with the nature of the rock and the natural forces to which they have been subjected. Britain is fortunate in having many extensive stretches of sea cliffs and numerous steep-sided, flat-topped islands suitable for nesting seabirds. To attract nesting seabirds a cliff must be sufficiently high and steep to provide nesting sites out of reach of the waves and inaccessible to mammalian predators such as the fox, stoat and brown rat. Ledges must be firm and wide enough to hold nests and eggs. Certain species require vegetated stretches with enough soil to allow burrowing.

The variety of potential breeding sites on a cliff is considerable. The base may be strewn with fallen rocks offering nesting sites to species like the Black Guillemot between and under the boulders just out of reach of the sea. Elsewhere the lower faces may contain caves or wide vertical fissures into which the tide flows, protecting a hidden Shag colony. The main cliff face is invariably criss-crossed with ledges and vertical cracks, interspersed with vegetated patches in gulleys and on old scree slopes, attractive to a wide variety of species. Towards the cliff top come the grassy slopes on deeper soils into which Puffins can burrow and the bare plateaux on the summits of rocky stacks afford excellent conditions for the Common Guillemot. The cliff top and land immediately adjacent provide yet another interesting sub-division of habitat, subjected to on-shore winds and spray drift.

Gulls

There are six species of gull which breed regularly in Britain. Four of these, the Herring, Greater and Lesser Black-backed Gulls and Kittiwake, are primarily coastal nesters. The Common Gull, while also nesting on some coasts, commonly breeds on moorland and is discussed in the chapter on Upland Habitats (page 16) and the Black-headed Gull, which has the widest inland distribution, is discussed under the Freshwater Habitat (page 103). Of the four coastal breeders, the Kittiwake is almost exclusively a cliff nester. The other three are more adaptable and will use a variety of coastal sites including saltmarsh and sand dunes. They are also able to breed successfully inland and scattered, occasionally large, colonies still exist on moorland. Increasingly however they are being restricted to sea cliffs and islands to escape disturbance and persecution.

All four species will nest in the same locality, often in close proximity, but their selection of nest sites and food and feeding techniques differ, reducing competition. The Kittiwake prefers vertical faces and is a marine feeder taking small pelagic organisms. The Greater Black-backed prefers rocky prominences and in addition to taking large seafish will kill other species of seabirds. The Herring and Lesser Black-backed are more omnivorous, feeding at sea, on the beach and (more particularly the Herring Gull) inland. The Lesser Black-backed Gull commonly nests in groups on grassy slopes, while the Herring Gull may be widely scattered amongst the boulders and ledges on both rock or grass cliffs.

The **Kittiwake** is the most numerous British gull and almost exclusively restricted to the open sea and coast, only rarely venturing inland. Until the turn of the century, it was heavily persecuted but following protection has steadily increased and the British breeding population has now reached about 470,000 pairs. The main colonies are situated along the north sea coast, extending from Bempton in Yorkshire northwards to Orkney and Shetland. More scattered and usually smaller colonies are found along much of the west and south coast wherever suitable cliffs occur.

A medium-sized (41cm) grey-backed gull, distinguished by the plain black tips to the wing, black legs and lemon bill, it has a most distinctive call 'Kitti-w-a-a-k, kitti-w-a-a-k'. In contrast to other British gulls, the immature plumage is white and grey rather than brown and there is also a distinct black band across the neck and diagonally along the wing. Adult plumage is acquired after two years and the food comprises small marine fish and a variety of marine invertebrate species. It feeds by pecking from the surface while in low buoyant flight or when swimming and will also plunge dive or land and dive, occasionally going right under.

Prospective breeders may begin to visit the cliffs in late February and March and colonies are located on sheer faces with nests in close proximity. The nest is a substantial, neat cup, often built on a surprisingly narrow ledge or projection and both sexes will take part in nest building, the main material used being seaweed whilst the cup will be lined with grass and moss. Breeding activities within a colony are closely synchronized. During nest building, the steady arrival of birds with beakfuls of brown seaweed, or a stream of birds to a favoured cliff-top site to pluck grass, can be very striking. In several localities colonies have become established on the window ledges of old warehouses and other waterfront buildings.

When displaying, the pair face each other, calling and showing off the orange interior to the mouth, and indulge in bill touching, bowing and gulping. The typical clutch of two pale brown, black-blotched eggs is laid at the end of May or in June. Both sexes share the twenty-one to thirty-one days' incubation and feed the young for up to five weeks before fledging. Colonies will be vacated during August when the birds disperse for the winter.

The **Herring Gull** is the second most common gull in Britain and the best known by virtue of its wide distribution, sedentary habit and close association with Man in such places as docks and holiday resorts. It is a large (56–66cm) grey-backed bird, with pink legs, yellow bill and white tips to the black ends of its wings. Juveniles have a mottled brown plumage which is gradually replaced during the first three years of life by the white and grey adult plumage. The British breeding population is steadily increasing and now numbers approximately 300,000 pairs.

Most British Herring Gulls do not migrate, but disperse outside the breeding season to suitable feeding areas. The British population is, however, supplemented in winter by the immigration of more northerly breeding birds. Winter feeding sites will include fishing grounds out at sea, sandy, muddy and rocky coasts, harbours, seafront towns, inland lakes and reservoirs, farmland and refuse dumps. The variety of food taken reflects this wide range of sites. It includes live fish and fish offal, crabs, shrimps, molluscs, carrion and scraps from tips. Feeding technique includes swimming and pecking, shallow plunge diving and searching by walking or flying over tidelines and beaches. They will fly up to drop molluscs onto the beach to smash the shells, puddle wet sand to bring worms to the surface and during the breeding season predate the eggs and young of other sea and shore birds. Inland they prefer meadows and recently ploughed fields. They are gregarious and often feed, flight and roost in flocks.

Most will return to the breeding areas in February and March and, particularly when nesting on sand dunes, shingle banks and salt marshes, will form compact colonies. By contrast, pairs on cliffs are usually thinly dispersed over long stretches. During the last fifty years some have become a nuisance to Man by nesting on roofs and chimneystacks in seaside towns.

Breeding display, sometimes involving several males on a standing ground, includes grass pulling, head bobbing and lowering the head while making a low moaning call. In one particularly characteristic action the gull bows until the bill is between the legs, then throws the head back and with vertical bill utters a yelping 'aow aow aow'. Other calls include chattering and yelps and the familiar 'Kee-ow, kee-ow kee owk owk owk'. Females will beg for food and occasionally fights develop when individuals grab each other's head, wings or tail.

The nest is often large, comprising a shallow scrape surrounded by a variety of vegetation, sticks and oddments collected from tidelines. The clutch is invariably three well camouflaged, blotched olive eggs and laying can extend from April to June but most eggs will be laid in May. Incubation, involving both parents, lasts for about a month and then both will feed the young at the nest site. The young have a plaintive 'puooo' food call and, when larger, often retreat into hollows in vegetation near the site. Fledging takes about thirty days and colonies will be deserted by mid-August.

The **Lesser Black-backed Gull** is similar in size (53–56cm) and general appearance to the Herring Gull, but can be separated from it by the black back. Its yellow legs distinguish it from the much larger Greater Black-backed Gull, which has white or pink legs. The immature plumage is similar to that of the Herring Gull and during the first two years, until some black feathers appear, the two are almost indistinguishable. The Lesser Black-backed Gull is less numerous than the Herring Gull and has a British breeding population of about 50,000 pairs. During the breeding season small numbers will be present round much of the coast, with the exception of the east coast of England. The densest populations are to be found in the Clyde and Forth in Scotland, in South Wales and south-west England and the largest single British colony is on the sand dunes of Walney Island, near Barrow-in-Furness, Cumbria, where nearly one-third of the population of the British Isles nests in association with Herring Gulls.

In contrast to the Herring Gull, the Lesser Black-backed Gull is migratory and few remain in Britain during the winter. Their southerly migration takes place during autumn when birds travel to the Mediterranean and Africa. Returning birds will arive on the south coast of Britain towards the end of February and during March but eggs are not laid until May and June, so that in mixed colonies of Herring and Lesser Black-backed Gulls the latter are often several weeks later in their breeding activity.

The display and nest are similar to that of the Herring Gull, although the Lesser Black-backed Gull prefers open and less precipitous sites and the nests are frequently in close proximity in colonies. The typical clutch of three brown, olive-blotched eggs hatches after about a month and the young are fed by both parents and fly in just under five weeks. Food and feeding techniques are similar to those of the Herring Gull, although the Lesser Black-backed Gull is less inclined to feed inland.

The **Greater Black-backed Gull** is easily identified by its large size (64–79cm), black back and pinkish legs. The juvenile plumage is mottled brown and gradually replaced until full adult plumage is achieved during the fourth year. It is the least numerous of the common

Greater Black-backed Gull

British gulls, but numbers are increasing and the breeding population now probably exceeds 20,000 pairs. During winter they are widely dispersed round the coast on cliffs, sandy coasts and saltmarshes and only small numbers venture inland. A few can often be seen in flocks with other gull species. The call is a deep bark 'uk uk uk'.

Breeding takes place throughout much of Shetland and Orkney, round the coast of Scotland and along most of the coast of Wales and south-west England. With the exception of one large colony containing about 2,000 pairs on North Rona, they breed in small colonies or more usually as isolated pairs. The large nest, built of sticks, seaweed and grass, is frequently placed on rocks, or on a small pinnacle or stack. Both birds build the nest and the display resembles that of the Herring Gull. The clutch of three brown-blotched eggs is laid during May or the first half of June. Incubation by both birds lasts for twenty-six days and the young are fed on the nest before flying after about eight weeks.

Because of their weight and long wings they make a short run along the ground before becoming airborne but once in the air they are strong fliers with slow steady wingbeats and glide well, skimming the waves or ground, and make good use of air currents. Large marine fish and fish waste are obtained by low flying and diving or by swimming and pecking. Carrion, crabs, molluscs, sand worms and other shore animals are sought by walking along the shore and tidelines and they will join Herring Gulls on coastal refuse dumps. Their powerful build and strong hooked bill enables them to kill rabbits, rats and voles when they encounter them and deliberate attacks are made on seabirds. They lack the speed or manoeuvrability of a raptor, so will take their prey when it is vulnerable or incapacitated. Thus Manx Sheerwaters are attacked on the ground because they are slow and clumsy in their movements, Puffins are caught as they surface after swimming and ducks and waders are attacked when sick or wounded.

Petrels, shearwaters and skuas

Superficially resembling a gull and nesting amongst them on cliffs is the **Fulmar**. A big bird (45–50cm) with rounded head, dark eye and strong, stubby, yellow bill with tube nostrils, it can vomit a jet of oil for a distance of a metre. Male and female are alike with ivory white upperparts and slightly greyer or speckled brown beneath. Unable to stand, it rests on the ground by lying on the full length of the tarsus but, once airborne, it is a superb and graceful flier, gliding low over the sea or back and forth along the cliff face on rigid, narrow wings with only occasional short bursts of stiff strokes or leisurely flaps.

The increase and spread of the Fulmar in the British Isles during the last 200 years has been phenomenal. The first pairs arrived in Shetland in 1878, following a marked increase in the Icelandic population. It has continued to increase, until the population of the British Isles now exceeds 300,000 pairs. Most occur in north-west Scotland, including the Outer Hebrides, St Kilda, Orkney and Shetland. However, small numbers are now present on all British coasts wherever there are cliffs. The cause of the increase is uncertain but has been attributed to the expansion of the whaling and fishing industries, climate changes and genetic variation. Waste fish, whale meat and blubber can form an important part of their diet and large flocks will gather round whaling vessels and trawlers at fish docks, feeding with other seabirds. Crustaceans, cephalopods and other marine invertebrates complete their diet.

Breeding activity usually begins in April, although some Fulmars remain at breeding sites in all months except September and October. Steep slopes and cliffs with ledges are preferred, but crevices, tussocks, ruins and stone buildings will also be used. Pairs are territorial within loose colonies and often the same pair will occupy the same site for several seasons. Patrolling birds glide back and forth along the cliffs in front of nest sites, hanging, turning and diving in the up-currents.

Courtship display includes billing and head waving with swollen necks, and pairs can be noisy with much cackling and crooning while a familiar call is a deep 'ug ug ug'. The single white egg is laid on a ledge or in a shallow depression in soil, usually during May. Both parents share the long incubation lasting about fifty-five days, the off-duty bird staying away from the nest, and some colonies will suffer heavy gull predation of eggs. The young are fed by both parents and obtain food by placing the bill inside that of the parent. Initially the chick is protected by an adult but later is left alone apart from infrequent visits for feeding. Fledging takes about seven weeks and from an early stage the young are able to squirt oil to defend themselves. Other cliff nesting species, including birds as large as Ravens and Peregrines, can be rendered flightless by a heavy coating of this oil. The juvenile Fulmar is whiter than the adult and spends much of its early life at sea before returning to breed when six to twelve years of age.

There are four species of seabird, associated with sea cliffs and islands, which for different reasons are less likely to be encountered. Two, the Storm Petrel and Manx Shearwater, belong to the same family as the Fulmar. The **Storm Petrel**, the smallest British seabird, (15cm) is a long-winged, blackish bird with a conspicuous white rump. Although the breeding population of the British Isles exceeds 50,000 pairs, they spend much time at sea and are restricted to a limited number of small, remote islands which they visit at night. The **Manx Shearwater**, a larger bird (35cm) with very dark brown, almost black, upperparts and white beneath, also has a large breeding population, probably exceeding a quarter of a million pairs, and likewise nests on remote islands which are visited at night, returning birds gathering offshore in huge numbers in the dusk.

The others are skuas – the **Arctic** and the **Great Skua**. These resemble large gulls, but are swifter fliers. In addition to taking a wide variety of prey, both hunt by harassing other seabirds until they are forced to disgorge food, which the skua then takes. The Great Skua also attacks and kills other birds such as small gulls and waders. The Great Skua is a larger (58cm) uniformly brown bird, while the smaller Arctic Skua has two colour forms, dark blackish-brown or light with white beneath. The total breeding population of the Great Skua is about 4,000 pairs and of the Arctic about 1,000 pairs and both are largely confined to Shetland, Orkney and north Scotland with small numbers in the Outer Hebrides and on the west coast of Scotland, but they may be seen outside the breeding season on migration elsewhere round the coast.

Auks

The auks comprise another group associated with cliffs and four species breed regularly in the British Isles. Of these, the Common Guillemot, Razorbill and Puffin are numerous and widespread, whereas the Black Guillemot is less common and more restricted in its distribution. They are medium-sized (30–42cm), fish-feeding birds, standing upright on land and using their wings to swim under water and the sexes resemble each other in appearance. In historical times the auks were persecuted and their eggs collected in huge numbers but populations now appear stable and may even be increasing, albeit gradually. Oil pollution of the seas and over-fishing represents a continuing hazard to their future numbers.

The four species frequently nest within the same colony as gulls and other cliff breeders, but differences in their choice of site reduces competition for space. Black Guillemots choose boulder-strewn shores at the cliff foot or crevices in small cliffs, Razorbills occupy scattered niches and platforms at higher levels, Common Guillemots cram onto long narrow ledges or crowd together on the flat plateaux of rock stacks and Puffins use burrows.

The **Common Guillemot** is the most numerous British seabird. The population of the British Isles is about 580,000 pairs and over three-quarters of these are in Scotland. In England and Wales, apart from long stretches of the flat coasts of east and south-east England, small scattered colonies can be found on cliffs round the coast. The important exception is the large seabird colony at Bempton cliffs in Yorkshire. The biggest British colony is on North Hill on Westray in Orkney which contains possibly as many as 70,000 pairs.

In appearance it is the slimmest of the auks, having a slender, pointed bill and long neck. The head and back are dark brown or black and the underparts white and in winter plumage the throat and cheeks will also be white. From southern Scotland southwards most tend towards the browner plumage, while northwards the plumage is blacker and this difference is sufficiently persistent to separate a northern and southern geographical race. Some individuals, referred to as the 'bridled' form, have a white eye ring and white line behind the eye. Bridled birds are uncommon in the south but become more numerous further north with as many as a quarter being bridled in some of the Shetland colonies.

Winter is spent at sea with only exceptional visits to land. The diet is almost exclusively fish and the Sand Eel is a major constituent. They fish by diving while swimming on the surface and underwater both the large webbed feet, positioned towards the posterior of the body, and the paddle-shaped wings will be used. Because of the dual function of the wings, aerial flight is simple and direct with continuously beating wings, the feet as well as the tail being used to aid manoeuvrability. Towards the end of December, and thereafter with increasing frequency, Guillemots will begin to visit their breeding colonies and by the end of May breeding will have started.

At the colonies there is a constant movement to and fro between flocks on the sea and large numbers jammed together on the ledges and plateaux. The groups on the sea occasionally erupt and simultaneously thrash over the water with much wing splashing. Most of the nuptial display is performed on the breeding sites where males and females bow to each other and crane their necks or take part in mutual preening of the partner's head and neck plumage. Mating is also performed on the ledges. They can be noisy, uttering a raucous, growing 'arrrrr' which reverberates up the cliff face.

There is no nest, the single, large, pear-shaped egg being laid from mid-May onwards on the bare rock, its shape preventing it from rolling into the sea. The eggs are highly varied in colour, the bright greeny-blue to white background being beautifully blotched and etched in a rust colour or in black. Both birds incubate the egg for about a month after which both will feed the chick, usually by bringing a single fish in the bill. After two weeks, when half grown, the young will flutter down to the sea where the parents continue to look after them as they move out to deeper water. The breeding cliffs will be finally deserted in August.

The **Razorbill** is similar in appearance and habits to the Common Guillemot. The head and back are black and the underparts white and in winter the throat is also white. They do not separate into distinct northern and southern races like the Guillemot, so in southern colonies the black of the Razorbills contrasts with the browner Guillemots. The main distinguishing feature between the two is the bill shape. The Razorbill has a large, deep, laterally compressed bill, crossed with a noticeable white line.

They are less common than the Guillemot, the total population of the British Isles numbering about 150,000 pairs, approximately a quarter of that of the Guillemot. However, something like three-quarters of the world population of Razorbills breeds in the British Isles so, from a conservation standpoint, they represent an international responsibility. Their distribution round the coast parallels that of the Guillemot and

Razorbill

the two are usually present in the same colonies. They winter well out at sea and, although the different bill shape suggests different feeding techniques, their diet and method of fishing are much the same. They dive while swimming on the surface, following a quick flick of the wings and feet. Small fish, usually swallowed under water if they are not feeding young, form the major part of the diet and their dives last just under a minute. Flight is rapid and direct and low over the surface. Like all the auks, they do not venture inland, although during prolonged winter gales flocks may be driven into coastal waters and occasionally individuals are blown inland.

The gradual build-up of numbers at colonies will start early in the year and eggs are laid towards the end of April and during May. A preference for crevices and niches, rather than the straight open ledges used by the Guillemot, enables the Razorbill to occupy a greater variety of cliff types. This also results in its wider dispersion in small groups through the colonies. As with the Guillemot there is a constant flying back and forth between flocks on the water and the nest sites. Simultaneous thrashing over the surface by the flocks at sea occurs, but again the main display is on land. This includes bill touching and rubbing, mutual preening of head and neck and raising bills in unison. Mating also takes place on land. The single brown to white egg, not so pear-shaped as the Guillemot's, is laid in a crevice or hollow. Incubation is by both parents and lasts a month and after hatching the parents feed the young by bringing a fish held crosswise in the bill. When about half grown, the young flutter down to the sea during the hours of darkness, presumably to escape predation. The parents continue to look after them while they move out to deeper water.

The **Puffin** is the smallest (30cm) of the four auks. It is gregarious but groups are easily overlooked in mixed colonies amongst the more widely distributed Razorbills and Common Guillemots. Once seen, however, its large, brightly coloured triangular bill and bright orange feet make it unmistakable. The bill is at its brightest during the breeding season, with much of the red being lost during winter when grey and yellow predominate. Flight is direct with rapidly beating small wings and when landing on water it splashes down head first, frequently going under.

The British breeding population probably contains between half and three-quarters of a million pairs. Puffins winter at sea, usually far out from land in deeper water. Throughout the year small fish provide the staple diet, supplemented with molluscs and crustaceans, including shrimps. From a surface dive, prey is pursued and swallowed underwater and both wings and the large webbed feet will be used to obtain maximum speed and manoeuvrability. It is not known if individuals from the same colony remain together during the winter, but birds returning in spring are generally paired. There are breeding sites round much of the coast on suitable cliffs and islands and general distribution coincides with that of the Common Guillemot and Razorbill, the major part of the population occurring in the northern half of the British Isles.

Nuptial display is simple, consisting mainly of head shaking, bill rattling and nibbling. Much of it, as well as mating, takes place on the sea within sight of nesting localities. Although they will nest under boulders in rock screes and in natural crevices, most Puffins lay their eggs in burrows. Typically these are excavated by both birds digging into the soil with their bills and grass-topped islands or grassy slopes near cliff tops are favoured locations. Where rabbits are present, Puffins will make use of their burrows.

The usually single, whitish egg is laid towards the end of May in a shallow depression in the ground some distance from the entrance. Incubation, which lasts about six weeks, is shared by both parents which then co-operate to feed the chick, bringing several small fish, carried across the bill, at a time. Feeding will be continued until about the fortieth day when the parents stop coming. The deserted youngster fasts for several days before leaving the burrow under cover of darkness and fluttering down to the sea.

The **Black Guillemot** (34cm) is only slightly larger than the Puffin. In summer it is a distinctive black, apart from large white wing patches and red legs; in winter the barred black and white back helps to single it out. The British Isles are at the southern limit of its breeding range, so it is the least numerous and most restricted of the auks, the total breeding population being under 10,000 pairs and largely confined to Shetland, Orkney, the north and west of Scotland, Ireland and the Isle of Man. In Wales it only occurs on Anglesey, and its only English locality is St Bees Head in Cumbria. It is a sedentary bird of boulder-strewn coasts and local colonies remain throughout the year in the vicinity of the breeding sites. Essentially a small fish feeder, it pursues its prey underwater in shallow coastal regions, inlets and bays.

Cormorants and Gannets

There are three species belonging to these two families associated with cliffs – two cormorants and the Gannet. They are amongst the largest birds on cliffs and this, together with their distinctive plumage, readily distinguishes them. The two cormorants – the Cormorant and the Shag – are dark and similar in appearance and obtain food by swimming underwater. They are ecologically distinct, however, nesting apart and feeding in different areas on different prey. The Gannet by contrast is predominantly white and dives from high to catch fish. It occupies discrete nesting colonies either amongst other seabirds or apart and will travel far out to sea to feed.

The **Cormorant** is the least numerous of the three, with a total British and Irish breeding population of under 10,000 pairs. Primarily a marine species, most colonies are located on rocky coasts in the western half of Britain and Ireland. It is resident, but disperses to different parts of the coast in winter. Coastal feeding is in shallow inshore waters, estuaries and bays but it will travel inland to lakes and large rivers. Flat fish form a major part of the diet and in fresh water both coarse and game fish are taken. When hunting it will swim low in the water with head erect and bill inclined upwards, before giving a small jump and vanishing head first. Dives usually last under a minute and only the strong webbed feet are used for swimming. Large fish are brought to the surface before being swallowed head first.

On land its size (90cm), uniformly dark plumage, erect stance and long neck distinguish it from all other species except the Shag. Throughout the year the Cormorant has a distinct white chin and sides to the face and in summer it also has white thigh patches. These are lacking in the Shag which, unlike the Cormorant, grows a crest in the summer. In the water the heavy hooked bill helps to separate them from the divers. It is less easy to separate the immature Shag and Cormorant as both are a uniform brown, but the Cormorant has a dull white breast. Flight is direct with steady beats, usually low over the water with neck outstretched, and resembles that of a goose. When travelling overland, they will fly at considerable height, sometimes in formation, and will perch and roost on trees, posts, boulders, ledges and on flat, sandy coasts, often holding their wings outstretched to dry.

Birds are present at the colonies from March to mid-September, although eggs will not usually be laid until late April or May. Early in the season a male will occupy a nest site and initiate an advertisement display involving slow flapping or partially erected wings which emphasizes the white thigh patches. Mutual display follows, which includes head waving, bill gaping and stick presentation and during incubation birds will greet each other by erecting their tails and throwing back the head.

Nests are located on broad ledges near the cliff foot, sometimes in caves, or on buttresses and small rocky islets. In Ireland some still nest in trees. Nests are mainly built by the female which uses sticks and seaweed brought by the male and they are usually found in groups with individual nests close to one another. Three or four chalky eggs are incubated for a month by both parents which then share in feeding the young for a further seven weeks. Food is carried in a pouch and the young feed by thrusting their bills into the parent's open mouth. At first the young are naked and need brooding, but are soon large and strong enough to defend themselves and quickly become independent after fledging.

In appearance and general behaviour the **Shag** closely resembles the larger Cormorant. Individually they vary in size (65–80cm), males on average being larger than females. At close range the smaller size, more slender appearance, dark green plumage and (in summer) the recurved head crest distinguishes the Shag. It has the same upright stance and goose-like flight as the Cormorant but is more a bird of rocky coasts and deeper water and avoids shelving sandy coasts, bays and estuaries. Numbers have increased in recent years and the population now exceeds 30,000 pairs, well over three-quarters of which are in Scotland.

Less gregarious than the Cormorant, it favours narrow, sheltered

Shag

71

ledges just above the sea's reach, fissures, caverns and caves and, where small colonies occur, the nests tend to be well spaced. Males arriving on the breeding cliffs will select nest sites and attract a mate by repeatedly stretching and withdrawing their necks and gaping to display the yellow mouth interior. Mating occurs on the nest site where the female frequently encourages the male by displaying with upright tail, head and neck thrown along the back and at intervals darts her open bill at the male. Both birds build the nest using sticks, seaweed and flotsam. They are silent birds but occasionally throat clicking, grunts and hisses are to be heard.

Egg laying starts in March, the three chalky eggs being incubated by both birds for just over a month. The young are naked and brown at birth and fledge at about eight weeks. They are fed by both parents, the young obtaining food by thrusting their bills down the parents' throats and the same pair will often breed together for several seasons in succession. Juveniles quickly become independent and, like their parents, disperse round the coast during the winter. Throughout the year they are almost exclusively marine feeders and only very exceptionally venture into fresh water. Fish are taken live under water, the Sand Eel forming by far the most important prey and the surface dive is frequently preceded by a small jump before fish are brought to the surface for swallowing.

The islands round the British coast hold some of the largest gannetries in the world and almost three-quarters of the world's **Gannet** population. The total breeding population of the British Isles now exceeds 140,000 pairs and all but 5,000 of these are included within nine huge colonies. Four are in Scotland, one each in England (Bempton Cliffs, Yorkshire) and Wales (Grassholm, off Pembrokeshire) and three off the southern coast of Ireland. The largest gannetry in the world with about 60,000 pairs is on St Kilda in the Outer Hebrides. The British population has been increasing slowly in recent years.

The largest British breeding seabird (90cm), the Gannet has a wingspan of almost two metres. Adult plumage is white apart from the golden head and neck and black wing tips. Males and females are similar, but juveniles are dark brown, faintly speckled white and the immature plumage is gradually replaced during the first four years of life. Flight is strong and direct with steady flaps interrupted by short glides. When fishing, typically it flies at a height of about ten metres, searching the sea below, before suddenly going into a steep plunge dive with wings gradually closing behind the body as it nears the surface. A speed of 100 kilometres an hour is reached during the dive, which often carries it over five metres below the surface and fish are grasped in the bill and brought up to be swallowed. Gannets are exclusively marine and take a range of the commoner small to medium-sized fish as well as dead fish thrown from fishing vessels.

Gannets start to breed when five or six years old, but once established a pair tends to remain together for several seasons using the same nest site. Arrival at the breeding colonies begins in late January and February and nests will be built on level or gently sloping ground, on stacks, smooth-topped islands or on wide ledges towards the foot of precipitous cliffs. While breeding, they are highly gregarious with nests almost touching and it is the male that first occupies a site and then attracts a female to join him. A substantial nest is formed from seaweed, grass and flotsam, cemented together with droppings. A central cup, eventually lined with feathers and finer material, is produced by the bird pressing the unconsolidated mass with its breast. Display includes bowing, nape-biting, headshaking and bill-fencing and, particularly near the beginning of the season, there will be fighting when individuals grab each other's bills while trying to push and pull one another from a site. The call is a harsh 'urrah'.

A single pale blue egg is laid in late April or May, both sexes undertaking long periods of incubation lasting at least thirty hours. The egg is brooded under the webs of the feet and hatches in just over six weeks, after which the chick is brooded for a further fortnight. Throughout the entire period in the nest, which lasts for just under thirteen weeks, the chick will be guarded by one or other or sometimes both parents. It begs for food and will feed by partial regurgitation, thrusting its bill into the parent's mouth. After fledging it is independent and, like the adults, disperses out to sea for the winter, ranging widely in the north Atlantic. Gannets are less gregarious outside the breeding season, only gathering to follow shoals of fish and while fishing will rarely come ashore unless storm driven.

Rock Dove

The true **Rock Dove** is a medium-sized bird (33cm) of coastal cliffs, distinguished from other pigeons by a prominent white rump and two black wing bars which stand out from an otherwise grey plumage. The grey is paler on the back and at close range a green and purple sheen is visible on the sides of the neck. Its natural distribution and purity of plumage has been altered through interbreeding over most of its range with dovecot and racing pigeons that have reverted to the wild. These feral pigeons and wild/feral crosses are now extremely common on most coasts, as well as being abundant in towns and cities. Indeed, it is now only in the north and west of Scotland and Ireland that many pure Rock Doves survive and the total breeding population of the British Isles is put at about 100,000 pairs. The plumage of feral pigeons varies greatly, from those closely resembling the Rock Dove to chestnut and pied birds. The Stock Dove, a farmland pigeon, many also occasionally occur near the coast and care is necessary to avoid confusion with this species also.

Rock Dove

Rock Doves have a rapid dashing flight and will fly low over the sea. When disturbed suddenly they clatter out of crevices and plunge downwards, but they can also make good use of rising air currents to glide and circle at the cliff face. They travel singly, in pairs and in small flocks and possess a characteristic exhibition display when they rise with slow beats before circling with wings held at a steep angle. Food consists primarily of seeds and grains, obtained by ground feeding on rough or cultivated land behind and adjoining cliff tops. They most usually perch on ledges, boulders and buildings.

Most breedings occurs from April to July, but the breeding season can be protracted and nesting is not infrequently recorded as early as March and can continue well into September. Nests are typically grouped in small colonies on ledges in caves and crevices or amongst steep boulder scree. During display, the cooing male erects its head, before continuously bowing with swollen throat as it rotates. A fairly large but ill-formed nest is built with twigs and the typical clutch is two white eggs. Both adults share incubation which lasts for eighteen days and then both feed the young by regurgitation whilst the young bird inserts its bill into the parent's mouth. Initially they are fed on 'pigeon's milk', a curdlike substance formed from cells of crop lining. Fledging takes five weeks and then the young quickly become independent and the parents frequently nest again to produce further broods.

Crows

The inclusion of the **Jackdaw** as a bird of coastal cliffs is arbitrary as it is present throughout virtually the entire British Isles in farmland, woodland, towns and cities, in ruins, on moorland cliffs and quarries, as well as round the coast. The population of the British Isles probably exceeds half a million pairs and it is only in north-west Scotland that it is rare or absent, although even here it appears to be extending its range. It is particularly evident on coastal cliffs and often present in large numbers and for this reason is discussed in association with them.

A small black crow with a stubby, sharp bill and strong black legs, it can be singled out by its small size (33cm), light grey nape and nearly white iris. Juveniles are browner and the grey less evident. Gregarious throughout the year, normal flight is steady with regular rapid beats of small wings but it can glide well on rising currents and flocks will often erupt into aerial gyrations when individuals will dive steeply and swerve and twist in an unexpectedly violent and rapid manner. Flocks and individuals can also prove very noisy, uttering in unison a barrage of sharp, metallic 'tchack' notes. Food is found on the ground and the bird will walk rapidly over the surface with quick, jaunty steps. Much of the year is spent feeding on meadows, often in association with Rooks and Starlings, foraging for insect larvae and seeds and occasionally eggs and young birds.

Breeding will start during the second half of April. The preferred nest site is in a hollow or cavity, so in woodland they are restricted to large deciduous trees or dead and dying trunks with broken branches and in quarries, cliffs and buildings they will congregate where there are broken faces or ruins. Less frequently, chimneys, dense scrub, ivy and rabbit burrows are occupied. A substantial twig nest is built with a large central cup deeply lined with hair, wool and grass and the same site will be used in subsequent seasons so that individual nests become huge. Both birds co-operate to build the nest, but the clutch of four to six greenish-blue eggs is incubated by the female only which is fed at the nest by the male. Nest sites are selected early in spring and pairs will perch together near the entrance, males displaying with raised crowns and wings and tails outspread. Hatching takes two and a half weeks and the young are then fed for almost five weeks by both parents which bring food in a throat pouch. Jackdaws are single brooded and immature birds will remain with the flocks which usually roost in winter in the vicinity of the breeding colonies.

The **Chough**, a second member of the crow family and of similar size to the Jackdaw, is confined almost exclusively to sea cliffs. It is a much rarer bird and the population of the British Isles is now under 1,000 pairs. Previously it was more widespread, but is now only found on the south and west coast of Ireland, the Welsh coast, the Isle of Man and Islay while a few breed inland on some northern Welsh uplands. Its decrease appears to have coincided with the loss of maritime heaths and other rough uncultivated ground along the coast.

When perched, its glossy black plumage, thin downcurved scarlet bill (yellow in juveniles) and scarlet legs distinguish it from the Jackdaw. In the air, its black silhouette and superb buoyant flight on broad wings with splayed tips is unique. Individuals, pairs and small flocks rise and plunge in the air, often calling noisily with a high pitched 'kwee-Ow'. If perched, the wings and tail are usually flicked vigorously when calling. There is little competition for food with the Jackdaw as the Chough confines itself to tidelines and rough uncultivated heaths and sheep-grazed turf near the coast. Using its fine bill, it will probe into soft ground, heaps of rotting seaweed and cushions and tussocks of coarse vegetation, extracting ants and a range of other insects and their larvae as well as seeds and berries. Long spells of deep snow or frozen ground cause starvation. Breeding will start at three years of age and substantial twig nests are built on ledges in caves, old mine shafts or wedged in clefts. Three eggs are laid in late April or May and incubated for two and a half weeks by the female which is called from the nest to be fed by the male. Both parents feed the young during the five and a half weeks of fledging, by regurgitating food into the mouths of the young.

Rock Pipit

The **Rock Pipit** is the only common and widespread small perching bird living almost exclusively on cliffs and rocky shores and its association with the coast is strong, with birds remaining on the coast throughout the year and only exceptionally being recorded inland. The breeding population of the British Isles probably exceeds 50,000 pairs.

Unobtrusive in behaviour and markings, it is not always easy without experience to confirm its identity. It has the same slim, generally olive-brown appearance of the more familiar Meadow Pipit, but is slightly larger (16.5cm compared to 14.5cm), darker, less strongly marked and has very dark, rather than brownish, legs and grey, not white, outer tail feathers. Present on most rocky coasts and islands, it is only absent from long stretches of north-western, eastern and south-eastern English shores where there is no suitable rocky habitat. The call is a short 'tsup' and feeding is largely restricted to boulders along the tideline, broken cliff faces and cliff tops, where they find a wide selection of insects as well as small marine worms, crustaceans and seeds.

Territories are maintained throughout the year and are often contiguous along a stretch of coast or cliff line. Pair formation will begin in March when males perform an aerial song flight, rising from and parachuting back to a rock in full song, much in the manner of the Meadow Pipit. The nest is hidden in vegetation amongst rocks, sometimes just above high water mark, or in cliffs, gulleys and crevices in a broken cliff face and will rarely be more than 500 metres from the sea. Four to five eggs are laid in April or early May and incubated by the female for two weeks, after which the young are fed in the nest on beakfuls of insects by both parents. Fledging follows in just over a fortnight and second broods are then laid.

This completes the species typically associated with sea cliffs. While some, like the Jackdaw, have been included although commonly also found in other habitats, others which may regularly be present have been omitted as they are considered elsewhere. Thus two further members of the crow family, the Raven and Carrion/Hooded Crow, nest on sea cliffs as do two raptors, the Peregrine and Kestrel. Even a pair of Barn Owls will occupy a sheltered coastal cove. It is always wise, therefore, to double check one's identification of a species and it will then be of interest to compare its occupancy of this habitat with that in another.

THE SHORE

Flatter parts of the coast support a different range of breeding birds compared with those found on cliffs, although several cliff-nesters feed on the shore and in the adjoining coastal waters. In addition, in contrast to sea cliffs, the shore supports large numbers of wintering birds that breed elsewhere, many outside the British Isles. Despite their differing feeding and nesting requirements, most shore birds, like most cliff birds, ultimately depend on the sea to provide food for their survival. A variety of food is available from different regions of the shore – from the sea itself, in deep or shallow water, from rocks, pools, sand and mud of the intertidal zone when exposed at low water and from the upper reaches subject only to occasional inundations during high spring tides. Muddy shores within the range of neap tides, covered and uncovered twice in every twenty-four hours, are the richest source of food in the form of invertebrate sub-surface dwellers. Sheltered rocky shores clothed in seaweeds and supporting rock pools and large stretches of stable moist sand come second, while exposed rocky coasts and unstable shingle banks unable to retain water are the least prolific.

BREEDING BIRDS

The waders

There are three common wading birds that breed widely on low-lying coasts round the British Isles: the Oystercatcher, Redshank and Ringed Plover. They differ in appearance, feeding technique and in selection of nest site. The largest and most distinctive, the Oyster-catcher, is adept at opening mollusc shells with its long, powerful bill and nests on open exposed ground. The commonest, the Redshank, is a bird of saltmarsh and damp meadows, where it hollows out a well hidden nest in grass tussocks and feeds by rapid probing in wet mud near the water's edge. The smallest and least numerous is the Ringed Plover which, using its short bill, takes small marine invertebrates from the surface of wet sand and mud and nests in a scrape on exposed ground amongst sand and shingle vegetation.

The large (43cm) noisy, conspicuous **Oystercatcher**, with its black and white plumage, long, bright orange bill and pink legs is unmistakable. Its flight is powerful and direct with quick, steady beats, low above the ground for short distances and rising higher, often in groups, for longer flights. During winter they will gather in large flocks and usually remain confined to the seashore. In England, Wales and Ireland most stay on the coast to breed, but in Scotland considerable

Oystercatcher

numbers will move inland following the river systems to nest on meadows, moorland and even cultivated land. The Oystercatcher has always been most numerous in Scotland, which contains almost three-quarters of the 20,000–40,000 pairs in the British Isles. The practice of breeding inland has long been established in parts of Scotland and appears to have intensified and spread to southern Scotland and northern England during the nineteenth century. Most of the inland breeders seem to be birds that winter on the west coast. The number of pairs going inland is still growing and is probably an important contributory factor in the recent general increase in the British Oystercatcher population as inland breeding birds tend to have a higher breeding success than coastal nesters.

Feeding on rocky shores and on sand and mudflats, they take a wide range of marine invertebrates, including limpets, cockles, mussels, periwinkles, crabs and the Lugworm. Inland, earthworms form the principal food. Individual Oystercatchers walk quickly over the beach, pausing to pull molluscs from the surface of a rock or to probe deeply for one before pulling it to the surface in preparation for opening. Like many waders, Oystercatchers have the ability to open the tip of the bill to catch and hold prey underground. Bivalves are either snipped apart by the bird inserting the flattened tip of its bill between the slightly opened valves or else hammered into bits and the mud can become strewn with broken and empty shells where large flocks have been feeding. Worms are obtained by probing deep into soft mud or soil. In winter, high tides will drive Oystercatchers from the shore and they then gather in huge flocks in high-water roosts with other shore waders.

The large coastal flocks break up early in spring when birds disperse to take up breeding territories. Some of the Scottish birds will be in territory as early as February and pairs will occupy adjoining territories and at intervals gather in small groups to perform a piping display. With hunched shoulders, neck thrust forward and bill pointing down, they burst into a cacophony of loud piping 'kleep kleep kleep-a kleep-a kleep-a'. Some will run forward while calling. Energetic aerial chases, sometimes of considerable duration and covering a large area, are also common, when two or more individuals will fly round and round, diving and swerving, calling all the time. Displaying birds also undertake a characteristic, slow-winged, so-called 'butterfly' display flight.

Breeding usually starts at the age of three. The exposed nest is a shallow depression, sparsely lined with broken shells and small stones, in shingle, sand, soil or on turf. Typically, three browny, blotched eggs are laid in late April or May with the female undertaking most of the incubation. Because incubating birds are conspicuous they are wary and leave the vicinity of the nest at early signs of danger, the loud piping alarm 'klee-eep klee-eep' frequently being given by the nearby off-duty bird. Hatching occurs in just under a month and the well camouflaged young leave the nest almost immediately to be tended by both parents which are vigorous in their defence, persistently mobbing humans who approach too near and avian predators such as gulls and crows, while the chicks crouch in cover. Oystercatchers are unusual amongst waders in that the chicks are fed by the parents. This probably reflects the experience needed to deal with mollusc shells and juvenile Oystercatchers take many months to become skilled feeders. Inland, earthworms are fed to the young which can swim strongly. Fledging takes just over five weeks and they are usually single brooded, but repeat clutches are not uncommon.

In contrast to the Oystercatcher, the slightly smaller (28cm) **Red-shank** is inconspicuous until it flies and calls, when its white rump, white hind edges to the wings and loud trilling 'Heu-hu hu' immediately attract attention. When standing, only the long reddish bill and long orange legs relieve the grey-brown plumage. Flight is strong, fast and twisting with quick, flicking beats and usually low over the ground.

After landing, the wings are momentarily held aloft and the bird has a habit of bobbing.

During winter, the Redshank, like the Oystercatcher, is a coastal dweller found in large numbers in suitable estuaries and bays. On rising and falling tides it will disperse across the mudflats to feed and at high tide gather into flocks to preen and roost, often with other waders such as Knot, Oystercatcher and Dunlin. To feed, it will walk quickly over the sand and mud, head down, pausing briefly from time to time to probe deeply for small molluscs, worms and crustaceans and will wade at the water's edge or swim across pools. The population of the British Isles is between 38,000 and 48,000 pairs. Widely distributed, the Redshank is commoner in the north than the south and scarce in south-west Britain and Ireland. There is little indication of any major overall population change but, being highly dependent on wet areas, locally it has been adversely affected by land drainge.

In March large numbers will move inland to take up breeding territories while the remainder disperse along coasts. From birth, the young feed themselves so nesting sites must be close to wet areas. Favoured inland sites include isolated marshes in grassland areas and wet meadows along river valleys. Coastal breeding is primarily restricted to saltmarshes or damp meadows on adjoining coastal plains. In rich inland meadows, breeding concentrations can be high and isolated from the next population, but the highest densities will usually be found on saltmarshes. In some seasons nests on saltmarshes are overwhelmed by high Spring Tides, but these sites continue to be used so the long term success must outweigh such occasional disasters.

Nuptial display is elaborate and attractive, a male arriving first to establish and then defend a territory and performing a song flight to attract a female. Rising on rapidly beating, almost vibrating wings, it quickly gains height before gliding slowly back to the ground with stiffly held decurved wings, fanned tail and raised head. The strident 'tloo tloo tloo' piping fills the air. Ground chases frequently precede mating, the male with fanned tail and lowered head pursuing the female until it crouches and then approaching slowly with wings extended vertically to display the brilliant white underside. The nest is lined with dry grass and hidden in a tussock, with an entrance through one side. Four buffish, brown-spotted eggs are laid during late April or May and incubated by both parents for twenty-four days before hatching synchronously. The young immediately leave the nest and both parents tend them closely for a month until they fledge when the whole family returns to the coast as second broods are not attempted.

Less obtrusive in size, colouring and behaviour than the two previous species, the **Ringed Plover** can easily be overlooked, particularly during the breeding season. Only two-thirds the size (19cm) of the Redshank and diminutive in appearance, it is distinctive on close examination for its prominent black collar (broader in front) and the

THE SEA COAST

bold black and white head pattern which contrasts with the brown body. The legs are orange-yellow and the rather short bill orange with a black tip. Confusion is possible with the much rarer, inland breeding, Little Ringed Plover from which it is most easily distinguished by the absence in the latter of a white wing bar. Although the British Isles are at the southern edge of the Ringed Plover's breeding range it is widespread round the coast, but commoner in the north and scarce in south-west England. The British population is just under 6,000 pairs with probably another 1,000–2,000 in Ireland. Most remain throughout the year on muddy and sandy coasts although recently, especially in parts of Scotland and northern England, greater numbers have started to nest inland. While feeding, it will run rapidly with raised head between pauses to peck at invertebrates on or near the surface. The call is a quiet melodious 'tooi tooi'.

Dispersal along sandy and fine shingle beaches begins in late February and initially pairs are aggressively territorial. In display the male crouches in front of a female with spread tail, half-open depressed wings and raised back feathers. Several scrapes are made in the soft substrate by the male before four inconspicuous, buffish, spotted eggs are laid in April. Incubation lasting twenty-four days is shared by both parents and when the young leave the nest shortly after hatching adults continue to tend them until they fledge in just under a month. Both parents will readily perform distraction displays to protect the young, fluttering over the ground dragging a weakly flapping, apparently damaged wing. Broods are vulnerable to crows and foxes and they, like the Redshank, are occasionally overwhelmed by exceptionally high Spring Tides but will readily repeat and second broods are common. During winter they will gather in small flocks, often in association with Dunlins, and there is a general southerly movement.

Avocet

The rare, graceful, black and white **Avocet** is now again breeding regularly on the east coast of England. A large wader (43cm), it is easily identified by its long, thin, upturned bill, bold plumage pattern and long blue legs; the sexes are alike. Until the mid-nineteenth century this species was apparently common along much of the east coast, but then became extinct probably as a result of habitat loss and human exploitation. It was almost 100 years later in 1938 before two pairs were recorded breeding in County Wexford. This first re-colonization did not persist but breeding attempts on the east coast of England in the early 1940s proved more successful and two major colonies are now well established in the Minsmere and Havergate reserves of the Royal Society for the Protection of Birds. It is assumed that re-colonization was by birds from Denmark and/or The Netherlands where the population of Avocets had been increasing.

The diet includes a range of invertebrates, in particular crustaceans, and shallow brackish pools provide important feeding sites in which the birds wade deeply, sweeping their bills from side to side in the water and plunging them into the soft mud. Breeding is in loose colonies with the clutch of four buff, spotted eggs laid during late April or May in a ground nest. The young leave the nest soon after hatching and are tended by both parents for about six weeks until they fledge. Minsmere now has over fifty breeding pairs and Havergate almost 100. Their success has resulted from extensive habitat management and protection from disturbance. Small numbers of Avocets are now starting to breed along other parts of the East Anglian coast so the future of this species seems assured.

Terns

Five species breed regularly in the British Isles – the Sandwich, Common, Arctic, Little and Roseate. The last two are uncommon. They are highly adapted to hunting by flying low over the sea and spend long periods on the wing during their migrations. This specialization is evident from their similarity in appearance, characterized by slender bodies, long, thin wings, long forked tails and slender, pointed bills.

Body coloration is light grey and white and all have black crowns. Flight is light and buoyant and terns hunt by quartering low above the surface with strong, flicking beats, pausing to hover with more rapid beats and downcurved tail before plunging headlong on half-closed wings to catch prey on or just under the surface. Extensive migrations are undertaken outside the breeding season with a return in spring to gently contoured islets and sand or shingle where they nest colonially. Differences in choice of feeding and breeding areas reduces interspecific competition.

In the context of north-west Europe, the British Isles are of great importance as breeding areas for all five tern species and have greater numbers of breeding pairs of all species than any other country except the Common Tern. This includes over three-quarters of the Roseate Tern population and over a third of the Sandwich and Little Tern.

The **Sandwich Tern** (41cm) is the heaviest and largest and most resembles a small gull in flight. Size, together with a black-tipped yellow bill and black legs, distinguish it from the others. The black crown feathers can be raised to form a slight crest and during the winter the forehead is white. Juveniles have a speckled crown and back. Its call is a loud, grating 'kirrick'. Sand eels and small sprats with other small marine fish predominate in the diet and fishing is usually undertaken well out from the shore.

Winter is spent off the west and south coasts of Africa, the birds returning to their largely traditional breeding sites in Britain in April. Numbers have increased by about 30 per cent in the last ten years, and the total population of the British Isles is now just over 15,000 pairs.

Sandwich Tern

Almost exclusively coastal in its selection of nesting sites, over two-thirds breed in England with 90 per cent contained within nine main colonies including both mainland and offshore sites. The largest concentrations are to be found in Norfolk and Northumberland. It is absent from Shetland, Wales (apart from Anglesey) and south-west England, apart from Dorset.

Breeding is highly synchronized with nests close to one another, often adjoining colonies of other tern species and Black-headed gulls. Colonies will be established on sand and shingle and less commonly on grassy islands. Aerial chases, with or without the birds carrying fish, are common and often of considerable duration with a pair turning and gliding in unison. Ground display will include bill raising with stretched neck and half open wings, as well as bowing and bill fencing.

The simple scrape forming the nest is often unlined and the two buffish, spotted eggs are laid towards the end of April or in May and incubated by both birds for about three weeks. The male feeds the female on the nest and then both birds will feed the young in the nest for the first week, after which the young gather in groups near the top of the shore before fledging in about thirty-five days and then migrating south with the adults during August and September.

The **Common Tern** (35cm) is the most widely distributed of the five tern species in the British Isles. It is similar in size and appearance to the Arctic Tern which predominates in the higher latitudes and in Britain the two overlap. In recent years the population of the British Isles has remained constant at about 15,000 pairs, over half of which are in England. It is widely distributed round the coast with the

83

Common Tern

exception of South Wales and south-west England, although it is present in the Scillies. Scattered pairs breed inland, particularly in eastern England and north-east Scotland, but almost half the population is contained in four coastal sites – one in Shetland, two in England in Norfolk and Northumbria and one in Northern Ireland at Strangford Lough.

The Common and Arctic Terns can be confused in the field, particularly during migration or when both are present in large colonies. Of similar size, their general body coloration is alike and both have a black cap, red legs and orange-scarlet bill, but the Common Tern has a black tip to its bill. In winter the forehead is white and the bill blacker although some red is usually retained. The back of the juvenile is barred with buff. They rest, often in groups, on sand, shingle, buoys and floating debris and rarely walk, only waddling for short distances. The call is a sharp 'kik-kik-kik-keerr-keerr-keerr'.

Winter is spent south of the British Isles and some travel as far afield as Africa. Returning birds reach the south coast of England early in April, after which numbers build up at the breeding colonies and coastal sites will include saltmarsh, sand dunes, sand and shingle banks, while inland they will use small islands and gravel spits in rivers, sand and gravel workings and small lakes. Aerial displays involve fish-carrying, when a bird of either sex will be joined by its mate which flies in front, frustrating attempts to be overtaken by the fish-carrying bird. The fish is rarely exchanged during these flights and similar flights without fish are undertaken, when the mode of flight may be varied with glides (sometimes with wings held in a V) and slow beats. On the ground birds will bow and elevate bills to each other with tails held erect.

The shallow, sparsely lined nest is formed by mutual scraping and the three olive, spotted eggs will be laid at the end of May or early June. Incubation lasts for just over three weeks when the sitting bird is fed by its mate which brings fish in its bill. The female broods the young in the nest for a few days fed by the male, after which both birds will feed them until they fledge at about a month. Second broods are not attempted. Avian predators and humans will be heavily mobbed by large numbers of the colony in the vicinity of the nest sites and another type of colonial behaviour involves almost the entire colony suddenly and simultaneously flying silently out to sea to return shortly.

Small fish, supplemented with crustaceans and worms, are taken by aerial diving. Flying buoyantly back and forth, bill down, low over the surface with flicking beats, they pause frequently to hover before plunging on closed wings and enter the water with a splash, often going under and, shortly after take-off, shaking the water from their plumage. They favour the middle zone some distance from the shore and will fish in groups.

The **Arctic Tern** (35cm), with a population possibly as high as 77,000 pairs, is the most numerous tern in Britain, but over 60,000 of these are equally divided between Shetland and Orkney and it is virtually absent from southern Britain apart from small numbers in Anglesey and on the north Norfolk coast, and two or three other scattered localities in Northumbria and Cumbria. With experience its distinctive screaming 'kee-arr-kee-arr' note can be used to distinguish it from the Common Tern, otherwise confirmation depends on close examination of the bill to ensure the absence of a black tip although, where the two species are roosting together in a good light, its shorter legs, deeper red bill and longer tail extending to the wingtips become evident.

During winter it makes an extensive southerly migration, which takes it as far as South Africa and Antarctica, before returning to the northern breeding grounds in May. Its fishing technique parallels that of the Common Tern with small fish and other small marine organisms forming the diet. Colonies are situated on sand and shingle banks and grassy and rock strewn islands and it will share colonies with the Common Tern although showing a greater preference for islands far out at sea. Display is similar to that of the Common Tern and the nest, thinly lined with grass and shells, is a hollow scraped out by the female, or a small depression on a rock. The two buff and brown eggs will be laid at the end of May and incubated by both birds for three weeks. They are single brooded and fledging takes about a month, but feeding continues for about a week after the young are on the wing, both young and parents deserting the colonies by the end of August which is earlier than the other tern species.

The small size (24cm), black-tipped yellow bill, yellow legs and white forehead to the black cap distinguish the **Little Tern**. During winter most of the black cap is lost and the juveniles have a speckled crown and back. They feed close inshore at the edge of the tide or in muddy creeks and channels, hovering for long periods with quick wingbeats before plunging with a splash to obtain small fish and crustaceans and call 'kik-kik' and 'kirri-kirri-kirri-kik' recurrently. During the last ten years, numbers have decreased slightly and the population of the British Isles is now just over 2,000 pairs, two-thirds of these being on the Lincolnshire and East Anglian coasts.

Breeding is in small, rather scattered, coastal colonies on shingle and sand just above the high tide mark. They are noisy and conspicuous at the nest sites which are not infrequently overwhelmed by high Spring Tides and predated by foxes. Disturbance by holiday makers was a problem but breeding sites are now fenced off and usually guarded during the season. Display is similar to that of other terns with aerial chases involving gliding with wings held aloft in a V. Two brown, blotched eggs are laid at the end of May or June in a shallow unlined depression and incubated for three weeks by both parents. The young leave the nest the second day after hatching and settle again nearby where, for some days, they are brooded by the female while being fed by the male, before eventually the female helps with the feeding. Fledging takes a month and birds begin to leave the colonies by the end of July to return again next April.

The rarest of the British terns – the **Roseate** (38cm) – is still declining. Less than 1,000 pairs now breed in the British Isles whereas there were over twice this number ten years ago. Most are included within nine surviving off-shore island colonies, all of which are now rigorously protected as this small number represents 80 per cent of the north-west European population. Largest numbers will be found on three Irish sites, Green Island, Strangford Lough and Lady Island Lake, and the other notable colony is on Anglesey. Winter migration takes them to West Africa and trapping at these winter localities is considered to be a factor in their decline. Very much a maritime species, it is similar to the Common and Arctic Terns in size, appearance and general behaviour, but distinguished from them by a predominantly black bill. The pink flush on the breast from which the name derives can only be seen at close quarters.

Duck on the coast

Only two species of duck breeding in the British Isles are largely confined to coastal breeding sites – the Shelduck and Eider Duck. Male Eiders and both sexes of the Shelduck are conspicuous, appearing predominantly black and white. Molluscs form an important part of the diet of both, but whereas the Eider obtains these by diving in deep water out at sea, the Shelduck feeds by wading or up-ending in shallow in-shore waters. Consequently the Shelduck is usually found along low-lying sandy and muddy coasts or in bays and estuaries, while the

Eider is also present off rocky coasts, cliffs and steep sided islands. The two contrast in their breeding distribution, the Eider being very much a northern species with few breeding outside Scotland whereas the Shelduck is found all round the British and Irish coasts.

The large size (58–67cm) which gives the **Shelduck** its goose-like appearance, and the generally black and white plumage distinguish it from other coastal species. Males and females are alike except that the male has a conspicuous knob at the base of the scarlet bill which contrasts with the dark bottle-green head. The overall black and white effect is relieved by a broad bright orange round the forepart of the body. Juveniles have a dark grey-brown head, nape and back. Local

Shelduck

flights are made in pairs or small numbers low over the water with slow, heavy beats and the head is characteristically drooped on take off which, when made from land, is preceded by a short run. Long distance flights are undertaken in flocks in formation or lines at high altitude. During winter, about 50,000 individuals are present round the coasts of the British Isles and it is thought about 12,000 pairs remain to breed. The number breeding has increased slowly during the last fifty years and more are beginning to breed inland although this practice is still the exception.

First breeding begins in the second year when pairs select nest sites in sand dunes, on low grassy islands and coastal marshes during March and April. At the same time territories are formed on the feeding areas adjacent to the nesting sites and territorial chases are frequent with birds uttering the characteristic, chattering 'ag-ag-ag-ag-ag' call and occasional dramatic squabbles are fought out in shallow water with much splashing. Groups of displaying males will chase a female in display flight and individual males will swim or walk with erect necks, flicking the head vertically upwards. Successful pairs will remain together for several seasons and nesting will usually be underground, most commonly in rabbit burrows, although holes in walls, under tree roots, in buildings or large pipes and culverts are all used with the nest of pale grey down typically about two metres from the burrow entrance. Nests may be in close proximity.

A large clutch of up to sixteen creamy white eggs is laid in May and incubated by the female, which is called off three or four times a day to feed. Hatching follows in a month after which the pair will lead the young, sometimes over considerable distances or possibly several kilometres, to the water. In densely populated areas the territorial system is disbanded at this stage and the young from several broods will gather together in crèches guarded by only a small number of the original parents. The young start flying and become independent after about two months and then gradually disperse from the breeding areas.

Throughout the summer, the immature one-year olds and non-breeding older birds gather into flocks and during the crèche period these flocks will be supplemented by breeding adults no longer involved with guarding the young. During July and August small groups of birds from these flocks from all parts of the British Isles, and indeed from all the north-west European countries, move to assembly points from which, in suitable weather conditions, they will leave in large flocks to fly to the German Waddenzee area. Here in shallow off-shore conditions tens of thousands of Shelduck undergo a moult during which they are flightless and will escape predators by diving and swimming underwater. The return moult migration flight back to the breeding areas is made gradually through the autumn. In Britain the main exception to this pattern is the use made of Bridgwater Bay in Somerset by a few thousand, possibly Irish, Shelduck as their moulting site and smaller numbers in the Forth and Wash.

The **Eider Duck** is almost exclusively marine and only exceptionally recorded inland. It is one of the most numerous ducks in the world and the European winter population alone is estimated at about two million. The British breeding population has been increasing gradually and now numbers over 20,000 pairs, almost all of which are confined to Scotland and the north coast of Ireland, but it is slowly extending southwards and outlier populations are well established in North-umberland and Cumbria.

Much the same size as the Shelduck (50–71cm) it appears smaller because of its heavy build, thick neck and habit of holding its head retracted. The male is conspicuous with a white back contrasting with black below and the black crown and lime green on the nape are clearly visible at close quarters. The female is uniformly brown, mottled black, and in the absence of distinguishing plumage features, is most readily identified by the heavy build and unusual wedge-shaped head with the top of the bill merging smoothly into the forehead. Immature males are mainly dark brown, although some white gives them a piebald appearance. First breeding begins when three years of age.

During winter Eider Duck will assemble in large flocks which may include several hundred birds, often well out from shore. They come ashore in estuary mouths and on boulder-strewn coasts to rest and preen, and the flight is low over the water in lines or V formation. British breeders are thought to remain in the vicinity of their breeding areas throughout the year although some populations undertake short, post-breeding, moult migration flights. Particularly in the spring, but not uncommonly also in winter, the characteristic low crooning note 'a-ooo a-ooo oo oo oo' draws attention to their presence.

Nesting is colonial and females begin to prospect for sites on rocky shores and islands by mid-April. Much of the pair formation will have taken place during autumn with small groups of males cooing and head flicking round a female. The nest is a hollow amongst boulders and vegetation, further shaped by the female before a basal lining of seaweed and grass is covered by a huge mound of down and small feathers (the much sought after eiderdown). Although often sited in exposed situations, the camouflage of the female which sits tight throughout the month-long incubation is highly effective. Loose territories are sometimes held along the shore close to nest sites but no nest territories are established although an area round the nest will be protected from intruding pairs. The four to six pale olive eggs are laid in late April or early May and the females, now deserted by their mates, incubate them for a month, only occasionally leaving the nest for short feeding periods at sea. In the early morning of the day after hatching the female leads the young to the water. Neighbouring broods join to form crèches which in densely populated areas sometimes include hundreds of ducklings guarded by a small number of females, initially often not their own parents which have to feed to compensate for the lack of feeding during incubation. A further two months elapses before the young, which are covered in pale grey down and can feed themselves, fledge. The areas used for feeding may be several kilometres from the nest sites and the young disperse from these over short distances to join the wintering flocks.

Stonechat

The **Stonechat** is the only small perching bird closely associated with low-lying coasts. It favours rough, uncultivated land, commons and heaths with shrubs and sand dunes, coastal plains and low vegetated

Stonechat

cliffs, particularly those with extensive areas of gorse and bracken and rough pasture. In times of high population numbers it will spread inland to rough field corners, railway embankments and young conifer plantations and onto moorland where it may overlap with the Whinchat. It is very susceptible to severe winters and avoids cultivated land and this largely dictates its westerly and southerly coastal dispersion within the British Isles and preserves its separation from the Whinchat. It is widely but generally thinly distributed, being most common in the north-west and south-west of Britain and Ireland and absent or uncommon along much of the east coast of England. The total breeding population of the British Isles is between 30,000 and 60,000 pairs.

It is a small (12.5cm) but conspicuous bird with a habit of perching with erect posture on fence posts and tops of bushes. While perched it spreads and flicks its wings and tail in a restless manner, uttering a sharp, clear 'tsack tsack tsack' alarm. The male has a black head and back, relieved by white patches on the neck and wings, a white rump and buff-chestnut underparts. Females and juveniles have brown-streaked upper parts and are paler beneath and the white patches are less conspicuous and the rump dark. Insects and spiders, supplemented with worms and seeds, form the diet and these are obtained by short foraging dives into the undergrowth.

During winter there is a generally southerly movement and although some emigrate, most will remain in the British Isles, often in pairs although not necessarily in their breeding territories. In mild conditions nesting can begin as early as mid-March and in good seasons three broods may be reared with the last young flying in August. The song is a short, soft, unremarkable double note and, like most birds of open habitat, it is the song flight which attracts attention to them at the start of the season. During this the male will rise vertically for twenty metres or more and then flutter rather clumsily before dropping to the ground. The nest of grass and moss is built by the female and is lined with hair and feathers. Placed in the foot of a thick bush, preferably gorse, it often rests on the ground and has a run or tunnel through the vegetation leading into it. Incubation of the five or six pale green eggs takes two weeks and is primarily by the female which will leave the nest to feed. The young are only in the nest for about a fortnight, where they are fed by both parents which bring insects in their bills and they then remain together as a family for a short time before the parents start a second brood.

WINTERING BIRDS

The other significant and exciting aspect of the coasts of the British Isles is their value and importance as overwintering areas for hundreds of thousands of wading birds, duck and geese. These are birds from their breeding areas in British uplands, inland marshes and lakes or returning from distant, largely uninhabited, breeding localities in Arctic regions. Early arrivals begin to appear in groups or large flocks in the late summer and early autumn while others will delay their arrival until the onset of winter, having paused elsewhere in Europe.

It is less easy to distinguish the subtle ecological differences of numerous species of wading birds massed on a seashore than it is to consider the ecology of breeding sites. It is also usually more difficult to identify birds in winter when they are less approachable, viewing conditions can be difficult and most have assumed a duller, more uniform, winter plumage. To complicate matters, some will be juveniles in immature plumage and others adults still displaying remnants of breeding plumage, while in the early spring, before departure, individuals may already be moulting into breeding plumage. And although it may be exciting to see a Knot in August with bright rufous underparts, it complicates the task of the beginner who is trying to distinguish one species of wader from others if it is represented by three different plumages.

Patience, careful observation and frequent reference to a field guide is essential, but there are ecological aspects and behavioural traits which can be applied in addition to noting differences in appearance. First, there is the simple separation into waders, duck and geese. Waders are highly dependent on the tide and feeding is primarily undertaken on falling and rising tides with different species favouring distinct parts of the shore – some occupy the tide's edge, others concentrate higher up the shore, while still others use the channels. Duck also separate into deeper water, shallow water and shore feeders.

Unfortunately, in practice it rarely works out as simply as one would hope and conditions can change along short stretches of coast but, taken in conjunction with other factors, the feeding preference can help. All species rest and preen sometime during the twenty-four hour cycle and this usually occurs on high tide roosts during the turn of the tide. These roosts provide excellent opportunities to study a range of species concentrated together which, if approached carefully, are often susceptible to extended periods of relatively close observation.

The waders

Well over a million wading birds winter in the major estuaries and bays round the British coast. A good starting point to help distinguish one from another is by size as they divide conveniently into large and small species. In addition to the Curlew and rare Whimbrel, considered under Upland Habitat, and the Oystercatcher covered earlier in this chapter, there are two other large waders – the Bar-tailed and Black-tailed Godwit. The latter has recently become re-established as a British breeding bird, but has been included as a winter bird because of its larger numbers and wider distribution at this time of the year. The larger waders with their long legs and long, probing bills tend to feed at the water's edge or in tide and deeper channels.

The commoner small waders present on the shore in winter, in addition to the Dunlin, discussed under Uplands, and the Redshank and Ringed Plover already covered, are the Knot, Sanderling and Turnstone. The Redshank, mainly singly, favours the tide edge, channels and pools, Knot usually feed in flocks which disperse over the middle shore, Sanderling run in small groups just in advance of the breaking waves, Dunlin and Ringed Plover (sometimes together in small flocks) favour higher, drier stretches of mud and sand while, highest of all, are the Turnstones on the tidemark, high shingle or seaweed-covered rocks exposed at low tide.

Godwits

The **Bar-tailed** and **Black-tailed Godwit** are similar in size and appearance with a uniform brownish-grey winter plumage. Although smaller than the Curlew, their large size (38–41cm), long, straight bill and long legs help to single them out. They wade deeply and plunge their heads below the surface and on the exposed shore will bury the full length of the bill into the mud for worms. Both tend to remain in small flocks and are silent most of the time. The Bar-tailed Godwit is much the commoner, being widespread round the coast with peak numbers for the British Isles of about 50,000. The Black-tailed Godwit has been increasing slowly since the middle 1950s but the winter population is still under 5,000, most occurring on the south coast of England and Ireland in a few favoured sites including Langstone and Chichester harbours, the Exe estuary and Ballymacoda and Dungarvan in Ireland. An important northern exception is the Dee estuary which holds over 700 birds.

Distinction between the two is made possible by the broad white wing bar and white tail with black terminal bar of the Black-tailed Godwit, contrasting with the uniform wing and barred tail of the Bar-tailed. Both have chestnut red heads, necks and breasts in summer and traces of this are often present in some of the fresh arrivals during autumn passage and in departing birds in early spring. The Bar-tailed does not breed in the British Isles, whereas the Black-tailed bred until the nineteenth century before becoming extinct through habitat loss and collection of both their eggs and specimens for taxidermy. Small numbers re-colonized the Ouse Washes in East Anglia in 1952 and from these the British population has gradually built up to about fifty pairs.

The **Knot** is the biggest of the small waders and the second most numerous wintering wader with a peak number in good years approaching a quarter of a million birds (the Dunlin is the most numerous). About half the Knot are concentrated along the west Lancashire coast from Morecambe Bay to the Dee, with the Humber and Wash providing important sites on the east coast. It does not breed in the British Isles but, like most of the non-breeding waders, it leaves during mid-March for the plateaux and marshes of the high Arctic, returning again after mid-July. It rarely ventures inland, but favours extensive open areas of gently shelving mudflats.

A small (25cm) stockily built bird with a short, straight black bill and nondescript greyish plumage, pale beneath and with a faint white wing bar, it is not easy to identify except that in its favoured areas it remains in huge flocks comprising hundreds and sometimes thousands of individuals. During feeding spells these flocks blanket areas of the mudflats and, if disturbed, rise with a roar of wings in a dense cloud, sometimes appearing dark, sometimes light, as they present their upper then lower surfaces. Generally silent, they have a quiet double whistle 'tooit-wit'. The summer plumage is red beneath and mottled black on the back and the early arrivals and late leavers often display traces of this brighter plumage, as do some of the small number of non-breeders that sometimes remain on British coasts during the summer. Before their plumage becomes worn, the newly arriving juveniles appear paler on the back from white edgings to their feathers and are buff below. Dull as its winter plumage may be, the aerial evolutions of a large flock of Knot, particularly if reacting to a Peregrine Falcon, is undoubtedly one of the outstanding sights of the shore.

The **Sanderling**, like the Knot, is almost exclusively coastal in its winter distribution, favouring large expanses of gently shelving mudflats and stretches of wet sand devoid of vegetation. It is widely distributed, but nothing like as common as the Knot, and peak numbers usually remain under 5,000. It also contrasts with the Knot in

Sanderling

its behaviour by usually forming only small flocks and its feeding is characterized by a restless activity. It will move with astonishing speed on twinkling legs in a series of continuous dashes along the very edge of the tide, dodging the breakers and darting left and right to pick up surface-dwelling invertebrates, and has been compared to a clockwork toy. At times it associates with Dunlin, Ringed Plover and Knot, particularly at high tide roosts, and at low tide it will feed at pools left on the shore. It calls frequently when feeding and in flight with a characteristic 'wick-wick'.

A plump little bird (20cm), slightly larger than the Dunlin, it has a short, straight, black bill which contrasts with the latter's somewhat larger, slightly decurved bill. It often appears very pale, almost white in some lights, having a pale grey back and the whole of the underparts and much of the head being white. It displays a prominent white wing bar in flight and the front of the wing when folded appears as a black spot. In summer plumage the upper parts become golden brown and traces of this are often present at both ends of the winter season while in juveniles the upper parts are chequered black. It does not breed in Britain but small numbers may remain along the coast in summer, the majority leaving in mid-March to breed in the barren Arctic Tundra.

The **Grey Plover** which, unlike the closely allied Golden Plover, does not breed in Britain, remains almost exclusively on low lying, sandy coasts throughout the winter. By contrast, the majority of British breeding Golden Plovers, supplemented by northern immigrants, occupy southerly inland agricultural areas. In size (28cm) and shape the Grey Plover resembles the Golden Plover but can be distinguished from it in winter plumage by its white rump and, when seen from the side or underneath in flight, by the small patch of jet black axillary feathers located at the base of the underside of the wing. Both are uniformly greyish above and pale beneath, but the grey of the Golden

Plover still retains a slightly golden tinge which is evident in good light. In the late summer, newly arriving adult Grey Plovers can be startlingly obvious through the retention of the vivid black underparts of the breeding plumage.

The Grey Plover does not migrate in large flocks and usually stays isolated from other species, remaining either singly or in small groups. While feeding, it favours the middle or higher parts of the shore, making short sorties with long pauses as it searches for invertebrates picked from the surface with the short, rather thick, black bill. The total winter population rarely exceeds 15,000 birds and most of these are farily evenly distributed between southern British localities, the Wash holding most with between 1,000 and 1,500 individuals.

Because of its bold body and wing patterns, the **Turnstone** (23cm) is the most readily identifiable of the small waders. The term 'tortoiseshell' is often used to describe the upper parts, which are browner in winter and bright orange-brown in summer. There is a broad black band across the breast which extends to the side of the face and it appears pied in flight from the double white wing bar, white rump and tail with black band. The bright orange legs are another noticeable feature. Habitat selection and behaviour help to confirm its identity. Favouring rocky and stony shores, it feeds on shingle and old tidelines at the upper reaches and amongst rafts of seaweed on boulder patches and mussel beds exposed at low water. Rarely going inland, in recent times it has been reported more frequently from some sandier coasts

Turnstone

and is now widely distributed round the British Isles with peak winter numbers exceeding 10,000. It does not breed in Britain but small numbers remain in the summer. The short pointed bill is used to flick over debris, small stones and fronds of seaweed to expose invertebrates sheltering beneath. If disturbed while feeding, it will fly only a short distance, keeping low over the ground, and likes to rest on boulder tops, jetties and harbour walls. It will associate with other small waders, but generally keeps apart as singles or in small scattered flocks. It has a sharp metallic call followed by a drawn out, twittering 'wiiiiiick'.

Many of the British breeding waders, supplemented by northern immigrants, contribute significantly to the numbers of wading birds present round the coasts in winter. The Dunlin, with peak wintering populations in some years exceeding half a million birds, is the most numerous shore bird; Oystercatchers can number over 200,000, Lapwing 100,000 and Redshank and Curlew up to 50,000. Several other species of wader occur from time to time in small numbers, particularly at the time of the autumn and spring passage. In addition to the larger Whimbrel, Avocet and Greenshank, these include smaller species such as **Curlew-Sandpiper** and **Little Stint**. Some of the more northerly estuaries and coasts carry small but regular winter populations of the **Purple Sandpiper**. This dumpy, very dark plumaged wader is associated with seaweed-covered boulders and can be identified by its yellow legs and the orange base to its long, slightly decurved, dark bill.

Geese

The Greylag Goose is the only indigenous goose to breed in Britain (see Upland Habitat). The relatively small number of British breeding birds is joined in winter by large numbers of immigrant Greylag, as well as large wintering populations of the Pink-footed, Barnacle and Brent Goose and smaller numbers of the White-fronted Goose. Although the Greylag and, to a slightly lesser extent, the Pink-footed Goose feed on agricultural land, all wintering geese are discussed together under Coastal Habitat to enable comparisons to be drawn.

All geese are vegetarian and while superficially resembling each other in appearance and general behaviour, their plumage, individual behaviour, distribution and feeding habits are sufficiently different to enable relatively easy distinctions to be made. Using general coloration they can be separated into the larger 'grey' geese and the smaller 'black' geese, the plumage of the first being predominantly light or medium grey which contrasts with the dark greys and blacks of those in the other group. The Greylag, Pink-footed and White-fronted Goose come into the former category and the Brent and Barnacle in the latter. The Brent is essentially a maritime species, feeding in the edge of the tide or on the exposed shore on marine vegetation, while the Barnacle and White-fronted Goose are also associated with the coast but feed on grass on saltmarsh or adjoining pastures. The Brent is more usually seen in small flocks, whereas the Barnacle and White-fronted Goose remain in large flocks. All three are restricted in their distribution to a limited number of well established sites.

The Greylag and the Pink-footed are more easily confused as both are widely distributed in northern Britain and spend much of the daylight on farmland. The Greylag had its origins in marshland and from this it developed the habit of feeding near its roosts in small flocks. The Pink-footed Goose, however, was originally associated with open estuaries and so developed the habit of travelling in large flocks to feeding grouds some distance from its sandbank roosts. Although both are now largely dependent on the same agricultural crops, these differences in behaviour still reduce competition between them to their mutual benefit and so will presumably persist. Even where the two species roost together, small parties of Greylag will leave the roosts to feed locally at an earlier time than the larger flocks of the Pink-footed Goose depart for more distant farms and the Greylags return later to the roosts in the afternoon.

Grey geese

Immigrant **Greylags** wintering in Britain come from Iceland, arriving in October and November and staying until the following April. Most remain in central and east Scotland near agricultural land. They feed during the day, initially concentrating in the early autumn on barley and oat stubbles and later turning to potatoes, turnips and carrots, supplemented throughout the winter with grass. Local feeding parties will assemble in the late afternoon at roosts on lakes and estuaries. Numbers have gradually increased since the 1960s and now fluctuate around 60,000–70,000 individuals. The **Pink-footed Goose** (61–76cm) is smaller than the Greylag (76–89cm) and has a shorter, shallower bill. The head and neck are dark in comparison with the lighter grey of the body and the bill is black and pink in contrast to the yellow bill of the Greylag. Juveniles are darker and more mottled. The voice is a far-carrying 'wink-wink' which quickly draws attention to a huge skein sweeping across high up in V or extended line formation. There are two separate populations, those from Spitsbergen wintering in the Low Countries on the mainland of Europe while those from the tundras and river valleys of Iceland and Greenland come to Britain. The number in Britain has increased since the 1950s and now fluctuates around 70,000, largely in response to good or bad breeding seasons.

First arrivals appear in early September with the majority reaching Britain in October and staying until April or early May. Initially they concentrate in central Scotland, before some move further south, many to the most important southerly roost on the Ribble estuary in Lancashire. During the first part of the winter they will remain together in large flocks usually containing several thousand birds and feeding

Pink-footed Goose

takes place during the daytime. Like the Greylag, they concentrate during the early part of the season on corn stubbles, followed later by potatoes and carrots before finally turning to winter cereals and grass in the early spring. By the end of the season, presumably because food is harder to find, they tend to break up into smaller flocks assembling in the later afternoon on sandbanks and lakes to roost.

The less numerous and more locally distributed **White-fronted Goose** is the same size as the Pink-footed Goose and can be distinguished by the white forehead, from which its name derives, and the broad black barring across the belly. Small numbers from two separate breeding populations winter in the British Isles, those originating from Greenland remaining in Ireland and west Scotland and those from northern Siberia coming to England and Wales. The Greenland population now numbers about 16,000 birds and most of these are concentrated at two main localities – the Wexford Slobs in Ireland, which at times has held up to 10,000, and Islay in the Inner Hebrides. The greater part of the Siberian population winters elsewhere in Europe and the number reaching Britain, which rarely exceeds 7,000–8,000, is to a considerable extent dependent on the severity of the winter across the Channel. The most regular flocks which together contain over three-quarters of the birds reaching Britain are at Slimbridge on the River Severn and on the Powys/Shropshire border.

Black geese

The rather small (58–69cm) **Barnacle Goose** can be readily identified even at long range by the black bill, head, neck and feet which contrast with the white face and underparts and light grey back with bold black and white bands across the wing coverts. Juveniles are paler and the voice is a short 'yap'. Once again those wintering in Britain originate from two separate breeding populations, those from east Greenland settling in west Scotland and Ireland and those from west Spitsbergen concentrating on the Solway Firth. The Greenland birds, which in total now number about 50,000, arrive in October and over half pass the winter in Islay in the Inner Hebrides. The Solway flock, whose numbers in the late 1940s had fallen below 1,000 birds, has now recovered to over 8,000. Feeding in daylight on the short grass, clover and seeds of saltmarshes and coastal meadows, they tend to remain in their large flocks, roosting on sandbanks in the estuaries.

The smaller sized **Brent Goose** (56–61cm) has a more compact appearance because of its short neck and legs and, apart from the pale underparts, appears uniformly dark, having a black bill, head, neck and legs and dark grey back. There is a thin white collar just below the head and juveniles have noticeable white edges to the wing coverts and initially lack the white collar. During the breeding season, it is widely distributed across the High Arctic and on a world scale is divided into

Brent Goose

three races, referred to as the Dark-bellied and Light-bellied Brent and the Black Brant. With experience the first two, both of which occur in the British Isles can be separated by the very dark grey belly of the former. The Dark-bellied Brent breeds on the coast and islands of Arctic Siberia and winters in Denmark, The Netherlands, France as well as in England. They leave the breeding grounds in August and early September, earlier than most other geese, reaching the Baltic by October. About 140,000 will continue the journey as far as England, settling initially on the south-east coast, and smaller numbers will disperse north later to the Norfolk and Suffolk coast and west as far as Chichester and Langstone Harbours.

Virtually all the birds of the light-bellied sub-species that come to the British Isles, about 6,000–12,000, are part of the Greenland and Canadian breeding populations which remain throughout the winter dispersed round the Irish coast with the biggest numbers in Strangford Lough in the north. Small numbers of the light-bellied race also occur in most winters in Lindisfarne on the Northumberland coast, but these are outliers of the Spitsbergen breeding population, most of which winter in Denmark with substantial numbers crossing the North Sea only in severe winters.

One of the major food items of the Brent Goose is eel grass, a saltwater plant growing in sheltered muddy bays. The birds, grouped in flocks, forage for this when it is exposed at low springs or up-end for it. This, with the bright green seaweeds popularly known as sea lettuce, forms their staple diet. Towards the end of the winter when these plants become scarce they will go onto farmland adjoining the coast to feed on grass and cereals. Following serious population declines in many parts of the world in the early part of this century as a result of excessive hunting and extensive die-back of eel grass, the Brent Goose has been protected in Britain.

Divers, grebes and ducks

During winter several species from these groups are present on the coasts of the British Isles. Some, like the Black- and Red-throated Divers, Great Crested Grebe, Red-breasted Merganser and Wigeon, are native breeding birds which have migrated to the coast from inland breeding sites, although the numbers are often greatly increased by an influx of more northerly and easterly breeding birds of the same species which have travelled south and west to avoid the harsh northern climate. Others, however, are truly northern birds from the high Arctic and northern Europe which do not breed in any numbers in the British Isles and so are only to be seen in winter. As with the wading birds, they can present problems of identification. The winter plumage of many species is dull and uniform and under conditions of poor visibility when the birds are being tossed about far out on a rough sea their identification will require patience, good telescopes and binoculars and careful reference to the field guides. It is not uncommon to find that conditions have been so difficult that even the experts have returned home having failed to confirm the identity of a distant group of dark blobs appearing and disappearing on the crests of distant waves.

Most species are widely dispersed round the coastline of the British Isles, but except for parts of the Scottish coast and a few notable exceptions further south such as the concentration of several thousand Common Scoters in Carmarthern Bay, the numbers present are generally small. In several Scottish localities, however, such as the Moray Firth and the mouth of the Tay, the concentrations can be huge with mixed flocks containing tens or even hundreds of thousands of birds. Favoured sites are broad, sheltered, gradually shelving shallow bays and estuaries with a sandy substrate. Deep waters off rocky, exposed coasts are shunned. The drabness of winter can suddenly be lifted if one is lucky enough to find one of these huge concentrations in conditions of clear weather and calm seas. The concern to identify individual species quickly becomes less important than the sheer enjoyment of the spectacle of so many birds swimming, diving and flighting low over the incoming tide.

In addition to the native Black- and Red-throated Divers, there is a third species – the **Great Northern Diver** – that winters regularly, albeit in small numbers, round the coasts of the British Isles. Breeding in the Western Palearctic is limited to a few hundred pairs in Iceland and it is probable that most of our winter birds are from this population, although they may include some from Greenland and even the Canadian Arctic. The first birds begin to arrive in late August and return to the breeding grounds during May and early June.

Their bulky appearance and large size (69–91cm), horizontally held dagger-like bill, steep forehead and thick neck are good field characters. Should the bird be in summer plumage the black head and bill stand out, but the winter plumage is a nondescript dark above and white below.

Likewise, when the native Great Crested Grebe (see Lowland Freshwater Habitat) moves to the coast in winter it is joined by smaller numbers of a somewhat similar bird – the **Red-necked Grebe**. This species does not breed in the British Isles but can be seen between October and March, mostly along the east and south-east coast of England. The winter plumage of both species is grey-brown above and whitish beneath and confusion is all too easy. The slightly larger size of the Great Crested, its pink bill, white line over the eye and white neck are best characters to separate it from the Red-necked which has a yellowish bill and dark neck. The slighter build and erect slender neck help distinguish the larger grebes from divers.

Two smaller grebes (30–33cm), the **Slavonian** and **Black-necked**, also winter in our coastal waters. Both can be found on the southern coasts of England and Wales, while the Slavonian also occurs off the west coast of Scotland and Ireland, along stretches of the east coast of Scotland and round Orkney and Shetland. Most of the Slavonian Grebes come from Iceland and Scandinavian breeding areas, but since the first nest was found in Inverness-shire in 1908 a small breeding population has become established in Scotland on remote freshwater lochs and now numbers just over fifty pairs. The Black-necked Grebes are also almost exclusively winter migrants with only three or four pairs breeding in most years in the British Isles. The two resemble each other in their grey-brown and whitish winter plumage, but the white cheeks and straight bill of the Slavonian contrast with the grey cheeks and slightly uptilted bill of the Black-necked.

Five species of essentially northern Arctic breeding seaduck winter along the coasts of the British Isles – the Common and Velvet Scoter, Long-tailed Duck, Scaup and Goldeneye. They are often found in association with auks, divers and grebes. A sixth northerly species, the Smew, also winters in the British Isles and while it will use estuaries and sheltered bays it prefers fresh water and is described under that habitat.

Scoters and Long-tailed Duck dive for bottom living mussels, worms, crabs and shrimps. They feed during daylight in shallow water before moving further out to sea to rest at night. **Scoters** are large (48–56cm) dark birds, the males jet black with yellow bills and females dark-brown with light cheeks. The Velvet Scoter can be distinguished both at rest and in flight by a white wing bar. From the mid-nineteenth century small numbers of Common Scoters have bred in the British Isles and the breeding population now numbers about 200 pairs with the majority located in Ireland and the rest in Scotland.

By contrast the **Long-tailed Duck** is small (body length 30cm). Males are easy to identify because of their pied appearance produced by white head, neck and flanks contrasting with the dark-brown back and the long, needle-like tail (13cm). Females lack the long tail, but have a white face with a dark cheek mark and a dark-brown body.

Scaup and Goldeneye reach the British coasts in October and **Scaup** numbers are estimated to reach 50,000. A large duck (48cm), the male can be distinguished by a black head and breast, grey back and white flank and the uniform dark brown female by a very evident white patch round the base of the bill. They dive for molluscs which are often brought to the surface and swallowed whole.

Goldeneye often congregate round sewage outfalls, feeding on waste grain and vegetable matter from canning factories and domestic waste in addition to molluscs, crabs and shrimps. In the southern half of the country they will also occupy freshwater lakes. Only slightly smaller (46cm) than the Scaup, the black and white flanks of the male provide a striking contrast to the dark green head with its prominent white spot in front of the eye. The head of the female is brown and lacks the white spot and the body is grey-brown. In flight the wings make a character-istic singing note. Both species now breed in the British Isles in small numbers, mostly in Scotland, the former irregularly and the latter, a hole-nesting species, in increasing numbers in response to the provision of nest boxes.

·4·

Lowland Freshwater Habitat

The major components of this habitat are lakes, large rivers and marshes. As severe winters with associated periods of prolonged ice are infrequent the value of these components is enhanced as they usually remain hospitable to birds throughout the year.

Food available to birds in freshwater habitats includes vertebrates, invertebrates and vegetation. The vertebrates are represented primarily by a variety of species of fish, some amphibians (the frog, toad and newts), a more limited selection of small mammals (principally the bank vole and water shrew) and one reptile (the grass snake). Invertebrates are varied and abundant in all freshwater habitats and include many aquatic insects, larvae and bottom-living animals as well as others associated with the vegetation floating on the surface over deeper water, growing in shallow water near the banks or lining the banks. Vegetation also provides roosting and nesting sites for freshwater birds. A few, such as the Great Crested Grebe, make use of vegetation as an anchorage for a floating nest, many more use the reedbeds and other emergent vegetation, nesting both amongst the bases of the stalks at water level or in the stems well above the water surface. Still others will occupy trees and bushes lining and overlapping the bank or in the ground vegetation of adjoining marshes.

RIVERS

These differ from lakes in several important characteristics and so are attractive to different species of birds. The water is constantly moving, sometimes, over shallows, very rapidly, or more slowly where there are pools. Adjoining stretches differ, often suddenly, in depth and, following heavy storms or periods of drought, the overall depth can alter within a few days, sometimes within only a few hours. They are usually shallower than lakes and contain more protruding boulders, small islands and shingle banks and their twisting courses enable birds to remain hidden from predators. The flow limits the extent of vegetation and of particular significance is the absence of extensive reedbeds or other tall emergent vegetation and this, with their greater changeability, makes rivers less suitable for nesting birds. Indeed the lower reaches of large navigable rivers with deep muddy water and tall vertical sides often devoid of vegetation can be very poor for birds and the main ornithological interest will be found on adjoining river meadows and marshes rather than on the river.

We have already seen in the Upland Habitat how the smaller, gushing mountain streams, with long, frequent stretches of rapids and few small pools are characterized by the presence of the Dipper, Grey Wagtail and Common Sandpiper. As the stream broadens into a small river, its flow becomes less rapid, the pools larger, deeper and more numerous and the shallows linking them less violent and it becomes increasingly attractive to two species – the Kingfisher and Grey Heron. Both are fish-feeding species but differ very markedly in appearance and ecology. The Heron is one of the largest British birds, a wader which snatches medium-sized fish in its large bill with a thrust of the head and neck. The Kingfisher is small and dives for small fish. Clear, moderately flowing water of about half a metre in depth with abundant fish provides excellent conditions for both. Shallow torrents and rapids carry few fish of suitable size for the Heron and make diving conditions difficult for Kingfishers, large rivers are too deep for both species which consequently are able to use only limited stretches adjoining shelving banks. Competition between the two species is avoided by the selection of different-sized prey and different methods of feeding.

The **Kingfisher** is the most brilliantly coloured of all British birds and this, with its short-tailed, dumpy appearance, long, sharp bill and small size (16.5cm) makes it easy to identify. The head and back appear cobalt blue or emerald green depending on the light conditions, the underparts are orange-red and the short legs and diminutive feet are sealing-wax red. Males and females are indistinguishable and juveniles are similar to the adults but less vivid. Flight is swift with whirring wings and usually low over the water although they will rise to cut corners or when crossing land to reach a pond. While medium-sized rivers offer the best conditions, they also live on ponds, lakes and canals and in dispersal during autumn and severe weather will venture to estuaries and tidal channels in coastal marshes.

In spite of their brilliant plumage Kingfishers can be surprisingly difficult to see when perched amongst stream vegetation dappled with sunlight and shadows and if disturbed their speed and directness of flight quickly takes them out of sight round a bend in the river. They rarely fly far however and with care can be re-located and observed. In addition to small fish such as stickleback and minnow, they will take the young of a wide range of larger fish species as well as water beetles,

Kingfisher

tadpoles and insect larvae. When fishing they perch on a branch, post or stone about half a metre or a metre above the surface, gazing intently at the water beneath, before suddenly diving vertically downwards and plunging beneath the surface. They emerge quickly to fly back to their perch carrying prey which is swallowed head first or carried in the bill to the nest. Less commonly they will hover with rapidly beating wings low over the surface with the body almost vertical, head uppermost, before diving.

Kingfishers have a southerly distribution and are absent from most of northern Scotland and only thinly distributed in south Scotland. Elsewhere in the British Isles they are fairly common and widely distributed and the total population is estimated to be between 5,000 and 9,000 pairs. They are badly affected by severe winters, but recover quickly because of a long breeding season which extends from March to mid-September, during which most pairs usually raise two and sometimes three broods. In some areas the absence of suitable breeding sites appears to limit their numbers and the canalization of rivers as part of drainage schemes is often to their disadvantage. Severe pollution also reduces their numbers, but the current national policy of ensuring no river is allowed to become more polluted than at present and all are to be gradually improved will undoubtedly produce a benefit.

Pairs will occupy a territory on a length of river or lake shore, the male displaying to the female using a slow wing beat 'butterfly' flight and the pair engage in extensive aerial chases which on occasion take them well away from water. The shrill 'cheeee' flight call is much used in the chase and the male will feed the female. The male also has a soft trilling song, but this is rarely heard. A steep, tall, sandy face is required for the nest and usually a river bank site is chosen, although locations over 200 metres from water have been used. Both birds will be involved in the excavation of a metre-long horizontal tunnel into the face, terminating in a nest chamber lined with fish bones. Incubation of the six or seven white eggs extends over three weeks and is shared by both birds. The young fledge in just under a month and both male and female bring fish in their bills to the nest. The young soon become independent when the parents start a second brood, often using the same nest.

The **Grey Heron** is easy to identify, being the only common storklike bird in Britain, with large, pointed bill, long neck and long legs. One of our largest birds (90–98cm), adults have a white head and neck and grey back and a noticeable bright yellow bill and black crest.

Grey Heron

Juveniles are more uniformly grey, the crest is lacking and the upper mandible is brown. Their apparently heavy, slow flapping flight with large, rounded, hollow wings, retracted neck and extended legs distinguishes them in the air. They are found throughout the British Isles with densest concentrations in eastern and south-east England and Ireland. Numbers fluctuate in relation to hard winters and following the particularly severe winter of 1962–63 the British breeding population was down by about a half, but recovery in the absence of subsequent cold winters takes only a few seasons. The total population of the

British Isles is about 8,000 pairs. In the British Isles, with few exceptions, Herons are colonial and tree nesting and many colonies are traditional sites. In remote treeless regions they will nest on sea cliffs in low bushes or on the ground and a few small reedbed colonies exist. The typical heronry holds between fifteen and thirty nests, the largest in Britain with 200 pairs being in the Northward Hill reserve of the Royal Society for the Protection of Birds in Kent. Breeding starts early when males gather in a field near the heronry during daytime in late January and early February and soon afterwards females will start to roost in the trees near the old nests. Pairing, nest selection and building is at its height in the early morning and evening in the colonies when displaying males call as they stretch their necks skywards and then bow to attract a female.

The first clutches of four blue eggs are laid in late February, although most eggs will be laid during March and early April. Males incubate during the day and females at night for the twenty-eight days before the eggs hatch. Both parents brood the young for a few weeks and feed them by regurgitating small fish and partially digested larger fish into the bottom of the nest. Fledging takes place after seven weeks, but towards the final stages the young clamber into the branches round the nest. Both adults and young are noisy throughout the season. The young hatch at intervals and differ in size so that in times of food shortage the smallest often perish in the competition for food. On average two young will fledge from each nest and second broods are not attempted although the replacement of lost clutches is normal.

On leaving the nest the young quickly become independent and, like their parents, are largely solitary feeders. Food includes a wide range of medium-sized coarse fish, game and seafish as well as amphibians, young birds and small animals and indigestible bones, scales and fur will be regurgitated as large pellets. British Herons are largely sedentary and most will remain within 100 kilometres of their colony of birth. The favoured method of hunting is to wade along shallow stretches of rivers and ditches, pausing to fish from the bank as they walk round deeper pools. They can swim and can catch fish when standing on stumps, posts and rocks and even occasionally drop and grab them in their bill while flying low over the surface.

LAKES AND PONDS

Lakes and ponds include a variety of waterbodies, ranging from small shallow meres with extensive reedbeds in the shallows and thick vegetation overhanging the banks, through marshy regions where reedbeds and tree growth cover larger areas than the scattered stretches of open water, to large lakes of great depth in the middle, with a variety of bank types including inhospitable stony beaches, woodland, riverside meadows and marshes. The range of birdlife associated with lakes is consequently varied and includes diving birds that feed in deep water, dabbling and wading birds occupying the shallows, numerous reedbed species and still others dependent on adjoining meadows and alder and willow scrub that quickly invades inland waterbodies.

The most common diving birds, feeding on fish, micro-organisms and bottom-living plants and animals and thus associated with the deeper parts of meres and lakes, include the Great Crested Grebe, Pochard and Tufted Duck. The **Great Crested Grebe** (48cm) is the largest of the three and widely distributed over most of England, southern Scotland and northern Ireland, the total British population numbering about 5,000 pairs. It prefers open water of between one and five metres in depth and will occupy large lakes, meres, reservoirs and gravel pits over two or three hectares in area. It is essentially fish-feeding, taking a wide range of species supplemented by aquatic invertebrates such as crayfish, shrimps and dragonfly and stonefly larvae in its long sharp bill. Highly adapted for swimming under water to catch live fish, it has a slim body with legs placed well back and the toes broad and fat to provide propulsion. Dives are typically of thirty seconds' duration and the birds plunge head first with a slight splash as they disappear. They are disinclined to fly and will escape danger by swimming under water.

The return from the coast to inland breeding sites is usually completed by April and by this time they will be in their attractive summer plumage when both birds display a black crown, double-horned tufts and a broad chestnut frill round the top of the neck. Their nuptial display is varied, dramatic and fascinating to watch and includes head shaking when the pair face each other, upright on the water, and a so-called 'penguin dance' in which the two birds dive for weed and then swim at each other, carrying the weed in their bills and rising breast to breast.

Nests are usually well separated and a pair will defend a territory. Both birds bring weeds to build a floating nest which is anchored and usually well concealed in emergent vegetation and both will share the incubation of the three or four eggs which are laid in May. If disturbed on the nest, the incubating bird will cover the eggs with weed and leave the vicinity, swimming under water. The eggs hatch after a month after which the grey and black striped young are tended and fed by both parents, often resting nestled on the parent's back. Fledging is not for ten or eleven weeks and during this time the young remain close to the parents, persistently uttering a rather plaintive 'pee-a pee-a' food call whenever a parent surfaces with a fish. Adults are generally silent, but will occasionally utter a far-carrying bark 'rah rah rah' and a grunting 'gaaaaaa------'. Movement to the coast precedes the onset of hard weather during the autumn.

The **Pochard** and **Tufted Duck** are of similar size (46 and 43cm) and generally similar in their habits. Both dive for a variety of plant and animal food but the former is more specialized as a vegetarian and prefers large natural lakes and ponds whereas the latter takes predominantly molluscs and other invertebrates and, as well as occupying large lakes and ponds, will also live on smaller pools, gravel pits and reservoirs. Both are widespread in the British Isles but while the total population of the Pochard is restricted to only a few hundred pairs, that of the Tufted numbers over 7,000. The Tufted only started breeding in the British Isles in the mid-nineteenth century, whereas the Pochard was present before this although in small numbers. Both populations are still increasing, probably as a result of better protection. The greater success of the Tufted appears to derive from its wider selection of habitats and the spread of its principal food item, the zebra mussel.

The male Pochard has a chestnut head and neck, black chest and greyish-white body. Females are less distinct with a brown head, neck and breast and grey-brown body, but have a noticeable blue band across the bill. During winter they are sociable and many pairs are formed during communal courtship in February and March when the birds are still in flocks. Aerial pursuit flights are common and on the water males will engage in head shaking and head flicking or throw their head right back, calling much of the time. They are not territorial and several pairs may breed in close proximity. Nests are built on the ground by the female, usually within a few metres of the water's edge or sometimes in the water. The single brood of eight to ten eggs are laid in mid-April and will be incubated for about a month by the female, which is deserted at this stage by the male and so subsequently has to tend the young alone for seven or eight weeks until fledging.

Tufted Ducks have a dumpy appearance, emphasized by a large round head. Males are black with contrasting white flanks and belly and display a drooping black crest at the back of the head. The females have only a short crest and are uniformly dark brown, flecked with yellow-brown, although many often have a white band at the base of the bill. Juveniles resemble females. Like the Pochard, they are good divers, giving a slight jump before vanishing with a flick of the webbed feet and a 'plop' beneath the surface. They frequently re-surface quite suddenly, almost bouncing on the surface, and during dives can reach depths of up to 14 metres.

Throughout winter Tufted Ducks will remain in flocks, often in association with other duck species. Communal courtship in the flocks may start as early as November and December, but usually it is not until February and March that groups of excited males can be seen swimming rapidly back and forth, shaking and flicking their heads. Considerable numbers are often found nesting in the same area and the greatest concentrations, involving possibly as many as 1,000 pairs, are on Loughs Beg and Neagh in Northern Ireland. Islands are favoured sites and nests will be grouped in loose colonies on some of them, the best example being Serfs Island in the Loch Leven National Nature Reserve with over 500 pairs. Nests lined with grass are built by the female in depressions in deep vegetation and may be as much as ten metres from the bank. The female alone incubates the eight to ten eggs which are laid from mid-April onwards and then, alone, protects the free-swimming self-feeding young for seven weeks until they fledge.

Another species that feeds extensively by diving is the **Little Grebe** or **Dabchick** but it will remain in shallower water, usually about one metre in depth, and thus is associated with stretches along the shore or adjoining reedbeds. Its food includes small fish, insects and their larvae, amphibian larvae, crustaceans and molluscs. When diving for these it jumps slightly with a flick of its broad, semi-webbed toes and usually remains submerged for about a quarter of a minute. It will also feed while swimming on the surface by submerging its head and will take insects from floating and emergent aquatic vegetation. Fish are usually brought to the surface before swallowing, but smaller prey may be swallowed under water. They feed singly or in pairs but most usually the Little Grebe will remain solitary, many birds retaining a territory throughout the year. Broadly distributed throughout the British Isles, it occurs on a wide variety of lakes and ponds ranging from very large lakes with vegetated, shelving banks, to gravel pits and even small farm ponds and ornamental waters in town parks. On larger lakes it may be present with Great Crested Grebes as the two species apparently do not seriously compete. The population fluctuates in relation to hard winters, but is possibly increasing slowly in the longer term and the total population now exceeds 10,000 pairs.

It is the smallest European grebe (27cm). The body colour remains uniformly brown throughout the year, but in summer plumage the cheeks and throat of both sexes become bright chestnut and there is a noticeable white patch at the base of the bill. Unlike many grebe species courtship is rather simple, calling playing as important a role as either plumage or behaviour. If a pair have not remained together during the winter, pairing appears to be complete by February. This is in preparation for the long breeding season which extends from March to July during which two and sometimes three broods are raised. Displaying birds will face one another, simultaneously uttering a loud extended trilling note, interspersed with head shaking.

The nest, formed from heaps of water weeds, is built by both birds amongst emergent aquatic vegetation close to the shore or amongst branches of the bank vegetation overhanging the water. The four to six eggs are laid in April in a simple cup in the centre and the incubating bird covers them with leaves before leaving. Incubation by both birds lasts about three and a half weeks and then the free-swimming young are tended by both parents for about nine weeks unless the female starts to nest again. They are reluctant to fly and when they do, remain low over the water and become airborne for only a short distance. When they disperse in winter some birds move to large, slow moving rivers and others to the coast where small flocks may be formed.

Surface feeders include the common and widespread Mute Swan, Mallard and Teal duck and the less common Shoveller duck. Because of its semi-domesticated status, the **Mute Swan** is tame and easy to approach and hence one of our best known water birds. Its large size (*c.* 152cm) and white plumage single it out from all the others with the exception of the Bewick's and Whooper Swan which both winter in the British Isles. Both of these, however, have knobless, black and yellow bills, in contrast to the orange bill and black knob of the Mute Swan and much of the time they hold their necks straight, whereas that of the Mute is usually held in a gentle curve. The male Mute can be distinguished from the female by its larger knob and juveniles are brownish with grey bills until the end of their first winter, after which they gradually assume adult plumage.

Mute Swan

It is a sedentary species which is widely distributed, although uncommon in north-west Scotland and absent from Shetland. In summer it will occupy lakes, reservoirs, large gravel pits and slow flowing rivers and canals, where it feeds on bottom vegetation by neck dipping or up ending in water of up to a metre in depth. It will also take vegetation from the water surface and bank and less commonly come ashore to graze on wet meadows and young corn. On land it is ungainly and even on water is reluctant to fly, requiring a long take-off. In flight, its size, extended neck and the throb of the wings make it unmistakable and groups will fly in V or line formation. It is gregarious in winter and flocks will form in shallow coastal bays and estuaries as well as on inland sites. In contrast to the other two species, as its name suggests, it is usually silent, although it will hiss and snort. The breeding population in Britain probably remains under 5,000 pairs, with a greater number in Ireland. There are many non-breeding birds, the numbers equalling or possibly exceeding the breeders and these will often remain in flocks throughout the year.

Breeding begins at three or four years of age and pairs are often formed the year before breeding is attempted, remaining together then for many seasons. At the start of the breeding season in February they become highly territorial, with pairs separated by several kilometres along rivers or distributed round large lakes. A notable exception in Britain to this is the swannery at Abbotsbury in Dorset where large numbers nest colonially. During courtship pairs will face each other with fluffed necks and indulge in mutual head turning. Immediately prior to mating, both birds alternately dip heads and preen until the movements gradually become synchronized and mating follows.

The huge nest of one to two metres in diameter is formed from a mound of fresh and dried vegetation and built by both birds, usually in deep vegetation on the bank or an island close to the water's edge or in shallow water. The same nest may be re-occupied in subsequent seasons. A clutch of five to eight pale green eggs is laid in May and incubated almost exclusively by the female, the male only taking over for short spells while she is absent feeding. Incubation lasts five weeks and the young immediately take to water where they are guarded by both parents. Mute Swans are determined and aggressive in defence of their young, facing human and avian interlopers with wings arched and, neck retracted, hissing as they lunge forward using both feet simultaneously to obtain maximum effect. Throughout the long fledging period which can last up to five months the young feed themselves, although at first they are helped by their parents stirring up bottom vegetation with their feet or bringing it to the surface in their bills. Initially also they are brooded at night by the female and frequently ride on the parents' back. Second broods are not attempted but replacement clutches may be laid.

The **Mallard** is the commonest and most widely distributed duck. Occurring throughout the British Isles, it is frequently simply referred to as the Wild Duck. It is found in an extremely wide variety of freshwater, brackish and marine sites, including coastal bays and estuaries, lakes, rivers, reservoirs, gravel pits, ponds, ditches, marshes and even in city parks. Largely sedentary and making only local movements to the coast and large lakes in severe weather, it is gregarious outside the breeding season and commonly seen in flocks numbering hundreds or even thousands. Its wide distribution is reflected in its omnivorous diet and varied feeding techniques, which include upending or dabbling for aquatic vegetation, grazing on meadows and young corn and grubbing for invertebrates or rotten potatoes.

The largest British duck (57cm), the male is distinctive with its yellow bill, green head, white neck band, rusty breast and silver-grey body. Females are mottled brown with a greyish-green bill and so are difficult to identify except for the bright purple speculum. Both sexes have bright orange webbed feet. Males in their so-called eclipse plumage during midsummer and early autumn resemble the female, although the yellow bill is retained. Juveniles also resemble females, apart from the bill colour which is a reddish brown. They are strong fliers and leap almost vertically from land, shallow or deep water, flying strongly and quickly with rapid, shallow beats. The call is the familiar 'quack', the female's being softer. It is difficult to estimate the population of such a common species and the situation is confused locally with the introduction of hand-reared birds in attempts to improve sport, but it seems likely that the current breeding population of the British Isles is at least 150,000 and possibly as high as 300,000 pairs. The native population is supplemented by northerly breeding birds during winter.

The Mallard's selection of nest sites is also catholic and includes river and lake shores, islands, hillsides, woods, stumps, trees, farmland, roofs and specially provided nest baskets. Nests are formed from depressions in the vegetation, lined with grass and hidden in thick cover. Most are well spaced, although on certain islands they are so close they can be considered to form a colony. Pairing follows communal courtship in the winter flocks and is at its height in October and November or February and March. A typical display involves a party of males swimming rapidly but erratically with heads sunk onto their shoulders, interrupted by head flicking, bill dipping and tail wagging. Aerial chases of females by one or several males are common, and fights between males which will charge aggressively with extended necks, jab one another with their bills and bite each other's necks are also frequent occurrences. Immediately prior to mating which takes place on the water, a pair will engage in mutual vigorous head bobbing. Sexual maturity is achieved during the first year of life, many birds breeding when well under twelve months in age.

In mild springs nest building can begin in early February, but because cover is sparse a high proportion of these will be predated. Repeat clutches are, however, quicky laid. The usually large but varied clutch of between four and eighteen eggs is incubated for a month by the female alone and during feeding spells away from the nest the eggs will be covered with down. Males remain close to the nests during the initial stages of incubation and join the females as they feed, but then desert the nest site, leaving the female to care for the young. Newly hatched young leave the nest within twenty-four hours, but remain with the female which broods them at night. They are self-feeding, diving for vegetation and catching swimming insects and often stray only to be summoned or rounded up at intervals by the loudly calling female. They become independent and start flying after about eight weeks.

Like the Mallard, the **Teal** is widely distributed, but numbers are generally smaller and the breeding population of the British Isles is estimated to be between 3,500 and 6,000 pairs. Breeding in many areas is thought to be spasmodic, but during winter the population is increased by northerly migrants. Outside the breeding season they are gregarious and commonly form small flocks of usually fewer than fifty individuals. Omnivorous in their diet, they take a variety of vegetation, seeds and invertebrate food in shallow water by up-ending, swimming with head submerged and diving and they will also graze and dabble in mud. Their selection of feeding grounds is equally varied, ranging from shallow coasts and estuaries, through saltmarshes to vegetated ponds, small streams and ditches.

The plumage is not boldly marked and its small size (36cm) and fast flight with rapidly beating, small, pointed wings in compact flocks are often the best guide to its identification. At close range the male's chestnut head and bright metallic green eye patch outlined in white stand out from the grey body. The uniformly brown female resembles a small female Mallard except that the scapulars are green rather than purple. Both males in autumn eclipse plumage and juveniles resemble the female. They readily take flight, springing from the water before sweeping about like a flock of waders. Males have a whistling 'crrick crrick' call and females a soft quack.

Favourite breeding sites are ponds or shallow, well vegetated parts of larger meres, but moorland pools and streams are also used. The nest is a hollow lined with grass, formed by the female in thick vegetation close to or in the water, often under overhanging branches. Teal start breeding in their first year and the sequence of events is similar to that of the Mallard, pairing starting while the birds are still in their winter flocks. Several males will gather round a female, swimming erratically while head shaking and flicking, whistling loudly much of the time, and short pursuit flights are common.

Pairs disperse to breeding sites in the early spring and the clutch of eight to eleven eggs is laid during April. Incubation for three weeks is by the female only which covers the eggs with down when leaving the nest to feed. Males desert the females during incubation, moving short distances to undergo the moult. The young leave the nest soon after hatching and throughout the following month are guarded by the female. They are self-feeding but when small are brooded during the night by the female. Throughout this period they will remain in deep cover and in contrast to Mallard families are difficult to locate. Second broods are not attempted but repeat clutches are common.

The last relatively common, surface-feeding duck is the **Shoveller**, which derives its name from its large, flat, spatulate bill. The sides of both upper and lower mandibles are lined with large numbers of thin lamellae which form fine combs. Water taken in through the broad tip is expelled through the lamellae, which trap zooplankton, seeds and plant particles. Nutrient-rich lowland meres with muddy, vegetated shallows are favoured feeding sites, but lowland swamps in meadowland and brackish coastal marshes are also used. When feeding, the birds, singly or in small groups, wade belly deep sifting liquid mud, or swim with head thrust forward sweeping from side to side. Upending and diving are uncommon.

Shoveller

A medium-sized (48cm) duck, most readily recognized by its large bill and compact, short-necked appearance, the colouring of the male is vivid, the dark green head contrasting with the white chest and bright chestnut flanks. Females, however, are a nondescript brown and resemble a large-billed Mallard, although the speculum is green rather than purple and in flight the pale blue forewing is noticeable. During early summer males begin moulting and in their eclipse plumage resemble females. The moult is drawn out and often not completed until November or December and in the initial stages they are flightless for almost a month. Juveniles resemble females. They swim low in the water with the bill characteristically inclined downwards and are strong fliers, springing from the water's surface and flying swiftly with rapid wingbeats which frequently produce a whistle. The large bill is usually evident even in flight. Males have a soft 'took took' call and females quack.

British breeding Shovellers are migratory, flying south in August and September to France and Spain. They are replaced by more northerly breeding birds which winter in the British Isles and pass through on migration. Outside the breeding season they form flocks, typically containing less than fifty birds, but sometimes numbering hundreds. During the first half of the twentieth century breeding numbers in Britain increased, but appear to have levelled off with about 1,000 pairs now breeding in the British Isles. These are widely but generally thinly spread, with the largest numbers in south-east England and very few in the south-west, Wales, Scotland and Ireland.

Like many duck species, pairing takes place while the birds are still grouped in winter. The display is less spectacular than in many duck species, small numbers of males rapidly paddling round females while engaging in head bobbing, head shaking and ritualized feeding. Short courtship flights are common. Breeding pairs are strongly territorial and returning pairs take up their territories during February and March. Females will hollow out a shallow cup in vegetation close to the mere side or in tussocks in meadows and line it with grass. The clutch of nine to eleven eggs is laid in May and incubated solely by the female for twenty-three days, the male remaining in the vicinity until hatching time and then leaving to moult. The self-feeding young which leave the nest shortly after hatching are cared for by the female for about six weeks until fledging. Only one brood is attempted, but repeat clutches are common.

In addition to the common breeding species just described, there are three other categories of waterfowl that may be encountered in smaller numbers on inland freshwater bodies. The first comprises breeders whose main areas lie outside the British Isles, the second introduced species that have become established in the wild and the third winter visitors.

There are three duck outstanding in the first category – the Pintail, Gadwall and Garganey. Probably fewer than fifty pairs of **Pintail** breed in the British Isles and most of these are thinly scattered throughout Scotland and northern and eastern England. It has been found breeding on moorland pools and small lochs as well as freshwater lakes and marshes. A large duck (56cm), the silver-grey male is distinctive with chocolate-brown head and greatly elongated central tail feathers, but the elongated tail is lacking in the uniformly mottled brown female which is difficult to distinguish. Pintails are widely distributed in northern tundra regions and birds from Iceland, Sweden,

Finland and Russia winter in the British Isles, most favouring sheltered estuaries or lakes close to the coast. Large resident flocks, comprising several thousand birds, are present in most winters on the Cheshire Dee and the Nene and Ouse Washes in East Anglia, while elsewhere they may be found in smaller, scattered groups.

There are also fewer than fifty breeding pairs of **Garganey** and most of these are confined to south-east England. Britain forms the extreme western edge of their wide breeding distribution and British birds winter in Africa, returning to breed on freshwater and brackish lakes in April and departing again during September. A small duck (38cm), the male has a distinct white eye stripe on an otherwise brown head and the female is uniformly mottled brown.

The **Gadwall** is the commonest of the three with about 500 pairs breeding in the British Isles, most of which nest on shallow, well vegetated, freshwater lakes in East Anglia. This small resident population is supplemented by small numbers of winter migrants from Europe and Iceland, but the main breeding area for this species is the USSR. A large duck (51cm), the females are uniformly mottled brown and even the males appear a rather dull brown-grey, but at rest and in flight both display a distinct white wing mark.

The most notable of the introduced waterbirds are the Ruddy and Mandarin ducks and Canada Goose. The small (41cm) **Ruddy Duck** is a North American species that has become established on small lakes and reservoirs in Cheshire, the West Midlands and Gloucestershire and the present breeding population is probably still under fifty pairs although it may be increasing. The white cheeks of the males stand out from the otherwise reddish plumage and the longish tail is evident in both sexes. The **Mandarin Duck** comes from East Asia and several hundred pairs are now breeding on small lakes in Surrey and East Berkshire. The males with their long crests, orange wing-fans and bright, variegated plumage must be the most striking in appearance of all ducks.

The **Canada Goose**, another North American species, is the most numerous and long established of the three. By the eighteenth century escaped pairs were reported feeding in the wild and numbers are now estimated to exceed 10,000 individuals. Most of these are on park lakes, meres and reservoirs in England. It is long lived, has few predators and a high breeding success, so numbers are still increasing. Recent attempts to reduce the size of flocks by transporting small parties to new localities appear simply to have accelerated the increase. Local flocks have shown themselves to be essentially sedentary, although one flock of 700 undertakes an annual summer migration to the Beauly Firth in Inverness-shire to moult.

A large (95cm) bird with uniform brown upperparts, the Canada Goose is most readily identified by its long, black neck and distinctive white throat patch, and the sexes are alike. It is reluctant to fly and has a loud trumpeting honk. A vegetarian, it feeds on the stems, leaves, roots, tubers and seeds of grasses and other meadow vegetation including sprouting corn. Breeding starts at the age of three years and the nest, a small pile of reeds and grasses with a down-lined cup, is built by the female on the ground close to the water's edge and often near a bush or tree. Islands are favoured sites and the five to six eggs are laid in April and incubated by the female for a month and then the self-feeding young are guarded by both parents for the seven weeks to fledging. Second broods are not attempted but repeat clutches are common and a high proportion of individuals in local flocks are non-breeding.

Winter visitors include the Smew Duck and the Whooper and Bewick's Swans. The **Smew** is a small (41cm) diving duck which breeds in Scandinavia and northern Russia. Winter migrants reach England during September and remain until May and highest numbers are recorded in January and February. Most are confined to small lakes, reservoirs and estuaries in south-east England, in particular the Thames valley. Males appear white with black face patches and other black markings, while females are greyish with a red head and white cheeks.

Most of the **Whooper Swans** probably come from Iceland. First arrivals appear in late September and initially may remain in large flocks but during winter they will disperse widely in small groups of generally less than fifty birds to shallow lochs and lakes and occasionally to the coast, mainly within central and southern Scotland, northern

Whooper Swan

118

England and Ireland. Later some will move further south into England onto flood waters on meadowland. In most winters the population of the British Isles numbers about 6,500 of which 2,000 are in Ireland. A larger bird (*c.* 150cm) than the Bewick's Swan (*c.* 120cm), it has a mainly yellow bill with black at the tip. **Bewick's Swans** nest in the Russian tundra and typically about 200,000–250,000 winter in the British Isles. Most are restricted to a limited number of regular sites in eastern England (the Cambridgeshire Ouse Washes being the outstanding locality) and on the river Severn in Gloucestershire. They are more widely scattered in Ireland. First arrivals appear towards the end of the year, but the majority arrive in January and February. The Bewick's has a mainly black bill with yellow restricted to the base and both species are vegetarians, grazing leaves, shoots, roots and tubers.

There is only one bird of prey closely associated with the deeper, open water of large lakes – the rare **Osprey**. A large (51–58cm) dark-brown bird, with a white, crested head and underparts, its distinctive plumage, together with its long wings and method of hunting by hovering over the water before diving and plunging to grab a fish in its talons, makes it distinctive. A migratory species wintering in Africa, it continued to breed in Scotland despite persecution until the early twentieth century when the last pair was killed. Recolonization occurred in the mid-1950s and since then, under strict protection, numbers have gradually increased until there are now over twenty pairs attempting to breed in most years in Scotland. Facilities are provided for the public to see the pair nesting at the original re-colonization site at the Loch Garten reserve of the Royal Society for the Protection of Birds and for another pair at the Loch of the Lowes reserve of the Scottish Wildlife Trust in Perthshire.

REEDBEDS, MARSH AND BANK VEGETATION

Reedbeds, with their dense forests of stems and deep shade, provide a marked contrast to the adjoining open water and birds living in them reflect the special conditions reeds provide. In contrast to birds of open water which escape by strong, rapid flight or by diving and swimming underwater, reedbed species rely more on camouflage and cover. Smaller ones, such as the Reed Warbler, slip agilely out of sight down the stems, the Bearded Tit flies dexterously and confusingly between the reed-heads, the larger Bittern, skulking in the shadows, freezes at the approach of danger, pointing its bill skywards to complete its camouflage, while the Moorhen sinks quietly out of sight beneath the water surface, leaving only its bill protruding for air.

Reedbeds are a transient habitat, occupying the shallows between the advancing vegetation and scrub of the land on one side and the deeper water of the lake on the other. They are also found fringing estuary shores above the reach of sea water. In Britain reedbeds have never flourished to any great extent in the north and west and elsewhere, in the face of a long history of drainage and reclamation, they are now a scarce and much reduced habitat with most of the major surviving ones located in East Anglia. Although still extensive in Ireland, their westerly location and impoverished nature limits their value for birds. In the absence of reeds the shallows may contain sedges, marestail and other aquatic vegetation, grading into lush marsh vegetation and alder and willow scrub.

Because reedbeds are scarce only four species are almost completely dependent on them. These are the Reed Warbler, Bearded Tit, Bittern and Marsh Harrier and only the first of these, a migrant from Africa, is relatively numerous. **Reed Warblers** arrive in south-east Britain at the end of April, the major part of the population dispersing to breeding areas in eastern and south-eastern England. Smaller numbers occur in scattered localities in central and southern England, very few are present in Wales and northern England and they are usually absent from Scotland and Ireland. Unobtrusive and secretive, it is difficult to estimate the total number breeding in Britain, but it is thought to lie between 50,000 and 100,000 pairs.

It is a small (12.5cm), slim, nondescript bird with slightly rufous, uniformly brown upperparts and paler beneath. It lacks the markings of the Sedge Warbler (see p. 122) with which it is most likely to be confused and its presence is most readily indicated by its monotonous, but distinctive, persistent song 'churr, churr, churr, chirruc, chirruc chirruc'. It also has a characteristic 'churr' alarm note, usually made from cover.

Most nest colonially in reedbeds although it will also nest amongst tall marshland vegetation, including plants such as meadow sweet and purple loosestrife, or in willow, hawthorn and other scrub on the bankside. Breeding birds usually fly considerable distances to feed and are often aggressive towards others from the colony feeding in the same area. Display is limited to fanning the wings and tail and raising the feathers of the crown and the neat, deeply cupped nest, supported by several reed-stems, is built of grass and reed-heads by the female. Four eggs are laid in June and incubated by both parents for eleven or twelve days and then both feed the young in the nest for a similar period, bringing compact 'balls' of insects in their bills. They are active feeders concentrating on insects and their larvae, although spiders and dragonflies are also taken. Most pairs are double-brooded, before beginning their return migration in August and September.

The resident **Bearded Tit** (or Bearded Reedling as it is often known as it does not belong to the Tit family) is uncommon and restricted in distribution and because of its dependence on reedbeds is affected by the severity of winters. In recent years numbers have fluctuated around

500 pairs, most being located in eastern and south-eastern England. During winter they are gregarious and re-colonization of depleted areas follows autumn irruptions from places with a high breeding success. Males are bright rufous with blue-grey heads and a black moustache while females are duller and lack the moustache. They have a characteristic 'ching' call. The nest is typically built low down in reeds, the birds flying up to 100 metres to feed on insects and their larvae. Both parents share the two weeks' incubation of the five to seven eggs and the feeding of the young by food brought in the bill.

The **Bittern**, which became extinct in Britain towards the end of the nineteenth century and then re-colonized in the early twentieth, is even less common with fewer than 50 pairs largely confined to East Anglia apart from the notable exception of the Leighton Moss Reserve of the Royal Society for the Protection of Birds in north Lancashire. A large (75cm) secretive, heron-like bird, it is almost invisible amongst the reeds because of its buff-brown speckled plumage. Solitary and territorial, its presence is confirmed by its extraordinary booming call which may be heard day or night from February to June. The nest, a mound of plant remains, is hidden in the reeds and the typical clutch is four or six olive eggs. The single brood is fed mainly on fish for over seven weeks before fledging.

One raptor is associated with reedbeds – the rare **Marsh Harrier**. The total breeding population of the British Isles is around twenty-five pairs and is confined to East Anglia. It is the largest (48–56cm) of the

Marsh Harrier

harriers and while it will hunt by quartering the ground in typical harrier fashion, dropping onto small birds and mammals, is more buzzard-like with a heavier, slower flight and broader wings. Appearing dark brown, males have grey, black-tipped wings and females and juveniles yellow heads. It hunts over open rough land but in Britain will nest exclusively in reeds, the female building a substantial ground nest of reeds and sticks. The three to eight eggs are incubated by the female, which is fed by the male which brings food in its claws, passing this in a flight-pass to the female in the vicinity of the nest. The spring aerial display involving high circling and spectacular dives is dramatic and the newly flying young remain in the breeding area for several weeks and provide good opportunities for observation.

Other species found in reedbeds, but which are equally suited to living in marshes and waterside scrub, are more numerous because of the larger number of sites available. They include the migrant, insectivorous Sedge Warbler which is similar to the Reed Warbler and occurs with it in reedbeds, although tending to favour the drier parts and readily extending its breeding sites to nearby scrub. Another insectivorous migrant warbler is the Grasshopper Warbler. The Reed Bunting, a widely distributed seed-feeder, is sufficiently versatile to occupy a variety of conditions in the vicinity of water and even open farmland considerable distances from it. The vegetarian Coot and Moorhen have different feeding habits – the Coot favouring more open shallow water and the Moorhen remaining in cover and on the bank. The secretive Water Rail, a shallow water and mud feeder, contrasts markedly with the noisy, obtrusive Black-headed Gull which, although it establishes its breeding colonies in marsh and lake vegetation occupied by Water Rails, will fly considerable distances to a variety of dry feeding sites.

Sedge Warblers arrive in Britain from Africa at the end of April and disperse to all parts of the British Isles except Shetland. Their presence is soon made apparent by their song, delivered from a high perch or in a conspicuous song flight in which the birds rise steeply for a short distance before dropping with outstretched wings and tail. The song itself is loud and strident and includes a mixture of sweet and harsh notes repeated several times. Their vocabulary also includes a harsh 'churr' and a sharp 'tuck' as alarm notes. A typical small (13cm), slim warbler, it is more distinct than most because of a noticeable white eye stripe and darkly streaked upperparts. The breeding population of the British Isles is thought to exceed half a million pairs.

They arrive at the breeding sites ahead of Reed Warblers and song can be heard from April to mid-July. In display males pursue females with extended, drooping wings and raised head feathers. Like the Reed Warbler and Bearded Tit they usually fly considerable distances from the nest to feed, but a limited territory encompassing the nest site will be defended. The rather bulky nest is well hidden in deep vegetation

Sedge Warbler

close to the ground and built by the female from moss and dry grass and lined with hair. Five or six eggs are laid in late May and incubated mainly by the female for two weeks and both parents feed the young by bringing food in the bill to the nest. Insects and their larvae form the main food items, but spiders and worms are also taken. Fledging takes two weeks and second broods are often produced.

The **Grasshopper Warbler**, like the Sedge Warbler, will nest in reedbeds and marshes but will also readily occupy dry scrub and the wetter parts of mature woods and more recently has been found nesting in young conifer plantations. It is small (13cm) and extremely secretive, spending much time low down in deep cover and hence is difficult to see. Even when seen, its olive-brown, streaked back and buff underparts are nondescript and its presence is usually only indicated by its unusual, far-carrying song – a long drawn-out, high-pitched, rapid, rather monotonous whirr, varying in pitch as the bird turns its head from side to side. Sometimes the song is uttered from an exposed branch, offering a glimpse of the bird with its wide open bill. The favoured singing times are dawn and dusk, particularly in overcast conditions, but the song can be heard at any time of the day.

Grasshopper Warblers arrive from their winter areas in north-west Africa towards the end of April and disperse to most parts of the British Isles, although they are uncommon in the northern half of Scotland and absent from Shetland. The total breeding population is thought to number about 25,000 pairs. Nests are sited very low down in reeds, rushes or in grass tussocks, often close to the outside edge of bushes or

Grasshopper Warbler

thick undergrowth. They are built with dead grass and finely lined and the clutch of six eggs is laid towards the end of May. Incubation, which lasts for two weeks, is shared by both birds and then both feed the young in the nest by bringing food in the bill for a further ten or twelve days. At this stage, although unable to fly strongly, the young leave the nest and the parents continue to feed them until they are strong on the wing. A second brood is rarely attempted. The food includes a variety of adult insects and larvae, including moths and caterpillars, and spiders and the return migration commences in September.

Three other rare and localized warblers which breed in lakeside vegetation are present in Britain. The migrant **Marsh Warbler**, with a population of just over fifty pairs, is almost indistinguishable, except by its song, from the Reed Warbler. It is decreasing and now restricted to a few localities with about three-quarters of the population in Worcestershire. The other two by contrast are recent colonists and both are increasing. **Savi's Warbler**, also a migrant, previously bred in Britain but became extinct towards the end of the nineteenth century. Recolonization of south-eastern England began about 1960 and the number of breeding pairs may now be as high as fifty and it has greatly extended its range. It favours wet areas and its presence is often first indicated by its loud, distinctive song which resembles the trill of the Grasshopper Warbler, but is louder, slower, lower pitched and lasts for shorter spells. It also has a harsh chatter. The last, **Cetti's Warbler**, was first recorded breeding in south-east England in 1972 and is now the commonest of the three with a breeding population probably exceeding 100 pairs. It is resident so numbers are affected by the severity of winters. A dark rufous, brown bird, it has an extremely loud staccato song 'chewee, chewee, pit, pit, pit' and nests in thick vegetation near water.

The **Reed Bunting** is widely distributed throughout the British Isles and the breeding population exceeds half a million pairs. Recently it has extended its distribution and now, in addition to its well known association with lakesides, rivers and marshes, it breeds in dry scrub and in low hedges and ditches on farmland more typically associated with the closely allied Yellowhammer (see p. 171). Reed Buntings are robust, streaky brown birds of 15cm length. The black head and throat of the male with its contrasting white moustachial stripes is distinctive. Females and juveniles have brown heads and a buff eye stripe and are less easy to identify but, like the male, both have white outer tail feathers. The call is a short 'tseep'. Most are resident and will disperse after the breeding season to form flocks on rough land, although there will be a general southerly movement and some will emigrate. Continental birds arrive in October to pass the winter in the British Isles.

Re-occupation of nesting sites begins in late March when males will take up prominent song perches. The song is a soft, tinkling trill 'tweek tweek tweek' terminating in a clear 'ti ti tick', the whole series repeated frequently with only short pauses. Displaying males engage in sexual chases and confront females with head feathers raised, throats puffed out and vibrating and partially opened wings and tail. The nest, built by the female in a tussock or close to the ground in a bush, is composed of grass lined with moss. The four to five eggs are laid in May and incubated for two weeks, mainly by the female and then both parents bring food in their bills to the young on the nest for the ten days to fledging. Two or three broods are undertaken in a season and the parents will readily perform distraction displays to divert attention from their young. Seeds form the principal food throughout the year, but insects and their larvae will be taken in summer.

The Coot and Moorhen are dark, rather similar, medium-sized (*c.* 37cm) birds. Superficially, with their small, erect, bobbing heads, short, sharp bills, high stepping gait and short upright tails, they resemble small domestic fowl. Both are, however, well adapted to waterside conditions, the Coot, with long, partially webbed toes, being a reasonable swimmer and diver and the Moorhen, with long, thin toes, moving easily over and through lush aquatic vegetation. Normally they are reluctant to fly, pattering with their feet on the water during take-off and then keeping low and flying straight for the nearest cover into which they make a heavy landing. Both are capable of sustained flight at altitude during dispersal.

The **Coot** is grey-black apart from a white forehead and bill and in flight it shows a white wing bar. Juveniles are duller and whiteish below. Gregarious, it is frequently found with duck in the shallows amongst or just beyond the vegetation. When swimming, the head is jerked back and forwards and it makes a slight jump before diving. A vegetarian, it commonly feeds by making shallow dives to pull vegetation from the bottom which it then brings to the surface to sort and swallow and it will also browse on floating vegetation and occasionally go ashore to feed in meadows. Often noisy and quarrelsome, its call is a sharp, loud 'owk kowk' or a shrill 'skeek' and confrontations with wildly threshing wings and feet and a great deal of splashing may end in sudden chases. Widely distributed, it is common everywhere apart from north-west Scotland where it is infrequent and Shetland from which it is absent. The breeding population is between 50,000 and 100,000 pairs and is largely sedentary except in hard weather when some will move to the coast.

During spring both displays and fights can readily be witnessed within groups of birds. Sparring males will face each other with half-open wings and erect tails, while displaying pairs face each other in similar posture with heads depressed low over the water surface. Mutual preening is also common. Both birds help to build the substantial nest, the male bringing much of the material. This is usually situated in water and well hidden deep within reeds or other vegetation. The clutch of four to eight buffish, black-speckled eggs is laid in April and incubation shared by both birds for just over three weeks. For the first few days the young will remain in the nest, protected and brooded by the female and fed by the male. The nest is then vacated and the young learn to feed themselves. Initially they are covered in black down, but have a rufous head and neck which distinguishes them from the otherwise similar Moorhen chicks. The chick's feeding call is a rasping 'creer' and fledging takes about eight weeks, after which second and sometimes third broods are undertaken.

The **Moorhen** is dark olive brown, relieved by white stripes along the flank and a bright red forehead and bill with yellow tip. When swimming the tail is jerked, displaying white under-tail coverts, and in flight there is no white wing bar which helps to separate it from the Coot. The sexes are alike and juveniles have dull bills and forehead but are less white below than juvenile Coots. It is a strong walker which, when disturbed, will bolt head down for cover uttering a loud sudden call 'curruc' and a trilling 'kik kik kik'. Widely distributed throughout the British Isles, the breeding population lies between a quarter and half a million pairs, fluctuating with severe winters. It is highly versatile, occupying aquatic sites from ditches, small ponds and streams to the banks of large lakes and rivers. Sedentary and often solitary and territorial throughout the year, it will form flocks during winter.

An extended breeding season lasts from March to August, although activity is greatest during April and May. The male will build a number of platforms hidden in vegetation within the territory which are used for display and mating before one is built up to form the nest. Fighting males fly at each other, striking out with wildly working legs and thrashing wings, causing considerable commotion. In display the pair meet with lowered heads and raised wings and tail, bow and undertake sexual chases. Mating is normally on land, but does occur on water. The nest, which can be in the water or on the land, is a well hidden, large, deep cup built of dead and fresh leaves and stems of reeds, sedges and other aquatic vegetation. Most of the work is done by the male assisted by the female.

The five to eleven eggs are incubated by both birds for three weeks and the young remain in the nest for the first few days, tended and fed by both parents, before they become active and gradually learn to fend for themselves. Initially they are covered with black down and after three weeks will wander widely, although they remain dependent to some extent on the parents for about five weeks before flying at six or seven weeks. Repeat clutches are readily laid and most pairs are double brooded, some occasionally producing a third brood. They are strong walkers from an early age and much of their feeding is done as they move agilely through the thick bank vegetation or while half swimming and walking amongst the lake shore plants. They regularly stray onto meadows and will swim into deep water. Seed, roots, fruits and stems of a range of aquatic and marsh plants are obtained by pulling and pecking with the short sharp bill.

The **Water Rail**, like the Bittern, is a solitary bird, relying on camouflage and secretive habits for protection. It tends to remain in

Water Rail

127

deep cover, crouching motionless if disturbed and when surprised in
the open will run, head down, for cover. Slightly smaller (25cm) than a
Common Snipe, it appears slim and generally dark brown. It is grey
beneath and heavily barred black along the flanks and its slim shape is
emphasized by a long, slender, red bill and short tail. In flight it trails
its legs, remaining low and appears weak and fluttering, although it is
capable of high, sustained flight. Its calls include a variety of squeaks
and grunts and a high pitched trilling whistle.

Widely but thinly distributed, it is absent from parts of north-west
Scotland and is particularly common in many parts of Ireland. It is
resident but because of its secretive nature numbers are difficult to
gauge and it is thought the breeding population of the British Isles
numbers between 2,000 and 4,000 pairs although, like many aquatic
species, these fluctuate in relation to hard winters. Provided there is
plenty of dense cover, it can be found in a variety of aquatic sites
including rivers and canal banks, lakesides, marshes and gravel pits
and many retain territories throughout the year. The long toes enable it
to cross floating vegetation and mud and it swims in muddy shallows,
taking a variety of small animals such as snails, shrimps, fish and frogs,
as well as a variety of insects for which it probes and picks from the
surface.

Neighbouring pairs and nests are separated by strongly defended
territories. Pairs engage in sexual chases and males have a short song
'tyick tyick tyick' terminating with a trilling 'tywirrr' and during
display the head is lowered and the white tail coverts exposed. The
ground nest, a deep cup of dead leaves and stems of reeds and sedges, is
well hidden in a tussock or amongst dense vegetation and the six to
eleven eggs are laid in May to be incubated by both birds for about
three weeks. Initially the young are fed and tended in the nest, but by
the end of the first week are active and feeding themselves although
they will remain with the parents for over a month and stay in the
vicinity of the nest for a further month while the parents normally start
a second clutch.

The **Black-headed Gull** is the smallest (35–38cm) and most widely
distributed inland breeding gull in Britain, establishing colonies in a
wide variety of sites from sand dunes and salt marshes to moorland
tarns, as well as on large numbers of small lakes and meres. During the
nineteenth century its population was smaller, but since then there has
been a steady increase and the number of breeding pairs in the British
Isles now almost certainly exceeds a quarter of a million. It is widely
distributed, although still absent as a breeding species inland in the
southern half of England but very common on the coast of East Anglia.
White with a light grey back, it is quite distinct in the summer with
chocolate-brown head, bright red bill and legs. During winter the
chocolate is lost apart from a dark spot behind the eye, but the white
forewing and black tips remain as a good characteristic. The sexes are

Black-headed Gull

alike and juveniles are mottled with pale bills. Small numbers of Common Terns (see p. 83) are beginning to nest on inland waters and superficially these may be overlooked amongst the Black-headed Gulls.

Flight is strong and buoyant and they are frequently noisy, uttering a short 'kraah' call or a raucous 'kwur-ir-up'. They will walk and search for food in flocks on arable and grass fields and will follow the plough and harass Lapwings to rob them of food. They will also quarter low over the incoming tide and dive to snatch food on or just below the surface, search tidelines, or puddle wet sand to bring worms to the surface and in late summer swirling flocks will gather to attack swarms of flying ants in mid-air. Omnivorous in diet, they favour animals ranging from insects and their larvae to soil invertebrates, small marine fish, crustaceans, molluscs and shore invertebrates.

Nesting is colonial, usually on tussocks in the marshes bordering lakes or in the vegetated shallows or on islands. Nesting birds are noisy and conspicuous, rising in unison to mob passing Herons and Carrion Crows and other predators. Nests are crowded together, colonies including a few pairs or many thousands and by March display and fighting will be in full swing. Displaying birds will stand with head erect and partially opened wings, flicking their head sideways or crouching with head and bill inclined and tail fanned. The nest is a scrape, sparingly lined with vegetation, and the three olive, blotched eggs are laid in April and incubated for three and a half weeks by both birds. The parents feed the young in the nest for five weeks to fledging and by August the colonies will be deserted as second broods are not

129

attempted, the birds dispersing locally and only small numbers migrating.

GRAVEL PITS AND WATERMEADOWS

Four species are so closely associated with specialized parts of the aquatic habitat that they should be considered separately – the Little Ringed Plover and Sand Martin with gravel and sand pits and the Yellow Wagtail and Common Snipe with watermeadows. The numbers and distribution of these species, with the exception of the Snipe which is less specific in its habitat selection, are to a considerable extent determined by the existence of these features. Gravel and sand winning is still expanding so the Little Ringed Plover and Sand Martin benefit but, by contrast, the continuing drainage and loss of watermeadows is proving detrimental to the Snipe and Yellow Wagtail.

Prior to 1938, when the **Little Ringed Plover** was first recorded breeding in Hertfordshire, it was an infrequent summer migrant to the British Isles. Since this first record numbers have gradually increased, closely linked to the expansion of the sand and gravel industry, until the total population is now about 500 pairs. It is almost without exception confined to England and is still absent from the south-west peninsula. It is smaller (15cm) than the Ringed Plover (see p. 80) and in flight the absence of a white wing bar in the Little Ringed Plover is a good distinguishing character while the mainly dark bill and pale, flesh-coloured legs contrast with the orange-yellow of those of the Ringed Plover. It has a distinctive 'tee-ū' call. The nest is a hollow

Little Ringed Plover

130

scratched in sand or shingle close to water and in spring the birds can be seen engaging in their attractive slow-flapping butterfly flight. Four eggs are laid in April and incubated by both birds for twenty-five days and the young leave the nest immediately after hatching to be tended by both parents for about three weeks. Food includes insects, spiders and molluscs taken from the water or ground.

The **Sand Martin** is one of the swallow tribe and, like the others, is an aerial feeder taking insects as it sweeps back and forth on the wing. Although it often feeds low over water, it is equally suited to feeding over land or at considerable heights and its link with sand and gravel pits lies in the opportunity they provide for nest sites. The smallest (12cm) of the swallow tribe, it is distinctive with its uniform light brown back and white underparts with a broad brown band across the chest. The wings are pointed and the tail slightly forked and it perches readily on telephone and fence wires or bushes and will cling to the vertical faces of the nest sites.

One of the earliest of the spring migrants, it begins to arrive at breeding sites early in April and is gregarious at all times – when feeding, nesting and during migration. It is one of the species thought to have been affected by the recent drought in the Sahel in North Africa and the present British population of about a quarter of a million breeding pairs is considered to be much lower than before. Clean, soft, stable sand and fine gravel faces provide ideal nest sites, the pair excavating a horizontal tunnel, which may be up to one metre in length, with a small chamber at the end. Artificial faces in sand and gravel workings or road and railway embankments are more widely used than natural faces on river banks. Colonies range in size from a few pairs to hundreds and other species, in particular the Tree Sparrow and Starling, will make use of the Sand Martin's burrows.

The breeding season is protracted with the first young fledged as early as the end of May and others from second and third broods flying for the first time just prior to the autumn migration in August and September. The song is a twittering repetition of the call note and there is always activity at the colony, birds diving and circling, clinging to the sand face or perched on the lip of their burrows. In common with other colonially nesting birds, the whole colony will suddenly and inexplicably rise simultaneously at irregular intervals as though alarmed, only to return shortly as though nothing had happened. The nest is sparsely lined with feathers and dry grass and the four to five eggs are white and incubated for two weeks. The young are then fed in the nest by both parents. Non-breeders and the early fledged young establish large roosts in reedbeds or scrub to be joined by most of the local population in preparation for the autumn departure.

The **Yellow Wagtail** is also a summer migrant from Africa which arrives in Britain from tropical West Africa in April and May and departs again during August and September. The total British breed-

Yellow Wagtail

ing population is considered to number 25,000 pairs and most of these are in England, seldom being found in the north and west of Wales and absent from most of Scotland and Ireland. A small (16.5cm), typical, slim, long-tailed wagtail, it has a pronounced swift, undulating flight and a fast walk or run with bobbing head and constantly flicking tail and will freely perch on posts, walls and bushes. Individuals may vary in coloration and numerous distinct geographical races have been described in different parts of its wide range throughout the Palearctic. In Britain they are generally greenish-brown above and yellow beneath with bright yellow heads. Females are duller and the yellow on individual males can appear startlingly canary-yellow bright. They have a clear sharp 'tsweep' call.

The drier parts of lush, damp river meadows are used as breeding sites and they will also occupy coastal marshes. Displaying males will engage in aerial chases both of rival males and potential mates and hover over females or approach with puffed feathers, emphasizing the yellow breast, and elevated tail. There is also a song flight, a musical trill, which is started from a perch and continued in an undulating, fluttering flight. Following the establishment of territories, females select nest sites and construct the nest which will be situated on the ground in tussocks or hidden under clods or amongst root crops and densely lined with hair and fur. The six eggs are laid in May and incubated for a fortnight by the female and both birds then feed the young in the nest for just under two weeks by bringing insects in their bill. Most pairs are double brooded.

Common Snipe

The **Common Snipe** (27cm) favours the wetter parts of river meadows, with rushy fields, marshes and bogs. They are widely distributed in all parts of the British Isles and the population is estimated at 100,000 pairs. Generally secretive, they are most active in the late evening although, particularly in winter, they will feed in full daylight. They rely on their camouflage for protection and typically crouch at the approach of danger, before suddenly springing into the air uttering a harsh 'creech' alarm note and zig-zagging vigorously in low flight for several metres before rising steeply in more direct rapid flight.

The dappled plumage appears striped and the principal diagnostic character is the long straight bill – the largest in proportion to body length of any other species. They are usually sedentary and solitary, but in winter disperse and will sometimes gather in small groups and in severe conditions make local movements to the coast. The food is a variety of soil invertebrates, snails, woodlice and, in particular, worms. These are found by probing deeply and vigorously into soft mud and soil, the bill often submerged up to the base and jerked up and down while the food may be swallowed without the bill being withdrawn.

Their presence on the breeding sites is readily demonstrated by their aerial drumming. This is done by both sexes, but more readily by the males, usually at dusk but sometimes at night and during the day as well. Displaying birds rise to a height of about 100 metres and then at intervals enter steep dives, regaining height between each dive while broadly circling the breeding grounds. During the dive the wings will be half-closed, the tail fanned and the outer tail feathers on each side extended beyond the others, vibrating to produce a loud, far carrying drumming sound. During the flight they will also turn onto their backs and glide for short periods. Territory holding birds engage extensively in a 'chip-per chiper-per' call uttered from the ground or from a fence post or wall and displaying males will approach females with drooped wings and tail.

In an extended breeding season, young hatch from May to August. Nests are on the ground, with the majority in wet grassland in hollows in a grass, rush or sedge tussock and lined with dry grass. The typical clutch is four with most laid in April and the eggs are incubated for 20 days by the female. The young leave the nest immediately they are dry and feed themselves. The parents sometimes divide the brood between them, each tending part, the adults perching on walls and posts and uttering alarm calls at the approach of danger. The parents have been recorded flying with the young held between their legs. Fledging takes three weeks and some pairs will undertake second broods. Predation and cattle tramping are the principal causes of nest failures.

In addition to suitable habitat for breeding birds, lowland freshwater sites also provide valuable feeding sites for spring and autumn migrants. During these times of the year they carry a different and changing bird fauna, including common species such as the Dunlin and Common Sandpiper that breed in the British Isles as well as rarer species such as the Little Gull, Black Tern and Spotted Redshank which rarely or never breed in Britain. They represent an interesting and valuable element of the bird habitats of the British Isles and one which is vulnerable to change – rivers may be deepened and canalized, marshes drained or overgrown and reedbeds dried out. Such losses are to some extent offset by the construction of new reservoirs, gravel and sand pits, and one of the most fortunate features of wetland is that it is one of the most readily re-created habitats.

·5·
Woodland

Nowadays woodland accounts for something like one-tenth of the surface cover of the British Isles and, with the intensively farmed land devoted to agriculture, replaces the vast, almost continuous, broadleaf woods that in prehistoric times covered most of the land surface. While some farmland birds, such as the Skylark and Partridge, are adapted to open plains and find a similar niche in flat, broad farm fields, most farmland birds are woodland species which persist in the remnants of woods, copses, scrub and hedges included in farmland. Almost half the regular breeding species of the British Isles evolved in woodland conditions, hence the importance of woodland and farmland as a habitat despite the impoverished nature of the latter.

The importance of woodland does not derive solely from its once extensive nature, but also from its composition. It includes a rich and diverse range of sub-habitats. A single mature tree supports a vast tangled canopy encompassing literally thousands of branchlets which, during a season, will sustain buds, leaves, flowers and fruit. These in turn support a teeming insect life. The larger branches and the main trunk likewise are host to further, often different, insects, living on the surface and in the cracks, crevices, holes and rotten patches. Beneath the canopy there is usually a sub-layer created by saplings and bushes, under which again lies a varied ground fauna and flora. When trees are grouped together in even a small piece of woodland, the space formed by glades, rides and at the woodland edge where it grades into scrub or open fields, present yet different opportunities for wildlife. This complex and diverse habitat is exploited to the full by a large, fascinating group of birds which finds food, shelter and nesting sites there.

It is possible to separate bird species linked more closely with different sub-divisions of this habitat, in particular those associated with broadleafed and mixed woodland rather than conifers, or those favouring the woodland edge, scrub, hedges and heath and finally those of the open farmland. Because so much of the land surface is taken up by this habitat, birds from other habitats are often dependent on it for parts of the year. Thus, as we have seen, wintering geese feed on farmland, flocks of waders, in particular the Lapwing and Golden Plover, spend most of the winter on lowland fields and some gulls feed regularly inland. Other species, such as the Heron, use woodland for their nesting colonies but otherwise have no links with it.

BROADLEAF
AND MIXED WOODLAND

Individual woods, even different parts of the same wood, will vary greatly. Such factors as soil type, drainage, aspect, age and variety of trees, their spacing and the extent or absence of an understorey, will all profoundly affect the type and range of sub-habitats present. Some species are less rigid in their ecological needs and can exist satisfactorily in a wide variety of conditions, varying from extensive mature woodland to scattered trees and scrub. Because of this they have fared best in the face of the loss of woodland and have most readily adapted to sub-optimal remnants such as copses, hedges, parkland and gardens. As a result, they have become some of the commonest and most widely distributed of all our birds and are amongst the best known. Four outstanding examples are the Wren, Robin, Blackbird and Song Thrush. Each is associated with low cover in the understorey of woods and this probably explains their ability to succeed in hedges and gardens. All are resident, found throughout the British Isles and have breeding populations numbered in millions of pairs.

The **Wren** is the smallest (9.5cm) British brown-coloured bird (the smallest bird is the greenish-coloured Goldcrest which is 9.0cm in length). Its small size, together with its rounded, plump appearance and cocked tail, readily confirms its identity. The sexes are alike. An active bird, it moves rapidly, almost shrew-like, through brambles, scrub and rank grasses searching for food, hopping when it emerges briefly in the open and making short, direct, low flights with whirring wings. When alarmed it will utter a loud, sharp 'tic tic tic tic' alarm. Insectivorous in its diet, it picks up a wide range of adult insects and their larvae from vegetation with its fine, slender bill and the diet of nestlings includes large numbers of caterpillars. Highly adaptable, it is found from sea cliffs to the uplands and is almost certainly the commonest bird with a population possibly as high as ten million breeding pairs, although this will be considerably reduced following harsh winters.

The start of the breeding season is proclaimed by a strident song, unexpectedly loud and harsh for such a diminutive bird. Uttered from low down in cover, it lasts for about five seconds and is often repeated several times. Display includes advances and singing with partially extended wings and tail and during this period the male will build a number of unlined 'cock's' nests, one of which is eventually selected by the female. Usually low down in hedge bottoms, or in coarse vegetation or ivy on earth banks or hidden in the thatch or crevices of outbuildings, they are domed and built of moss, dead leaves and grass. Having lined the chosen nest, the five or six eggs are laid in April and incubated for a fortnight by the female and then the young are fed by both parents which bring food in the bill for a further seventeen days. Second broods are usual and during winter the nests, or holes in stacks or thatch, are used for roosting by individuals, pairs and sometimes groups of Wrens.

The **Robin**, both because of its distinctive bright orange breast and tameness, is even better known than the Wren. Olive-brown above, it is small (14cm) and the sexes are alike. Juveniles, however, are speckled and lack the orange breast. It has an upright stance, moves with a sudden series of long hops and frequently bobs and bows when nervous, uttering a sharp, warning 'tic tic'. The diet includes a wide variety of insects, together with spiders, earthworms and some seeds and fruit. A favourite method of feeding is to dart to the ground from a low perch, pick up an item and return to the perch. The population of the British Isles is thought to number about five million pairs and it is absent only from Shetland. General dispersal and a southerly movement follow the breeding season and continental immigrants arrive during the autumn, some remaining to pass the winter in the British Isles.

Robins are aggressive and territorial and during autumn both sexes may hold a territory, expelling others by a threat display, the breast and throat emphasized by stretching and looking upwards while swaying at the same time and uttering snatches of song. The soft warbling song can be heard throughout the year, but singing is at its height during spring, dusk being a favoured time. Both sexes sing, although the males more so. A wide variety of nest sites is used – hollows in banks, thick ground cover, outhouses, old tree stumps. The nest is built by the female from dead leaves and moss and lined with hair and during display, the male will feed the female. In contrast to their tameness during winter, pairs are usually secretive in the nest vicinity. The five or six eggs are laid in April and incubated for two weeks by the female which is fed by the male. Both sexes then feed the young in the nest for a further fortnight by bringing food in their bills before a second or third brood is started, usually in a fresh nest.

The Blackbird and Song Thrush are larger birds (25 and 23cm). They are frequently found together in the same vicinity, share similar nest sites and their diets overlap. At times they are aggressive towards each other, but competition between the two is not severe and in most circumstances they co-exist satisfactorily. The **Blackbird** is the commoner of the two with a British breeding population possibly as high as seven million pairs. Both species suffer in severe winters but mortality in the Song Thrush is usually greater. Male Blackbirds have a glossy black plumage, long tail and bright orange bill, females are dark brown and juveniles similar but mottled. Albinism is not uncommon and pied Blackbirds are regularly reported. Flight is low and direct to cover from which it rarely strays far and the tail is characteristically flicked upwards immediately after landing.

The song, often at dusk, is beautifully mellow and far carrying and usually delivered from a high tree perch, post or building. It is superficially similar to that of the Song Thrush, but can be distinguished by the absence of any repetition of the notes. In display pairs will face each other with raised head and tail and flicking wings or with drooping, shimmering half-open wings and tails bent forward over the back and chases are common. Nests are built largely by the female assisted by the male which brings material. The nest, which does not have the mud lining of that of the Song Thrush, is lined instead with dead grass and typically placed low down in a bush or hedge. The four to five eggs are laid in April and incubated for two weeks by the female, after which both parents feed the young in the nest for two weeks by bringing food in their bills. Two or three broods are raised, often in the same nest.

In both the Blackbird and Song Thrush an autumn dispersal is particularly marked amongst juveniles and northern breeding birds tend to move south. Most are resident, but some migrate to the Continent and there is an immigration of continental birds of both species into Britain before the onset of winter. The Blackbird feeds by running over the ground or making a series of hops, with pauses in between, often with the head cocked to one side. It is usually solitary and favoured feeding sites will be under or close to cover, where it turns over leaves and pulls up moss and dry vegetation searching for earthworms, spiders and insects. They also readily feed on apples and pears and most soft fruits such as gooseberry, strawberry, raspberry, blackcurrant and cherry, as well as a wide variety of wild berries including holly, rowan, rose, hawthorn, yew and blackberry and seeds of wild plants. This catholic diet must be an important contributory factor in their ability to survive harsh winters, when they will also readily take advantage of scraps put out in gardens. On winter evenings communal roosts are common, which may also include thrushes. They have a loud characteristic warning chuckle 'tchook tchook tchook', which can be raucous and persistent when they are mobbing owls, cats and other predators.

The **Song Thrush** is distinctive because of its yellow buff breast, covered with large dark spots. Throughout the year confusion is possible with the larger Mistle Thrush, but this has a much paler breast, even bigger spots and whitish tips to the outer tail feathers. During winter there is also possible confusion with the large numbers of

Song Thrush

immigrant Redwing and Fieldfares. The Redwing, in addition to the red feathers under the wing, has a noticeable white eye stripe and the Fieldfare a generally richer coloration including a blue-grey head and rump and chestnut back. Although the Song Thrush, like the Blackbird, is usually solitary, in winter it will frequently form communal roosts with Redwings and Fieldfares. Less common than the Blackbird with a British breeding population of about three and a half million pairs, it is equally widely distributed, being absent only from Shetland.

The far carrying song with its repeated notes delivered from a high tree, perch or building can be heard for much of the year. In display males puff out their breast feathers and run and crouch with raised heads and expanded tails. The nest is built by the female low down in a tree, bush or hedge from leaves, twigs and grass and lined with a layer of mud. The four or five eggs are laid in April and incubated mainly by the female for about two weeks, after which both sexes feed the young in the nest for a further two weeks by bringing food in the bill. Two or three broods a season are common. Flight is direct with rapid, regular beats interspersed by short spells with closed wings. The stance is upright and feeding in the open on short grass is undertaken by a series of hops and short runs interrupted by pauses, when the head is often cocked to one side. Like the Blackbird, fallen apples and plums and a wide range of soft fruits are eaten together with spiders, worms and slugs. They specialize in taking snails and characteristically smash the shells on a favourite stone or step.

Two members of the Finch family are found in broadleaf woods – the Chaffinch and Hawfinch. The former is widespread in the British Isles, whereas the latter is largely confined to England where it is widely but thinly dispersed. Like all finches, they have short, thick, sharply pointed bills. That of the Hawfinch is particularly heavy and powerful, enabling it to crush hard seed cases, nuts and fruit stones, so that it tends to favour woods containing tree species with thick coated products. The Chaffinch has a larger, finer bill enabling it to take a wide variety of small seeds and insects and this less specialized diet no doubt contributes to its abundance and wide distribution. Both species are sedentary and may form flocks in winter and move to more open country.

The **Chaffinch** is absent from Shetland but is found in mature woods, shrubs, hedges and bushes throughout the rest of the British Isles. The British population probably exceeds five million pairs. About 15cm in length, it has distinctive white shoulder patches, wing bars and outer tail feathers. Males have grey heads and are bright russet beneath, while females have yellowish-brown heads and are paler below. They have a marked undulating flight and a distinctive 'pink pink' alarm call. In addition to small seeds, buds and blooms are taken as well as insects and spiders. On the ground they hop or walk with quick steps and will often join Yellowhammers, Greenfinches and Sparrows in winter flocks, while continental immigrants winter in Britain.

They are strongly territorial and territories are taken up in February, when the short, sharp, regularly repeated, rather shrill song is a common sound in woodland everywhere. It is usually delivered from a high perch and interrupted by sexual chases and fights when flashing white feathers will be much in evidence and displaying males will crouch with drooped, fluttering wings and spread tails. The beautiful, neat nest is built in April by the female, using grasses and roots which are then covered over the outside with a grey layer of lichen. Four to five eggs are laid in May and incubated for just under two weeks by the female, during which time she is fed by the male. Both parents then feed the young at the nest for a further two weeks and second broods are not normally attempted.

The **Hawfinch**, the biggest British finch, is a considerably larger bird (18cm) but secretive and elusive and tends to fly high and remain in the treetops which makes it difficult to find. It has a sharp 'tick' call and a shrill 'tzeep' which can help to locate it. The head appears big in relation to the body and it has a large, stout bill which is blue in summer and yellow in the winter and juveniles also have yellow bills. The generally chestnut and brown coloration is relieved by a jet black throat and wing tips and a white patch on the wings and border to the tail. It is not found in Ireland or northern Scotland and the British breeding population is put between 5,000 and 10,000 pairs.

Frequenting mature deciduous woodland, parkland and orchards, it feeds in the treetops or on fallen seeds on the ground. Fruits or wych elm, hornbeam, beech, wild cherry, sycamore and maple are all taken, also cherries and other fruit and some invertebrates. During the breeding season several pairs will nest in close proximity, flying some distance from the nests to feed. Pursuit flights are followed by bowing and bill touching. The song is weak and nests are built in April following pair formation in March. The nest, a platform of stiff twigs supporting a shallow cup, is placed high on a horizontal branch, apple and pear trees being favoured. The clutch of four to six eggs is incubated by the female for the eleven or twelve days until they hatch and then both parents feed the young, but a pair can be extremely secretive throughout the breeding period.

There is a woodland sparrow, appropriately named the **Tree Sparrow**. It is of similar size (14cm) and general appearance to the familiar House Sparrow but, in contrast to the latter, is rarely found in the proximity of human dwellings, favouring instead open woodland. It also occurs in parkland and scattered trees and in East Anglia colonies have been established in pollard willows. It is widely distributed throughout lowland Britain, but scarce or absent from south-west England, west Wales, the Highlands and Ireland. Numbers in local colonies fluctuate and the total British breeding population is about a quarter of a million pairs.

It is distinguished from the House Sparrow by its chestnut, rather than grey, crown and the black patch on its cheek. The sexes are alike and juveniles resemble adults. Its call also differs slightly from that of the House Sparrow, being a higher pitched 'chee-ip-chip'. It feeds on a wide range of seeds, but also takes insects and spiders and during the summer and autumn will take corn. A resident species, it disperses at the end of the breeding season to form flocks which roost communally on bushes or in holes in trees.

Holes and ivy-covered trees are favoured nest sites and they will readily take to nest boxes. Some heronries support colonies of Tree Sparrows where pairs will occupy the lower part of both occupied and unoccupied Herons' nests and they will also use old Sand Martins' burrows. The song is a rather monotonous, unmusical 'twit-it-it-it-chit' and displaying pairs run along boughs with bill and tail erect and wings extended. Both sexes help to build the big, rather untidy nest and the four to six eggs are laid in May. Both birds also share incubation which lasts for two weeks and then together feed the young in the nest. Two and occasionally three broods are reared.

THE TIT FAMILY

The tits form an important group of woodland birds which includes seven species – Blue, Marsh, Willow, Great, Coal, Crested and Long-tailed. All, with the exception of the Crested Tit, are widespread and common and share a similar lifestyle. They are resident, short-lived and during winter wander in flocks (sometimes including several species) and take up breeding territories in spring. Typically they nest in holes or cracks (the Long-tailed Tit being the exception) and lay large clutches of white eggs which are incubated by the female for fifteen days. The young are fed in the nest by both parents and only one brood is normally attempted. Their lightness, short legs and strong grip enable them to feed when perched on, or hanging from, thin twigs where they take a variety of insects and seeds.

Their feeding and nesting preferences differ, so the various species are found in different types of woods and within different niches in the same wood. Blue and Marsh Tits favour broadleaf woods, Coal and Crested Tits prefer coniferous woods (see pages 161–68), while Great and Willow Tits occur in both and also in mixed woods. Some feed in the high foliage, others on the larger, lower branches or on the ground under trees. These differences combine to reduce competition to the advantage of both individuals and species.

The **Blue Tit** is the commonest and most widely distributed of the tits, occurring throughout the British Isles with the exception of Shetland. It prefers broadleafed woods, in particular Oak, but is adaptable and is the commonest tit recorded in gardens and will venture into town and city centres. Continental Blue Tits migrate to the British Isles in winter, but the British population is resident, birds remaining close to their place of birth. The total breeding population of the British Isles is thought to exceed five million pairs.

Blue Tit

In appearance the Blue Tit is a typical, plump, small (11.5cm) tit, distinctive by virtue of its bright, light blue head, greenish back and yellowish underparts. The plumage of the male is usually brighter than that of the female and juveniles are generally duller. It has a distinctive 'tsee-tsee-tsit' call note. Its bill is short and deep, enabling it to take insects and quite large seeds, even including beechnuts. During summer, insects make up the greater part of the diet and feeding is concentrated in the upper part of the tree amongst the leaves. Breeding starts in April and nests are most commonly built in holes at heights of 15 metres or higher, although they will readily take to nest boxes and will nest in holes in walls. Existing holes are selected with little excavation done by the birds and the nest is built from moss, twigs, grass and bark and lined with feathers. The seven to thirteen eggs are incubated by the female which is fed by the male and later both birds feed the young. Repeat clutches are common, but second broods rarely attempted and family parties, after staying together for a few weeks, later join others to form winter flocks.

The **Marsh Tit** also favours broadleafed woodland, in particular open, dry woods of oak, birch, alder and ash with a thick under-storey, and not waterlogged areas as its name might imply. It is less common and widespread than the Blue Tit, being completely absent from Ireland and only just extends into the south-east corner of Scotland and has a total breeding population of about 100,000 pairs. Similar in size and shape to the Blue Tit, it can readily be told apart by its black cap, white cheeks and brown plumage. The sexes are alike. It is, however, extremely difficult to separate it in the field from the Willow Tit unless one is familiar with the calls and song. Indeed, it was not until 1900 that it was confirmed they were two separate species. In good conditions, with experience, the glossier black of the cap and smaller bib of the Marsh Tit can be distinguished from the browner cap and larger bib of the Willow Tit. The call note of the former is a loud 'pitchow' contrasting with the 'zee-zee-zee' note of the latter.

Many pairs will remain together holding a territory throughout their life. Breeding starts in April when holes close to the ground will be selected as nest sites. They do not readily take to nest boxes. Little or no excavation is undertaken and the nest is built from moss and lined with feathers. The clutch is between seven and nine and second broods are rarely attempted. Insects are taken in summer and seeds in winter and feeding is concentrated on the lower, larger branches and trunk and sometimes in the shrub layer or even on the ground. The bill is strong, enabling them to open hard seeds including Beech and Spindle, and larger food items than both Coal and Blue Tit.

The similar looking **Willow Tit** is less numerous than the Marsh Tit and has a British breeding population somewhere between 50,000 and 100,000 pairs. Like the Marsh Tit, it is absent from Ireland and from most of Scotland although, in contrast to the Marsh Tit, it is widespread in south-west Scotland. It is generally found in mixed woods, although in the northern part of its range it breeds in coniferous forests and in southern England is not uncommon in wettish areas supporting elder, alder and birch. The diet includes insects and seeds, obtained from the lower branches and underlying shrub layer, although they rarely feed on the ground.

The quiet warbling song contrasts with the sharper, chipping song of the Marsh Tit, although it is rarely heard as pairs tend to be widely spaced offering little competition. Both sexes sing. Breeding starts in April and, like the Marsh Tit, it will select a site close to the ground although, in contrast to all other tits apart from the Crested Tit, it excavates the nest chamber. Rotten stumps and decaying trunks are favoured sites and the female pecks away small flakes of wood, many of which are carried away from the nest vicinity, until an entrance hole and chamber have been completed. Nest boxes are rarely used. The typical clutch is seven or eight eggs and they are single brooded. The British population is sedentary.

The **Great Tit** is much the largest of the tits, being almost twice the size (14cm) of all others. Its size, black cap and yellowish underparts with a bold black line down the centre distinguish it. The colouring of adult males is generally brighter than that of adult females and juveniles are duller. It has a sharp 'chink' note and a churring 'cha-cha-cha'. Widespread throughout the British Isles, it is only absent from Orkney and Shetland. It is commonest in open, broad-leafed and mixed woods and because much feeding takes place on the ground, it has adapted well to scrub, hedges and gardens. The total breeding population is about three million pairs.

Insects taken from the leaves form the main summer diet and are largely replaced by seeds during the winter. Feeding is concentrated on the trunk, lower branches and ground. Its powerful bill and size enable it to take the largest of the food items exploited by tits and its diet includes beechmast, acorns, chestnuts and hazel nuts held in the foot and hammered open. The song is a variation of the familiar, bell-like 'teacher-teacher' note and both sexes sing. Existing holes at heights of between three and a half and seven metres are selected as nest sites and they will readily use nest boxes. The nest is formed from moss lined with hair or fur and the clutch varies between five and twelve eggs.

Woodpeckers
and allies

Another important and interesting group of woodland birds comprises five species highly adapted to feeding on tree trunks. All are capable of travelling with speed and dexterity up vertical trunks to obtain wood boring and bark dwelling insects which form a major part of the diet. All use holes in trees as nest sites. As would be expected with these specializations, the preferred habitat for all of them is extensive, mature, open, deciduous woodland or well wooded parkland which provide large numbers of feeding and nest sites. All five may occur in the same wood, but their difference in size, bill type, food preferences and feeding techniques allows exploitation of different niches within the woodland habitat and this reduces serious competition.

Three belong to the woodpecker family. These are sturdy, compact birds with short, broad wings, short, stiff tails, strong legs and strong, sharp bills. Their calls are loud and far carrying and their flight undulating. The toes are long and held with two forward and two back to provide a firm grip on the trunk, while at the same time the tail will be pressed hard against the trunk surface. They can travel upwards, round the trunk, along large branches, perch across branches and hop on the ground, but do not descend head first. All three species are widely distributed in England and Wales, less numerous in Scotland and absent from Ireland.

The largest (32cm) is the **Green Woodpecker** which, as its name implies, has a generally greenish coloration. The head is red and the rump a bright yellowish-green. Adult males have red moustachial stripes which contrast with the black ones of the adult females and juveniles are speckled and paler. It is still absent from the Highlands and present in smaller numbers in southern Scotland and northern England but over the last hundred or so years the population has increased and extended northwards and this trend appears to be continuing. The total British breeding population is now placed at about 15,000–20,000 pairs.

Of the three woodpeckers, the Green spends most time feeding on the ground. Its tongue is extraordinarily long and mobile, barbed in texture and can be extended into narrow holes and cracks to extract insects and their larvae. In many areas it takes large numbers of ants. Hopping agilely across the ground with head held high and tail dragging, it pauses to peck fiercely into an anthill, often tearing aside the vegetation to get at the ants within. In the summer, recently fledged young are often escorted to patches rich in ant mounds and the parents expose the ants to provide easy prey for the young. On trees, it takes wood boring and bark insects and spiders, together with acorns and pine seeds.

In contrast to the other species, the Green Woodpecker rarely drums, although hammering can be heard as it feeds and when excavation of the nest hole and cavity is being undertaken. During display and when alarmed, it makes a loud, distinctive laughing 'hellew-hellew-hellew'. Fighting males confront each other with swaying heads and partially spread wings and tail and displaying pairs pursue one another on tree trunks. A fresh nest hole is excavated each season, typically at a height of between three to five metres, and usually in the main trunk. Both sexes participate, first pecking out a horizontal hole of eight to ten centimetres in length just large enough to allow them easy passage in and out and then excavate a vertical nest chamber of about thirty centimetres depth and twelve centimetres diameter. Woodchips provide a soft lining for the five to seven eggs laid towards the end of April. Incubation is by both sexes and lasts for eighteen or nineteen days and then both parents feed the young in the nest by regurgitation of a milky paste. Fledging takes about three weeks and the young are noisy in the nest. Second broods are not attempted, but old nest holes will be used by other species as nest sites.

The other two species, the Great Spotted and Lesser Spotted Woodpecker, are smaller and appear generally black and white and there is no chance of confusion with the Green Woodpecker. The Great Spotted is considerably larger than the Lesser (23cm compared to 14.5cm) and has a black back with two large white wing patches, contrasting with the highly barred black and white back of the latter. The Great Spotted also has prominent scarlet under-tail coverts which are absent in the Lesser.

The **Great Spotted Woodpecker** is the most numerous and widely distributed of the woodpeckers, extending well into the Highlands (although absent from the Outer Hebrides, Orkney and Shetland) and with a total breeding population between 30,000 and 40,000 pairs. Its presence in a wood in spring is quickly indicated by loud drumming. This is done by both sexes and produced by rapid pecking (eight to ten pecks a second) near the end of a dead or decaying branch. Courtship can involve mutual display flights and spiral chases along and round branches and up trunks. The crown feathers are often raised and the sharp 'tchick-tchick' call loudly repeated. The nest hole, usually at a height of about fifteen metres in the main trunk, is excavated by both birds and the four to seven eggs laid in May. The entrance and chamber are similar to that of the Green Woodpecker but smaller.

Great Spotted Woodpecker

Incubation is mainly by the female and lasts just over two weeks and then for three weeks both birds feed the young by bringing food in the bill to the nest. In summer, feeding is concentrated on the larvae of wood boring and bark insects and spiders, while in winter beechmast, acorns, hazel nuts and berries are taken. The young call loudly in the nest prior to fledging and second broods are rarely attempted, although the old sites are used by other species such as Starlings, Redstarts and Pied Flycatchers.

The **Lesser Spotted Woodpecker** is finch-size, secretive and spends much time feeding near the tops of trees and so is difficult to find. Its presence is often best indicated by its high pitched 'pee-pee-pee' call. The sexes can be distinguished, males having a crimson crown and females a black crown with white forehead. Its light weight and small size enable it to cling to the smaller, higher branches on which it will search methodically for insects, fluttering to a neighbouring branch as it finishes the one it is on. It is frequently present in the same woods as the Great Spotted Woodpecker, but the separation in feeding sites in particular excludes competition. It is widely distributed in England and Wales, but absent from Scotland as well as Ireland and is the least numerous of the three woodpeckers with a total breeding population of between 5,000 and 10,000 pairs.

Pairs are largely sedentary and generally widely dispersed, so drumming and calling is less frequent than with the Great Spotted. When undertaken, the technique of drumming is the same, but the smaller size of the bird and the use of smaller branches results in a less strident sound. They also have an attractive 'floating' display flight, in which the bird appears to sail from branch to branch and tree to tree. Their preference for the tops of trees is perpetuated in the positioning of their nests which are excavated in decaying upper branches and can be as high as twenty-five metres. The entrance passage and chamber are similar in form to those of the other species but smaller, being about half the size of that of the Green Woodpecker and the entrance hole is not infrequently sited on the underside of a branch. Both sexes excavate the nest which is lined with wood chips before the four to six eggs are laid in May and incubated by both birds for two weeks. Both then feed the young in the nest for three weeks by bringing food in the bill. Second broods are not attempted.

The two other species with this specialized feeding technique, the Treecreeper and Nuthatch, are unlikely to be confused with a woodpecker. The **Treecreeper** (12.5cm) is even smaller than the Lesser Spotted Woodpecker and, in marked contrast to the bold pied appearance of the latter, is a dull brown, buff-streaked bird with a noticeable white eye stripe and silver underparts. It has a thin, curved bill which enables it to penetrate the narrowest of cracks and crevices in the bark to obtain small insects, their larvae and spiders. When feeding, it travels mouse-like vertically up the trunk and along side branches, moving in a series of short spurts, the stiff tail pressed against the bark. Having searched a tree it flutters rapidly down to the base of another trunk to continue feeding. It is more frequently found in conifers than others of this group but population densities in these are lower. Widely distributed throughout the British Isles, it is absent from Orkney and Shetland and colonization of the Outer Hebrides was as recent as 1962. The total breeding population is thought to number between 150,000 and 300,000 pairs.

Treecreepers become very vocal from February to April, making their faint, high pitched song as they search for food and occasionally interrupting the song with a clear 'tseee' call. They have a fluttering display flight and sexual chases occur on tree trunks and branches with wing shivering during encounters. Nests are well hidden and usually in mature trees, in slots or cracks or tucked in behind raised folds of bark and concealed behind old, dense curtains of ivy. Both birds build the nest on a base of twigs, using roots and moss lined with feathers and bark. The greater share of the two weeks' incubation of the six eggs is undertaken by the female and then both birds feed the young for two weeks to fledging by bringing food in the bill. Second broods are common. During winter they will roost in hollows and cavities behind bark, the deep folds of the soft bark of Wellingtonias providing an especially favoured site.

The **Nuthatch**, a bird of mature deciduous and mixed woods or well

Nuthatch

148

wooded parkland, prefers stands of beech, oak and sweet chestnut and only rarely lives in conifers. It is essentially a bird of the southern half of Britain, being absent from Scotland and Ireland, but numbers are increasing and it has recently extended its range northwards into Cheshire, Lancashire, Durham and Northumberland. The total breeding population is now possibly as high as 20,000 pairs.

Although of similar size (14cm) to the Lesser Spotted Woodpecker, it differs considerably from it in both shape and coloration, appearing rather slim, with a longish, straight bill and extremely short tail. The tail, in contrast to that of the others of the group, is not used to help support the bird when it clings to the trunk. Its back is blue-grey and the underparts orange-buff and there is a sharp black stripe through the eye. The cheeks and throat are white. Males and females are alike and juveniles generally duller. Flight from tree to tree or tree to ground is rapid and undulating and it has a sharp, loud, metallic 'chwit-chwit' and trilling 'pee-pee-pee-pee-pee', which can be confused with the similar call of the Lesser Spotted Woodpecker. When feeding, it is active, running both up and down vertical trunks and frequently darting to the ground, and it will perch across branches. In summer, insects taken from cracks in the bark form its main food, but during winter it will also take chestnuts, beechmast and hazel nuts. It is adept at jamming these in cracks and crevices to hammer them open with its sharp, powerful bill. It roosts in holes in trees.

Early in March Nuthatches become vocal and the search for nest holes begins. Holes with wide entrances in either the trunk or larger sized branches at a height of between three and ten metres are most commonly used, although occasionally they will occupy crevices in walls and buildings. Having selected a site, much time is then given to plastering the entrance hole with wet mud until it is reduced to a diameter of about three centimetres. The amount of mud applied may be considerable and much stabbing and probing with bills is required to work it into place before it dries into a hard, grey, uneven collar, They will use nest boxes and again mud is often applied to these. The nest chamber is lined with flakes of bark and woodchips. During display the head is turned from side to side while the wings are fluttered to expose the breast and the tail spread, revealing white spots. Six to eleven eggs are laid during May and about this time the pair will become quiet and secretive. Incubation lasting thirteen to seventeen days is by the female which is fed on the nest by the male. Both birds then feed the nestlings for twenty-three to twenty-five days by bringing food in the bill. Second broods are uncommon.

Birds of prey

The Tawny Owl and Sparrow Hawk are the two birds of prey commonly present in broadleaf woodland, Ecologically they are quite distinct, the Twany Owl being strictly nocturnal and feeding primarily on small mammals and the Sparrow Hawk taking birds during daylight.

Tawny Owls are medium-sized (38cm), have large black eyes set in a brown face and a rich chestnut plumage, beautifully marked with buff and black, together with white patches. There is a greyer plumage variety found in a small number of individuals. The sexes are alike and juveniles resemble adults. It is the most numerous owl in the British Isles with a total breeding population probably exceeding 50,000 pairs and in Britain is only absent from the Outer Hebrides, Orkney and Shetland and does not occur in Ireland. Favouring extensive broad-leafed or mixed woods, it is also found in parkland, suburban gardens and coniferous woods.

It has short, rounded wings and a heavy flight and its hunting technique is to drop from a low perch and grab prey in its talons. Studies have shown that Tawny Owls are extremely sedentary and remain confined to small hunting territories within a wood. Once selected, hunting perches will be regularly used and the two common woodland mammals, the Wood Mouse and Bank Vole, are important prey species. It will also take small birds, rats, earthworms and large beetles. Breeding begins early and hooting and calling, a soft 'hoo-hoo-hoo-hoooo' and sharp 'kee-wick', begins in late winter when territory boundaries are confirmed. Preferred nest sites are holes in trunks, but they will use old nests of Carrion Crows, Magpies, Sparrow Hawks, Grey Squirrel dreys and will occupy nest boxes. Two to four eggs may be laid as early as March and incubated by both birds for a month and then both birds will feed the young in the nest for a further four or five weeks and continue to help care for them for a further twelve or thirteen weeks after they have left the nest. They are single brooded and breeding is not attempted in years of food shortage. During daylight hours they roost on a side branch of an evergreen tree or bush, pressed close against the trunk, and if disturbed or when they become active at dusk are frequently fiercely mobbed by Blackbirds, thrushes, tits and Chaffinches.

In marked contrast to the Tawny Owl, the **Sparrow Hawk** is an active hunter, ranging widely over a large hunting area. Its short rounded wings and long tail provide quick acceleration, short bursts of high speed and manoeuvrability. Flying low, it courses down the sides of hedges and rides, across scrub and young plantations and through mature woodland, surprising the prey which is caught by a quick pounce or snatched in mid-air after a short, twisting chase. The toes are long and thin with needle-sharp talons, enabling it to retain a firm hold on struggling, fluttering prey. When moving from one hunting area to another, it rises high and drifts across country, circling with a characteristic series of quick flaps interspersed with glides. During these high flights it is commonly mobbed by small birds before it dives down to another hunting site. It rarely hovers. An extremely wide variety of birds is taken as prey, ranging from Blue Tits, Robins and finches to thrushes, Jays and pigeons.

Males are smaller (28cm) and have slate grey upperparts and orange-rufous barring below; females (38cm) are browner above and the barring is brown and both have yellow eyes and legs. Juveniles are a redder brown above and blotched, not barred. The call is a sharp 'kek, kek, kek, kek' or a softer 'kyow, kyow, kyow'. Juveniles have a mewing 'wee-oo, wee-oo' food call. They are found throughout the British Isles with the exception of the Outer Hebrides, Orkney and Shetland and, despite a long history of persecution, remained as one of our commonest raptors until affected by agricultural pesticides in the late 1950s. By the mid-1960s the population in the southern half of Britain had been drastically reduced and the recovery in east and south-east England is still incomplete. The breeding population of the British Isles is currently estimated at about 20,000 pairs and is largely resident, although there is dispersal outside the breeding season and passage migrants are numerous.

Occupation of a territory can be confirmed in early spring, when the male or both birds soar over the prospective breeding site, repeatedly crossing one over the other. Broadleafed, mixed woodland and pure conifer stands are all used for nesting, with conifers preferred as the nest tree if present. The large, bulky nest is built by the female starting with a base of long larch twigs, usually so placed that the finished nest abuts the trunk. In broadleaf woods other twigs are used. A smaller cup, composed of finer twigs and lined with bark flakes, is then added and during the course of the season the surface gradually becomes covered in white flecks of down from the female's breast. Four to six richly blotched eggs are laid in May and incubated for just under five weeks by the female which has food brought to the vicinity of the nest by the male. After hatching, the female feeds, broods and protects the young while the male hunts, calling the female off the nest as he arrives with food in his talons. Prey is plucked by the male close to the nest tree when most of the larger feathers, the bill, legs and wings are removed. Later, particularly if food is scarce, the female joins in the hunting. Fledging takes just over a month, but for some time after they can fly, the young continue to be fed by their parents and noisy aerial chases ensue with a parent pursued by juveniles.

Crows

Of the crow family, the **Jay** is the one most closely associated with woodland. In addition to nesting in woods, it spends much of its time feeding within them or close to them. A medium-sized bird (34cm), it is the most colourful member of the crow family in the British Isles, the soft, orange-pink ground colour being varied by a speckled black crest, a white rump, black tail and blue and white wing patches. When in the open, the flight appears rather weak with irregular wing flaps but the short rounded wings and long tail provide the desired manoeuvrability to enable it to slip from tree to tree, drop quickly to the ground and dart agilely from branch to branch. On the ground it moves with large hops and restlessly jerks its tail and flicks its wings and at any time of the day a wood may echo to its raucous, warning screech 'skaak-skaak'. It favours woods with oak and beech, but will readily inhabit mixed woods, venture into suburban parks or large gardens and occupy coniferous woods, in all cases preferring woods with a thick understorey. Widely spread in wooded areas throughout England and Wales, it is absent from the northern Highlands and patchy in its distribution elsewhere in Scotland and scarce or absent in western Ireland. More recently, presumably as a result of reduced persecution, it has been expanding its range northwards and the population has increased until the total British breeding population is now estimated to number about 100,000 pairs.

In spring, small groups of displaying Jays gather, calling excitedly, and engage in aerial chases and parade with drooped wings to emphasize the white rump and blue wing markings. The nest, formed from sticks and smaller twigs, has a thick lining of fine roots compacted with earth and is usually placed in a main fork or on a large side branch in a tree well hidden by foliage. They will also build in large bushes. Five or six eggs are laid in May and incubated for just over two weeks by the female, which is fed on the nest by the male. Both parents feed the young in the nest for three weeks and, after fledging, the family remains together for a further period. During the summer, large numbers of caterpillars, beetles and other insects may be taken, but the diet is varied and includes a wide range of fruits and seeds and, in spring, the eggs and nestlings of other birds. In winter it will take beechmast, hazel nuts and acorns, the last being of particular importance and the oesophagus is specially enlarged to enable it to carry considerable numbers at one time to hide them. They will be buried under dense mats of roots or in small holes pecked in the ground and recovered a week or more later. To eat an acorn, the Jay holds it in its feet and chips away the outer coat. It is a sedentary bird, but in winter will form small flocks and display locally.

Woodcock

Alone amongst gamebirds, the **Woodcock** is the one most closely associated with woodland, nesting, resting and spending much time feeding in woods or deep cover. It is commonest in dry, open broadleaf and mixed woods with a thick understorey of bracken, ferns and brambles, but will also be found in mature coniferous woods with rides and glades and will breed in young plantations. Although some northern birds move south in winter and migrate to France, Spain and Portugal, it is a solitary and sedentary species, widely scattered through wooded regions of the British Isles and absent only from the

Woodcock

Outer Hebrides, Orkney and Shetland. In autumn, in upland areas it may move from woods onto bracken and heather-covered slopes. It is severely affected by harsh winters and the total breeding population is probably under 50,000 pairs.

Medium-sized (34cm), it is plump, has short legs and a large head, large dark eye and long, narrow bill. The bright russet plumage is most beautifully varied with rich red-browns and black, and adult males, females and juveniles are indistinguishable in the field. Its wings are short and rounded and tail short and normal flight is rather slow with the bill inclined downwards, but when disturbed from cover it will rise with a rapid burst of twisting flight. Apart from the spring display it is usually quiet and secretive. Earthworms, other soil invertebrates and a variety of insects are procured by rapid, repeated probing in soft soil and mud, the bill often plunging to its full length.

Woodcock are more readily observed in early spring evenings during their roding display flight. In this males circle low over the breeding areas with slow, steady, wing beats, calling continuously with an alternating croak and squeaking 'tsiwick'. Having attracted a female in this way and completed mating, a male will resume roding to attract further mates and the process is repeated. Mid-March to mid-April is the peak egg-laying period with clutches of four eggs laid in simple depressions hollowed in moss and grass under deep cover, often close to the foot of a tree. Females sit tight on the eggs during the three weeks of incubation and then look after the young, which are led from the nest after hatching. Fledging takes about a month and second broods are usual and a female will fly with a chick held in its legs to remove it from danger.

SUMMER VISITORS

Hundreds of thousands of warblers arriving in the British Isles each spring are dependent on woodland or farmland for their breeding and feeding sites. Five species, the Willow Warbler, Chiff Chaff, Wood Warbler, Blackcap and Garden Warbler, are closely associated with broadleaf woods. All are small (11–14cm), slim, insectivorous birds which arrive in the British Isles from the end of March. They nest on or close to the ground and lay four to seven blotched and speckled eggs and as their nesting activity coincides with a period of insect abundance territories tend to be small and population densities high. The various species exhibit differences in feeding and nesting requirements, but since most woods are highly varied it is not unusual to find a wide overlap with several species nesting in close proximity. Much of their time is spent hidden in low, deep cover or feeding high in the foliage and, with the exception of the Blackcap, they lack distinctive plumage markings and are difficult to identify. The best means of separating them is by their calls and song and a preparatory study of recordings of their songs and field visits in the company of an experienced observer can save many hours of frustration.

The **Willow Warbler** appears to be the one best suited to woodland conditions now present in the British Isles and is the most numerous and widespread. The total breeding population is about three million pairs and it occurs throughout the British Isles with the exception of Shetland. The highest densities are in open woodland with glades and rides and a thick, shrubby ground cover. It is also common in regenerating woodland, damp areas with alders and sallows and can be surprisingly numerous in scattered remnants of birchwood on dry, gentle, upland slopes. The main arrival from their southern Africa wintering sites takes place during April and their presence is immediately indicated by their song – a gentle, almost plaintive, liquid trill growing louder near the end. They start singing as soon as they arrive while still *en route* to the breeding areas. In appearance they are olive-green above and yellowish-buff below and have a characteristic persistent alarm note 'hweet'.

The domed nest, which is well concealed and usually close to the ground, is built by the female from moss and grass and lined with feathers. In display both birds perch in an upright posture, slowly flapping their wings. The six to seven eggs are laid in May and incubated for thirteen days by the female and then both parents feed the young in the nest for a further two weeks, bringing food in the bill. Second broods are common before the birds set off to return to their wintering areas in mid-July.

The **Chiff Chaff** is almost indistinguishable in the field from the Willow Warbler which it closely resembles in size and appearance, the only clear difference being the blacker legs of the former which contrast with the light brown ones of the latter. Fortunately the simple song of the Chiff Chaff is markedly different, being an almost monotonously repeated double note 'chiff-chaff, chiff-chaff'. It has a similar 'hweet' alarm note. More restricted in its habitat than the Willow Warbler, it favours older, deciduous woods, copses and parkland with tall trees for song posts and rough undergrowth, in particular including evergreens, for nesting. It is uncommon or absent in upland birchwoods and coniferous woods. The total breeding population is about 300,000 pairs and, with the exception of the Highlands where it is sparse or absent, is widely distributed in the British Isles.

Breeding activity is indicated by males singing in the treetops, often moving from branch to branch as they do so. Displaying males with shivering wings pursue females and pairs will face each other in an upright posture with partially opened wings and spread tail moved from side to side. The spherical nest with a wide entrance in one side is built by the female from moss and grass and lined with feathers. It is usually less than one metre from the ground and hidden in a grass tussock, a clump of brambles or in the lower fringe of a bush. The six eggs are laid in May and incubated for two weeks by the female which then undertakes most of the feeding of the young in the nest for a further fortnight. Second broods are common. They feed most commonly in the high foliage where insects and their larvae are sought on leaves and fine twigs and occasionally snatched in mid-air in short flights. Return migration begins in August, but small numbers may still be present in autumn and part of the population apparently goes no further south than France and the east Mediterranean basin.

The **Wood Warbler** can, with care, be distinguished from the two previous species as the upperparts are distinctly greener, the breast yellowish, contrasting with the white of the remainder of the underparts, and there is a yellowish eye stripe. The song is also distinctive, taking the form of a shimmering trill. It is the least common of the three with a total breeding population of between 30,000 and 60,000 pairs and, although thinly distributed throughout Britain, is only exceptionally recorded in Ireland. The greater part of the population is located in mature Sessile Oakwoods in the western half of Britain, but they are also present in birch and pine woods in the north and in beech and chestnut woods in the south. Mature high forest or stunted mature oak on wet upland slopes with a closed canopy and short, open ground cover are the preferred habitat, the birds using the exposed, lower boughs as singing and observation perches. Because of the absence of this habitat, Wood Warblers are uncommon and absent from many parts of eastern Britain.

Following their arrival in Britain from Africa, males will establish

Wood Warbler

territories by singing from a number of alternative song posts, moving from one to another with a light, almost sailing, flight. In addition to the gushing trill for which the head is thrown back, they have a 'zeep zeep zeep' note. Displaying males posture in front of females, with slowly flapping, half open wings and crown feathes erect. The domed grass and moss nest, placed in a hollow in the ground and hidden by grass tussocks, bracken or under brambles, is built by the female which also incubates the six or seven eggs laid towards the end of May or early June. Incubation lasts for a fortnight and both birds feed the young in the nest for about twelve days and second broods are rarely attempted. Feeding is largely confined to the foliage, with occasional short flights to catch flying insects.

The two remaining species, the **Blackcap** and **Garden Warbler**, are close relatives and often found together in the same area. Their general distribution is much the same, both being widespread throughout England and Wales and becoming very much less common in southern Scotland and sparse or absent in the Highlands and Ireland. The Blackcap is the more numerous of the two with a total breeding population probably exceeding 200,000 pairs compared to less than 100,000 pairs of Garden Warblers. Both like open, mature, deciduous or mixed woodland, with dense undergrowth, although they will occupy scrub provided it still retains some, albeit scattered, mature trees or is adjacent to mature clumps of trees to provide song posts. Both are insectivorous, the Blackcap spending more time in the high canopy and the Garden Warbler preferring mature scrub. Of all the five species of woodland warbler the Blackcap is the most readily identifiable with the greyish-brown back, grey underparts and glossy black cap of the male and reddish-brown cap of the female. The Garden Warbler, on the other hand, is probably the least distinguishable with uniform brown back and buff underparts. Like other warblers, its presence is most readily indicated by its song – a sweet, musical warble, similar to that of the Blackcap but lower pitched and more sustained.

Male Blackcaps arrive in Britain from Africa at the end of March or early April about two weeks ahead of the females. Territories are defended by vigorously singing males and pairing quickly follows the females' appearance. The song is a beautiful, loud, clear warbling, similar to that of the Garden Warbler but with longer pauses between bursts. They also have a sharp 'tacc-tacc' call, which has been compared to two pebbles being struck together. During display, perched males erect their black crown feathers, spread their tails and slowly flap partially opened wings and fly from perch to perch in a slow flapping flight. The nest is mainly built by the female from grass and roots and lined with finer grass and hair. Most will be in bushes or brambles less than one metre above the ground and five eggs are laid at the end of April or in May. The nests are generally higher than those of the Garden Warbler and the eggs laid earlier. Both parents share incubation which lasts ten or eleven days and then feed the young in the nest for about a fortnight, bringing mainly caterpillars and spiders in the bill. Second broods are common and small but apparently increasing numbers now winter in Britain.

A similar pattern of migration from Africa is to be found in the Garden Warbler, males reaching Britain a week or two in advance of females but they do not arrive until late April or May. They go immediately to the breeding areas and will sing from deep cover in a bush or tree continuously throughout most of the summer, most persistently early in the season. Pursuit flights are common and displaying males will confront females with spread tails and fluttering wings. The nest is rarely over half a metre from the ground, hidden in brambles, low bushes or tussocks. Both birds take part in its construction from grass with hair for lining and males, like Blackcaps, will build cocks' nests. The four or five eggs are laid in May or early June and incubated by both birds for about twelve days and then both feed the young in the nest for a further ten days, bringing food (mainly insects and their larvae) in the bill. Second broods are not usually attempted before the return migration begins.

Another characteristic and eye-catching woodland species is the **Redstart**, a summer migrant from West Africa. Although small (14cm), its active nature and colourful plumage, particularly in the males, readily attracts attention. Males are grey above, have a white forehead, black throat and fiery red underparts and tail, while females

Redstart

are duller but also have the fiery red tail which, as in the males, is constantly flicked up and down. The call is a clear 'hwee tucc tucc' and a softer 'hweet' and the birds characteristically bob up and down when on the ground. Most commonly found in mature broadleaf woods and parkland with open glades and clearings, they also occur in pinewoods, on heathland and even on hillside scrubland. They are active feeders, flying from tree to tree, making short sallies from a branch to take insects and spiders.

Most of our Redstarts arrive in April and disperse widely but thinly throughout the British Isles, although they are uncommon in much of East Anglia, rare in Ireland and absent from the Hebrides, Orkney and Shetland. The breeding population is put between 50,000 and 100,000 pairs, but numbers have declined recently probably, it is thought, because of the drought in the Sahel region of North Africa.

Soon after their arrival in the breeding areas, males take up a number of high tree song posts and move between them, uttering their rather Robin-like, faint, warbling song. Displaying males chase females from branch to branch, displaying the bright breast and tail. Holes at varying heights in tree trunks, large branches or stumps provide nest sites and they will readily use nest boxes and occasionally crevices in walls. The nest is built by the female from grass and bark, lined with hair and feathers and the six eggs are laid in May. Incubation by the female lasts two weeks and then both birds combine to feed the young in the nest for a further two or three weeks bringing food, largely caterpillars, in the bill. The juveniles are heavily mottled. There are usually two broods raised and the return migration beings in August.

The **Nightingale** is another African migrant which soon draws attention to itself when it arrives in British woodlands. Unlike the previous species, it expresses itself vocally rather than visually and while its song, particularly when made after dark, is difficult to miss, the bird itself is rarely seen. Small in size (16.5cm), it spends much of its time, even when singing, in deep cover. It feeds primarily on worms and insects, foraging on the ground amongst dead leaves and vegetation beneath bushes and thick scrub and only rarely ventures into the open when it can be seen hopping with cocked tail. The plumage is nondescript, a uniform brown above and greyish-brown below only relieved by a rufous tail. Males and females are similar but juveniles are heavily mottled. It is a solitary bird and has a soft 'hweet' call and sharper 'tacc-tacc'.

Most arrive during April and disperse to breeding sites in mature, open, deciduous woods, copses, thickets, (in particular Blackthorn), scrub and wooded river valleys. It is a bird of lowland south-east England, with most of the population found south of a line from Humber to Severn. It is absent from Cornwall and from almost all of Devon. The British population is put at about 10,000 pairs and recently there appear to have been only local changes in its numbers and distribution.

The vigorous song is a succession of repeated phrases of a few seconds' duration with short pauses between each, some clear and bubbling and others harsh. They may sing at any time of the day or night but most commonly at dawn and dusk. It is, however, the night singing, when other birds are quiet and when the sound carries far in the still night air of the otherwise silent woods, that attracts most attention. In display the tail is spread to emphasise the rufous colour and then moved up and down while the wings are fluttered. The nest is built close to the ground in grass or thick ground cover by the female, starting with a foundation of leaves and then lined with dead grass. Four or five eggs are laid in May and incubated by the female for a fortnight, and both birds feed the newly hatched young in the nest for about twelve days by bringing food in the bill. They are single brooded and the return migration begins in September.

Two species of flycatcher come to our woodlands from tropical Africa during the summer – the Spotted and Pied Flycatcher. They differ in appearance as the former is a slim, brownish-grey bird and the latter plump and pied, but they share the characteristic hunting technique of flycatchers of making short aerial sorties from an exposed perch to take insects in full flight. The **Spotted Flycatcher** is the commoner of the two, being found throughout the British Isles with the exception of Shetland, and has a total breeding population of between 100,000 and 200,000 pairs. A small bird (14cm), the greyish-brown back and whitish underparts are varied by black streaks on the head and breast.

The sexes are alike but juveniles are paler and spotted. At rest, it holds itself upright, using exposed branches, twigs, posts, palings and walls as perches from which it watches for a wide range of flying insects up to the size of bees and butterflies. The sudden pursuit flight is fluttering and twisting and in still conditions the snap of the bill on the insect can be clearly heard, before it returns to the same or a different perch. Solitary, it has a soft 'tzee' call and a double 'tzee-tzee' alarm.

One of the latest arrivals, possibly conditioned by the need to ensure a copious supply of insects, it does not begin to appear until the end of April and the majority arrive in May. Open woodland with numerous rides and glades, orchards, parkland and gardens provide the necessary conditions for its nesting and hunting needs. It is also common in lake and riverside trees, presumably attracted by the abundance of water-side insects. The song is a faint, squeaky trill of about half a dozen notes and displaying males will offer food to females and indulge in aerial chases which end in confrontations with the bill held vertically while the tail and rump are flirted up and down. Nests are situated in cracks and openings in trunks, old stumps and stone walls, or abutting vertical faces such as walls and beams in outhouses and the females build them from moss, wool and hair held together with spiders' webs. Old bases of Song Thrush and Swallow nests are frequently used as foundations. Four or five eggs are laid in late May or early June and incubated for a fortnight by the female and then the young are fed in the nest for a further fortnight by both parents on insects brought in the bill. Second broods are common before the start of the return migration in late August.

The **Pied Flycatcher** is slightly smaller (13cm) but its striking plumage pattern, sharp 'whit' call and active hunting behaviour attract attention. In breeding plumage the male has a black back contrasting with a white forehead, white wing patches and white underparts. Females are greyish-brown above and lack the white forehead. Juveniles are spotted and in autumn males resemble females, although the white forehead is retained. When perched, the tail is moved up and down and the wings flicked and after completing an aerial chase of an insect, it will usually return to a different perch and will feed on the ground. It is restricted to deciduous woods in upland valleys and woodland alongside lakes and rivers and the general distribution is patchy. Its strongholds are Wales and northern England and it is locally common in north Devon and parts of southern Scotland, but it is only sparse and widely scattered in the Highlands, absent from most of East Anglia, south and south-east England and does not occur in Ireland. The total breeding population is about 20,000 pairs.

Breeding territories are occupied soon after arrival in late April and May and the simple song made from a high tree perch. Males select suitable nesting holes in trees, walls and buildings before the females arrive to line the cavity with bark strips, moss, grass and hair. The

Pied Flycatcher

displaying male will hold himself upright to exhibit the white breast. They will readily occupy nest boxes and their range has been extended and breeding densities improved through nest box projects, which indicates that a lack of nest sites can be a limiting factor in their numbers and dispersion. Four to seven eggs are laid during May and incubated for twelve to thirteen days by the female which is fed by the male. Both parents then feed the young in the nest for a fortnight. Second broods are not usually attempted before their departure in August.

PINE WOODS

Two species of tit are commonly found in conifers – the Coal and Crested. However, while the former is common and widespread and has a total breeding population of about a million pairs, the latter is rare, confined to a limited area of the Highlands and has a breeding population of only about 1,000 pairs. The black cap, white nape patch and white cheeks of the **Coal Tit** are the features to look for. Its upper parts are olive grey, the underneath buff and both sexes are alike. Juveniles are generally duller and both adults and juveniles make a faint 'tsee tsee' call. It can be found in most types of woodland, but populations are higher in pines, firs and larches and it has benefited considerably from the extensive planting of commercial conifer plantations. It is predominantly a northern species and, while less numerous

Coal Tit

in the British Isles as a whole than the Blue and Great Tit, it is commoner than either of them in both conifer and broadleaf woods in northern regions. It is particularly numerous in Ireland, possibly because of the absence of Marsh and Willow Tits. Generally sedentary throughout the year, the populations are supplemented by winter immigrants from the Continent.

The bill is relatively long and narrow for a tit, enabling it to probe for small insects deeply embedded amongst pine needles. Most feeding is carried out in the high foliage and seeds as well as insects are taken in winter and food will be stored. During spring, the presence of breeding birds is indicated by their repetitive 'teachoo, teachoo, teachoo' song, which may be confused with the song of the Great Tit. It is one of the earliest nesters among the tits, often starting in April, but the timing will be conditioned by spring weather. While it will occupy nest boxes, its preference is for small, natural holes close to the ground. The female builds the nest from moss lined with hair and an average clutch will hold as many as ten eggs. Second broods are usual.

Crested Tits prefer fine, mature Scots pine forest with its open understorey of heather and bilberry. They are largely confined to the Spey valley to the south of the Moray Firth and Easter Ross in the north. Before the destruction of the Highland forests they were presumably more widespread but at present are extremely sedentary, remaining in their pairs in the breeding areas during both winter and summer and, as a result, they suffer high mortality in severe winters. Increasing afforestation in north-east Scotland, if Scots pines are planted, may eventually provide opportunities for their spread, but so far there are no signs of any dramatic extensions.

Crested Tit

They are the rarest of the British tits and the most highly adapted to northern woodlands, breeding at heights up to 600 metres. On occasions they will occupy adjoining birch and alder woods and in the vicinity of towns can be tempted to bird tables. Because of their small size and quick movements patience is needed to locate them. Often the first sign of their presence is a purring trill and eventually they will be seen busily searching for insects among the dark-green needles of the larger branches of the canopy. There may be better glimpses when they perch momentarily on a bare twig or fly onto the trunk to feed like a woodpecker. During winter, conifer and other seeds and berries are taken and they will also feed on the ground.

Once a good view is obtained, there is little danger of confusion with other tits, the unique, pointed black and white crest, white cheeks and grey-brown upper parts singling them out. After a little experience, their characteristic trill, a high pitched 'tzee-tzee-tzee', quickly confirms their whereabouts. Adult males and females resemble each other. They are less sociable than most tits and rarely form flocks with other species.

Breeding usually begins at the end of April when males proclaim a territory with a fluttering treetop display flight, at the same time uttering a persistent, trilling call. Pairs are usually widely separated. Nest holes, typically just above head height in dead or decaying tree trunks or stumps, are excavated by the females. A fresh nest is used each season but they will occupy nest boxes. The single clutch of five or

163

six eggs is laid in the moss nest which is lined with wool and hair and the female incubates for about two weeks, during which time she is fed by the male. For two or three weeks after hatching the young are fed by both parents. They are single brooded and once fledged the family may remain together for some time.

Another small bird found at times in association with winter tit flocks and favouring the high foliage of conifers is the **Goldcrest**. With a length of only 9cm it is the smallest British bird. Its diminutive size, small fine bill and short tail help to distinguish it from a tit. The plumage is greenish above and whitish below, with a black bordered head crest, orange in males and yellow in females. An active feeder, it works its way along and round thin branches, often hanging tit-like in its search of the foliage for small insects, their larvae and spiders and making short flights between trees. While feeding, it flicks its wings and makes a 'zi-zi-zi' call which at times can be surprisingly loud and intense. It is found throughout the British Isles and has benefited from the planting of commercial conifer plantations and in winter will venture into areas of shrubs and gardens. The total breeding population probably exceeds one and a half million pairs, but the population is considerably reduced following harsh winters. After a series of mild winters and recovery of the population breeding areas will extend into broadleaf woodland.

Fir woods are favoured breeding sites and in spring the high pitched rather repetitive song indicates their presence and the crest is repeatedly raised and expanded in display. Both birds co-operate to build the nest which is typically placed towards the end of a branch hidden in the foliage and is made of moss held together with spiders' webs and lined with feathers. The seven to ten eggs are laid in April and incubated for just under a fortnight by the female and then both parents feed the young in the nest for about three weeks before a second brood is started.

Another characteristic bird of conifer woods – the **Siskin** – is also difficult to see as it, too, remains near the tops of the trees in its search for seeds. A small (12cm) finch, quick and buoyant on the wing, like the Crested Tit it is often first located through its call – a constant twittering, interspersed with a 'tsy-zi'. Rarely do they remain still for long but when a reasonable view is obtained, their greenish-yellow colouring gives an immediate clue. Confirmation will come from finding a male with the distinctive black crown and chin, yellow wing bars, yellow rump and yellow sides to the tail. The female is greyer and lacks the black on the head.

In most of the British Isles the Siskin is a winter visitor, but is now found breeding throughout much of Scotland, in many parts of Ireland and in widely scattered, isolated localities as far south as Hampshire and Devon. Until the mid-nineteenth century it was probably confined to the remnants of the Highland pinewoods and its spread is almost certainly associated with the planting of commercial and ornamental conifers. The total breeding population may now be over 20,000 pairs. In winter, Siskins are gregarious, often forming flocks with Redpolls and while they will feed in alderwoods in river valleys and elsewhere, they breed almost exclusively in conifers. During summer, spruce seeds form the principal food item, but in autumn and winter there is a change to birch and alder. Weed seeds such as dandelion and dock and some insects are also taken.

The small nests, built by the females, are extremely difficult to find, being usually well hidden in the needles near the end of a branch at the top of a tree. The simplest way to establish if they are attempting to breed in a wood is to watch for the delightful display flight of the males, in which they almost seem to float between tree tops with slow, exaggerated wing beats and spread tail, uttering their twittering call. The three to five eggs, laid during April, are incubated for just under two weeks by the female which is fed during this time by the male. Both parents then feed the young in the nest for about a fortnight before fledging and may then start a second brood. An unusual feature of the Siskin is that violent fluctuations can occur in breeding numbers, so one should not be surprised if in a subsequent year a previously favoured spot appears deserted.

The **Redpoll** is another finch associated with conifers and also birch and hawthorn scrub. It is slightly larger than the Siskin with a length varying from 13 to 15cm and its general coloration is brownish and

Redpoll

heavily streaked with dark brown. It closely resembles the Twite and the Linnet but can be distinguished from them by its red forehead, black chin, pink breast and rump. Males and females are similar apart from the absence of the pink in the female. There are several allied races which differ slightly in colour and size. It hops on the ground and has a distinctive flight note, 'chi, chi, chi'. Recently it has extended its range and in this it has been helped by the planting of commercial conifer plantations on lowland heaths and uplands. It is also found in chalk scrub, birch and alderwoods, particularly in winter when it will disperse widely in flocks and concentrate its feeding on birch and alder seeds. The total breeding population now probably exceeds 300,000 pairs and it is widely distributed, only being uncommon or absent from parts of south and south-west England, the Outer Hebrides, Orkney and Shetland.

The song is a brief rippling trill and far less dramatic than the rather beautiful sailing display flight in which males circle just above the canopy, flying with slow beats alternating with glides. Nests are rather ragged and well hidden in trees or bushes and built by the female from grass on top of a foundation of twigs and finally lined with down and feathers. The birds may be solitary or belong to small, loose colonies and four to five eggs are laid in May and incubated by the female, fed by the male, for ten or eleven days. Both parents feed the young in the nest for just under a fortnight and second broods are sometimes undertaken.

The **Crossbill** is aptly named, using its large overlapping bill to extract seeds from the cones of Scots pine, larch, spruce and other conifers. They feed on cones still attached to branches and so are not always easy to see, although the rustling of the needles, the cracking of cones and the cone falling at one's feet, combined with their distinctive 'jip-jip' call, can give them away. In spring courting males have a habit of perching on the topmost branches and from time to time will glide from one tree to another with rapidly beating wings and expanded tail. This is the best time to watch them and a red male Crossbill standing amongst dark green pine needles makes a fine sight. The females have the same characteristic large head and bill, but their plumage is olive-green although they have the same dark wings. A relatively large bird (16.5cm), it is generally gregarious and often quite tame.

Crossbills from distinct geographical regions have different sized beaks, related to the type of cone on which they feed. Scottish birds, specializing in the hard cones of Scots pine, tend to have heavier beaks than the common Crossbill found in Europe. At frequent intervals, following good breeding years, there have been invasions (often termed irruptions) of continental Crossbills and some have survived to breed in scattered localities in England. They do not breed in Ireland. The Scottish population is now regarded as a discrete species, restricted to the remnants of the old Highland forests in central northern Scotland.

The total breeding population in Britain in average years is put at about 5,000 pairs, but this will be higher in irruption years.

Like those of the Siskin, nests are placed at the end of high branches and are difficult to find, but Crossbills seem to prefer the more open parts of the forest or the forest edge. The three to four eggs, laid from March onwards, are incubated by the female for about a fortnight and the young remain almost a month in the nest where they are fed by the regurgitation of food by both parents.

The only gamebird strongly linked with conifer forests is the **Capercaillie** and one might suppose that because of its large size (males 94cm and females 67cm) it would be easy to see. Capercaillies can, however, be extremely elusive and much perseverance may be needed to find one. In summer they are most easily seen amongst the heather, whereas in winter they spend more time in trees feeding on the young shoots and pine needles which form their staple diet. Once seen, the great size of this, the biggest of all British gamebirds, its dark colour and large rounded tail as distinct from the forked tail of the Black Grouse, make it immediately recognizable. Males are adorned with a glossy, blue-green breast, white bill and scarlet skin over the eye. Females are lighter and browner in appearance and heavily mottled, with a distinct rufous patch on the breast. The flight is typical of a gamebird, a series of quick flaps alternating with long glides on downcurved wings, and for such a large bird they show great ability to twist between tree trunks as they disappear into a wood.

While now present throughout the east and central Highlands, Capercaillies were completely wiped out in the late eighteenth century. Although also present at one time in Ireland, they have not been recorded in historical times in England. Forest clearing and shooting brought about their demise and the present population is descended from Swedish stock introduced to Scotland, principally by Lord Breadalbane at Taymouth Castle, in the early nineteenth century. The establishment of commercial conifer plantations may have contributed to their wider distribution, and foresters and landowners are generously tolerant of the damage they can inflict on the tender shoots and buds of young trees, but there is evidence that Capercaillie populations in commercial conifer stands are not self-sustaining and rely on immigrants from more suitable breeding areas to sustain them. The total breeding population remains less than 10,000 pairs.

The nest, little more than a hollow scrape, is often to be found amongst the exposed roots at the foot of a Scots pine. The single clutch of five to eight pale, yellowish eggs is laid towards the end of April and incubated by the female for about a month before tending the young alone as they forage with her in the undergrowth. The male has nothing to do with family life and the young which are independent from hatching feed on insects, heather, shoots and berries, turning to pine needles in winter. The outstanding feature of the breeding season is the incredible noisy dawn display of the males which may occur singly or in small groups. With outstretched neck, fanned tail, drooped wings, bristled throat feathers and the whole body apparently expanded, they posture aggressively through the open vegetation, at the same time uttering a most extraordinary variety of calls, variously described as resembling twigs being banged together, the grinding of knives and the popping of champagne corks, and round the females up into a harem. A sight definitely worth experiencing.

The only bird of prey closely linked with coniferous woods is the **Long-eared Owl**. A medium-sized bird only slightly smaller (36cm) than the Tawny Owl, it appears taller and slimmer and at close range the ear tufts and orange eyes can be clearly seen. The upperparts are greyish-brown, beautifully marked with brown and black, and the buff underparts are heavily streaked and blotched with dark brown. In flight it closely resembles the Short-eared Owl, although the black wing patches are lacking and it appears greyer. Unlike the Short-eared Owl, it is strictly nocturnal, although in winter small wandering flocks roosting in long grass or scrub will fly strongly if disturbed. It will normally nest and roost in woods but, unlike the Tawny Owl, will hunt outside the forests over open country and include a wide range of small mammals, birds and larger insects in its diet. Previously more numerous, it is now thinly scattered throughout the British Isles and largely confined to coniferous woods, scattered clumps of pines on heath and shelter belts although in some places it is locally common in mature scrub and high hedges. It is absent from large areas of central England, from most of the south-west peninsula and the western Highlands and the densest populations are to be found in Ireland where it is the commonest owl. The total breeding population is thought to be somewhat in excess of 3,000 pairs.

Territories are established in late winter and early spring and are proclaimed by a triple hoot which is softer and more drawn out than that of the Tawny. In display it will fly through the trees in the vicinity of the nest or low over the canopy and clap its wings. It will use old nests of crows, Woodpigeons, Magpies and Sparrow Hawks and deserted squirrel dreys and so has greater flexibility in its choice of woodland and a considerable advantage in coniferous woods over the Tawny Owl which requires older timber containing holes and broken boughs. The four or five dull white eggs are laid in March and incubated by the female for a month, while the male roosts in a nearby tree, typically leaning against the trunk. The owlets are fed in the nest by both parents for just over three weeks and make a rasping squeak as a food call. Second broods are rarely attempted.

·6·

Woodland Edge, Farmland and Hedges

Over three-quarters of the land surface of the British Isles is devoted to agriculture. Part of this is represented by rough upland grazing and other marginal land, with the remainder comprising intensively farmed lowland ground. A wide variety of bird species is present in the latter, exploiting as food the large number of insects and tree and plant seeds available and using scattered trees, bushes and hedges for nesting. Many are more closely associated with the woodland elements during spring and summer, turning to the open scrub and fields in the autumn and winter.

One tit, the **Long-tailed Tit**, is commonly present in scrub and hedges, but may also be found in open woodland and occasionally in large gardens although they rarely go to bird tables. Its length (16.5cm) is deceptive as its body is extremely small and the apparent length is attributable to the long thin tail. This distinctive shape, together with the dark upper parts and pinkish underparts, make it unmistakable. The sexes are alike and juveniles duller and it has a 'tsup' call note.

The Long-tailed Tit occurs in all regions of the British Isles with the exception of the Outer Hebrides, Orkney and Shetland, but is scarce or absent in many parts of Scotland. A resident species, it suffers greatly in severe winters and will take several years to recover and the total breeding population fluctuates around 100,000 – 150,000 pairs. During winter, flocks of up to twenty or more birds, which probably represent several families, are formed and at night will roost in compact 'balls' with the tails sticking out. They feed among the thinner, higher twigs where a flock will move quickly and steadily from bush to bush or along a hedge. They will rarely go onto the ground. Exclusively insect feeders, the delicate, deep, narrow bill enables them to remove insects from narrow slits and fine cracks in the bark.

The earliest of the tits to begin breeding, nest building sometimes starts as early as February and it has a butterfly-like display flight, engaging in fast pursuit flights and adopting a hovering motion while searching for a nest site. The beautiful domed nest is a most complicated structure which takes over two weeks to construct. It is built from moss, held together with cobwebs and hair and finally covered with grey lichen and then lined with a mass of feathers. Blackthorn and hawthorn bushes or hedges are favourite sites, but nests will also be built in forks or against tree trunks at considerable heights from the ground. Eight to twelve eggs are laid in April and incubated for over a fortnight by the female and then the young are fed in the nest for a further fifteen or sixteen days by the male which brings food in the bill to be passed to the female to feed the young. Second broods are rarely attempted.

The **Dunnock**, or Hedge Sparrow, a solitary bird, is the second commonest bird on English farmland, favouring scrub or mature hedges with uncut vegetation and brambles. It is also commonly found along woodland edges, in open coppice, woodland and large, shrubby gardens. Widely distributed throughout the British Isles, it is only absent from Shetland and the total breeding population may exceed five million pairs. Many are resident, but there is some southerly movement in autumn and emigration to the Continent. A small (14.5cm), nondescript, brownish bird, it superficially resembles a sparrow (hence the alternative name) but is more delicate and has a fine, slender bill. On close inspection, the head and underparts can be seen to be grey. Holding its body horizontally, it skulks in the undergrowth, flicking its wings and never venturing far from cover, searching amongst dead leaves and vegetation for small seeds, supplemented by worms, spiders and insects. It hops and walks, tends to perch low down and flies for short distances with rapidly beating wings and has a shrill 'tseep' call.

In spring the high pitched warbling song is delivered from a song post in a tree or on a roof and sexual chases and standing displays, sometimes involving several birds with shivering wings and tail, are common. The well hidden, open cup nest is built low in cover by the female from moss, twigs and leaves on a foundation of twigs or sometimes on the remnants of a Blackbird or Song Thrush nest. The four to five eggs are laid in April and incubated by the female, which leaves the nest to feed, for twelve days, after which both parents feed the young in the nest for a further twelve days. Two and occasionally three broods are reared and Cuckoos often use Dunnocks as foster parents.

Two buntings – the Yellowhammer and Corn Bunting – are familiar birds of farmland, the former being more closely associated with woodland edge, scrub, hedges and young plantations while the latter favours much more open terrain and can live amongst sparse shrubs, remnants of hedgerows or in clumps of brambles and hedgerow weeds. Both have short, strong, thick bills and are primarily vegetarian, feeding on a wide variety of weed and grass seeds and fruits supplemented by worms, spiders, caterpillars and other invertebrates. While both nest low down, close to the ground in thick cover, they require a high song post and lay from three to five eggs which are incubated by the female.

The splashes of bright yellow and the white outer tail feathers draw attention to the **Yellowhammer**. Its body length is 16.5cm, the upper parts chestnut and the head and underparts predominantly yellow. Females and juveniles have less yellow and it has a 'tink' alarm note. A resident species, it is found throughout the British Isles except Shetland but is sparse in inland parts of the central and northern Highlands. The total breeding population is around a million pairs. In winter they will form flocks with finches and move onto old stubble and uncut field banks. Singing starts in February from a high song post, the short song immortalized as 'a little bit of bread and no-o-o cheese'. Although it will fly considerable distances from the nest to feed, the nest vicinity is defended vigorously. In display, sexual chases are frequent and males and females will confront each other on the ground with spread,

Yellowhammer

fluttering wings. The nest is formed from moss and lined with hair and fine grass and most of the clutches are laid in May although the breeding season extends from April to August. Both parents feed the young in the nest for a fortnight, in the early stages, when the young are small, carrying the food in their crops, and two and occasionally three broods may be fledged.

The **Corn Bunting** is bigger (18cm) and appears plumper and heavier with a large head and bill. An undistinctive brown above and with lighter, heavily streaked underparts, its identification is often best confirmed by its characteristic hovering flight with legs dangling, and by its jangling song. The distribution in England is irregular and patchy and it is absent from most of Wales and the Scottish Highlands, and confined to scattered coastal localities in Ireland. Numbers appear to have decreased recently and the total breeding population is now probably about 30,000 pairs. Males take up breeding territories as early as January and are joined by the females in April. The song is

Corn Bunting

usually made from a high song perch on a fence or telegraph post or wire and occasionally from the ground and males will also make a succession of short hovering flights. Ground display includes waving partially opened wings and tail. Most clutches are laid in June and incubated by the female for just under two weeks and she then feeds the young on the nest for about ten days. Males are polygamous and second broods are rarely attempted.

Four finches occur in marginal woodland conditions – the Greenfinch, Bullfinch, Goldfinch and Linnet. All are small and mainly seed eating and have stout conical bills and strong jaw muscles which enable them to deal with hard seed coats, although early in the season insects (in particular aphids and caterpillars) can also form an important part of the diet. In the course of a year a wide variety of seeds is taken but each species specializes in seeds of a particular size. These preferences are related to differences of bill shape and body size and reduce competition for food. With the exception of the Linnet, nestlings are fed on a mixture of seeds and insects which is formed in the crop from seed husks, crushed insects, water and grit and regurgitated into the mouth of the young. Young Linnets are reared entirely on plant matter. Nests are cup-shaped and built by the female, incubation lasts a little under a fortnight and the young remain in the nest for about a fortnight but are fed by their parents for a further one or two weeks after this.

The **Greenfinch** is the commonest, found along the edges of woodland, in open areas with scattered bushes and trees, parks and

Greenfinch

mature gardens. Recently the population has increased and expanded its range and it is now found throughout the British Isles except for the north-west Highlands where it is rare or absent and Shetland where it does not occur at all. It also breeds regularly in commercial conifer plantations and the continued planting of these areas previously devoid of trees should ensure further increases in numbers and range. The total breeding population of the British Isles may now be as high as two million pairs. Largely resident, in winter it forms flocks with other finches and buntings and spends much time in the open on stubble and arable fields. Winter numbers are increased by an influx of passage migrants coming to the British Isles.

It has a body length of 14.5cm and a general background colour of olive-green, relieved by bright lemon yellow patches on the wing and lighter greenish-yellow shading on the rump and breast. Females are duller with less yellow, juveniles are streaked brown and appear darker and males make a nasal 'zwee' call. They hop when on the ground and in flight appear rather plump, flying with a series of beats followed by a brief spell with wings closed, creating the effect of a bouncing flight.

Singing starts in January and is followed by pairing in February and March. The song is a medley of twittering made from a high perch, interspersed with a floating display flight in which the bird follows a wide circular course, weaving between the tree tops with exaggerated slow wing beats and making a wheezing 'dweee' note. Nests are built in April at heights from one to five metres, in bushes, often in evergreens, and in hedges. In areas of high population densities several may be found in close proximity forming a loose colony. Nests are bulky and built from twigs, dry grass and moss lined with fine roots and hair and the four to six eggs are laid in May. Second broods are usual. Juveniles disperse widely in the vicinity of the nest, but few will venture beyond a distance of five kilometres and there is no regular migration. The diet is varied, a short, broad bill enabling it to tackle tree fruits and cultivated cereals as well as seeds, taking them both from the stem and from the ground. Preferred weed seeds include chickweed, groundsel, dandelion and, during winter, charlock and persicaria. In woodland, dogs mercury and elm are favoured in summer, yew and hornbeam in autumn and rose and bramble during winter. They take few buds or insects.

The **Bullfinch** has also recently extended its range northwards and is now widespread throughout the British Isles, with the exception of much of the Highlands where it is absent or uncommon and the northern Isles where it is still absent. Considerably less numerous than the Greenfinch, the total breeding population is put at about 600,000 pairs. It, too, prefers the woodland edges, copses with a thick under-storey, thickets, old hedges and orchards. Most are sedentary, rarely venturing more than five kilometres from their place of birth. They pair for life and do not form flocks, although family parties may remain together for the summer and early autumn.

One of the bigger finches (14.5–16.0cm) it is unmistakable with its bright rose pink underparts, grey back, black cap, wings and tail and white rump. Females have a duller, greyer pink breast and juveniles are browner and lack the black cap. A secretive bird, it remains within the cover of bushes and hedges and rarely goes onto the ground and attention to its presence is often drawn by its far carrying whistle.

Nesting is confined to dense undergrowth in woodland, thickets and hedges. Its feeble piping hardly constitutes a proper song and in display the male puffs out its breast, droops its wings and vibrates the spread tail. The nest is built from rootlets and hair one or two metres above ground on a foundation of twigs and usually appears black. Three to six eggs are laid in May and second broods are common with third broods occasionally attempted. During the breeding season, adults develop a special pouch in the floor of the mouth in which the food mixture is carried to the young. The short, rounded bill has sharp edges and this enables the Bullfinch to deal with buds, tree flowers and berries as well as seeds and it will also take spiders and snails. Buds account for up to a third of its diet and as in fruit growing areas these come mainly from commerical orchards, locally Bullfinches are considered a serious pest. They usually feed direct from the plant, concentrating in spring when seeds are scarce on fruit and flower buds and then turning to a wide variety of weed seeds, in particular dogs mercury, bramble, nettle and dock. Later seeds of wych elm, silver birch and ash become important. Seeds, buds and berries are nipped off, crushed and then rotated on the tongue against the lower jaw which peels off the husk or flesh. It is the only finch to take snails and the shell is dealt with in the same way.

The **Goldfinch** is the smallest (12cm) and most colourful of the four. It has a scarlet face, separated from a black cap by a white border, brilliant yellow patches on black wings, a white rump and black tail. Females are duller and juveniles lack the red colouring. They have a dancing flight and a harsh 'geez' flight note. The total breeding population of the British Isles is about 300,000 pairs but numbers fluctuate, being considerably lower in cool summers. They are much commoner in the southern half of the country and absent from most of the Highlands. In autumn they gather into flocks and over three-quarters of the population migrates to western parts of the Continent.

Much of the time is spent in open country in low scrub, on waste ground, roadside verges, allotments and on coastal dunes and marshes where it feeds on tall weeds. A longer, thinner bill enables it to extract deeply embedded seeds not available to other finches and it specializes particularly on thistles which can amount to a third of its diet as well as dandelion, groundsel, ragworts, burdocks and hardheads. When flower seeds are scarce it will also take seed of birches and alder. While feeding it clings agilely to stems and hangs from flower heads, flitting easily from plant to plant, and in autumn will feed on the ground on fallen seeds. It breeds in much the same areas as the Greenfinch, although the nest is sited higher at between four and ten metres and, unlike the Greenfinch, it will use trees. The song is a twinkling 'tswitt wit wit' and males will defend a small territory round the nest site, travelling considerable distances to open ground to feed. Pairs form in April and will nest close together in loose colonies and the mating display consists principally of showing off the yellow wing patches. The nest is built from moss, roots and lichens, held together with spiders' webs and lined with thistle down. Four to six eggs are laid in May and second and occasionally third broods may be attempted. More young are fledged in hot dry summers.

The **Linnet** is the finch least associated with woodland, favouring rough, open, uncultivated land and gorse-covered commons. Generally chestnut brown in coloration, it can be confused with the Twite which takes its place in uplands and with the Redpoll which is more closely linked with mature woodland. Slightly larger (13cm) than the Twite and Redpoll, in summer the male Linnet has a grey head, red forehead and breast, but winter males, females and juveniles lack the red and are difficult to distinguish from the other two species. Winter is spent on stubble fields, open grassland and coastal marshes in flocks sometimes containing hundreds of individuals and often in association with other finches and buntings. Apart from Shetland and parts of the Highlands it occurs throughout most of the British Isles and the total breeding population lies between three-quarters and one and a half million pairs.

Some remain throughout the year in the vicinity of their breeding areas, but there is a generally southerly movement and many emigrate. Flight is wavering and dancing and it has a 'chichichichit' flight call and when on the ground will hop or perch low on wire fences or in bushes.

Almost exclusively seed feeding, its middle-sized bill is well suited to picking common weed seeds from the ground and while over fifty different species of seed have been identified in its diet, its specialization is common weeds of cultivated land, mainly from the cabbage, daisy, dock and goosefoot families. Frequently four to six pairs will nest as a colony, choosing breeding sites in bushes or hedges on heaths or downs and woodland edges. Several males will gather on exposed perches to sing the soft twittering song and displaying birds will sway with drooped wings and spread tail. Nests are placed low in bushes, often evergreens, or on the ground in tussocks and are made from dry grass, moss and twigs and lined with wool. Four to six eggs are laid, mainly in May, but some will be laid in April before those of other finches to take advantage of the early availability of fresh seeds for food. Two or three broods are frequently reared and the young will leave the nest and move into nearby cover after eleven or twelve days, possibly because of the vulnerability of their low nests to predators.

The **Mistle Thrush** is also common on lowland farmland with hedges, scrub or copses and will venture into town centres and large gardens. It is the largest British thrush (27cm) and is a greyer brown

Mistle Thrush

176

above and lighter below and has larger, darker spots than the more common and better known Song Thrush. The flight is characterized by a short burst of flaps followed by a longer pause with closed wings and when in the air the white under the wing and white patches on the outer tail feathers can be seen. It has a harsh, chattering flight call. Males and females are similar but juveniles are spotted white. On the ground it will stand with head held high and tail low and spend much time feeding in the open on rough pasture and arable land on worms, snails, insects and spiders. Cherries, apples, plums and blackcurrants and, in winter, berries including hawthorn, rowan, juniper, yew, holly and ivy are also taken. Until the eighteenth century it was restricted to southern Britain, but has now spread throughout the British Isles apart from Orkney and Shetland where it is still absent although it breeds spasmodically in the Outer Hebrides. The total breeding population is between 300,000 and 600,000 pairs. British birds are mainly resident but some will emigrate and continental migrants come to the British Isles during winter.

The loud, far carrying, rather harsh song can be heard from December onwards and is made from a high song post in a tree. During display, much time is spent in branch to branch pursuits, tails are spread to display the white patches and females open and shiver their wings. Nests are built high in a tree fork or on a large bough by the female from grass, roots and moss, compacted with earth and lined with dry grass. Four eggs are laid in March and incubated for a fortnight by the female, which leaves the nest to be fed by the male, and then both birds feed the young for a fortnight by bringing food in the bill. Second broods are common and pairs will be bold in defence of the nest, fiercely mobbing Jays and crows. Family parties remain together for some time and small flocks may be formed in winter.

Two crows, the Magpie and Rook, occur on lowland farmland. They differ markedly in appearance, behaviour and in the use they make of the habitat. Magpies are usually present singly or in pairs and their nests are isolated and sited in scattered trees, copses, scrub or high hedges. The Rook, by contrast, is gregarious, forming large flocks in winter and nesting in colonies in high trees in copses or small woods. The Rook's diet is closely linked to the crops being grown and much of its time is spent foraging in open fields and the use of trees is limited to resting, roosting and nesting. Magpies are more opportunist feeders and prefer grassland, tending to remain close to cover at the field sides and spending a great deal of their time in hedges and scrub.

The **Magpie** is medium-sized (46cm) and its bold black and white plumage and long, wedge-shaped tail render it unmistakable. Males and females resemble one another and juveniles are duller and have a shorter tail. On closer examination the black plumage can be seen to be beautifully glossed with purples and deep green. Its short, blunt wings and long tail produce a slow fluttering flight when in the open, but

Magpie

provide it with speed and manoeuvrability when travelling through the thick scrub or down a hedge. Recently its numbers have increased and it has extended its range, probably because of a reduction in persecution, and the total breeding population of the British Isles is now thought to exceed a quarter of a million pairs. It is widespread in England, Wales and Ireland and in Scotland is common in the central region and eastern Highlands but absent from the rest of the country.

Its diet is extremely varied but for much of the year it depends primarily on soil invertebrates found in pasture and arable land. During spring it will prey on the eggs and young of other birds, turning later to fruit and cereals, and at all times it will take advantage of any carrion that becomes available or kill small mammals caught unawares.

The Magpie is resident and throughout the year reveals its presence by a sudden, loud, raucous chatter. In spring small numbers come together and as they take part in short, excited chases in flight and on the ground, they make a softer, more musical chatter. Both sexes build the large stick nest which is usually domed and typically placed in the top of a large thorn bush or high in an isolated tree although the marginal trees of conifer plantations may also be used. It is lined with mud and grass and the five or six eggs are laid in April and incubated by the female for seventeen or eighteen days. Both parents then feed the young in the nest for a further three or four weeks. They are single brooded but family parties will stay together for some time and small flocks may be formed in winter.

Rook

The **Rook** has a similar body length to the Magpie, but looks considerably larger and heavier because half the size of the Magpie comprises the tail. In the distance Rooks appear black, but on closer examination the body can be seen to be beautifully sheened with purple and dark green. The chief difference from the similar Carrion Crow lies in its bare, light grey face, and a baggy appearance produced by loose flank feathers will also help to distinguish it. Juveniles lack the bare face and are extremely difficult to tell from young Carrion Crows in the field. Rooks walk strongly and occasionally hop, searching, probing and digging for worms, other soil invertebrates, insects, cereals, potatoes and roots. Flight is heavy with regular wing beats and gliding and soaring is rare except when use is made of rising air currents. Widespread and common throughout the British Isles, numbers still remain sparse in the north-west Highlands and northern Isles. Recently there have been local changes in densities apparently related to changing agricultural practices, but generally numbers remain high and the total breeding population is about one and a half million pairs. British birds are resident but winter numbers are inflated by continental immigrants.

Rooks return to their traditional rookeries in spring, their noisy cawing continuing throughout much of of the day as both on the ground and in the trees, displaying males bow with drooped wings to crouching, trembling females. Tails are spread and raised over backs and males undertake ritualized feeding of their mates. Both birds co-operate to build a large stick nest, often on the base of an old one, in

179

the thinner branches near the top of the tree before the leaves appear and the male collects and brings sticks for the guarding female to work into the nest. A central cup is consolidated with earth and three to five eggs laid in late March or April. These are incubated for two and a half weeks by the female which is fed at the nest by the male. Initially after hatching the young are brooded by the female while the male brings food, but later the female will also help to provide food carried in a pouch in the floor of the mouth which can be clearly seen. They are single brooded and the young are fed for some time in the fields after leaving the nest, before adults and young join large winter flocks, often in association with Jackdaws.

Only one gamebird, the **Pheasant**, is linked with marginal woodland habitat where it spends much time in open fields, seeking cover if disturbed and for roosting and nesting. It is the most widely distributed gamebird in the world, originating in Eurasia, and has now been introduced into many countries and was probably brought to the British Isles by the Normans in the eleventh century. It is widespread, being sparse or absent only in the north-west Highlands, Orkney and Shetland, and the total breeding population is about half a million pairs. Large numbers are reared artificially every year and released, but even without management it can sustain itself in the wild.

Readily recognized and well known because of its large size (53 –56cm), upright carriage and long thin tail, the plumage varies because of interbreeding between several races. Most males have metallic green heads, red wattles, a white neck ring and bronze, speckled body plumage. Frequently they run head down for cover without attempting flight, but when flushed rocket out with rapid wing beats, uttering a 'kuttuc, kuttuc' alarm note. After gaining height they enter a long glide on downcurved wings. interspersed with short spells of rapid beats. The food is varied and includes the stems, leaves and fruits of a range of plants, cereals and seeds of farmland weeds, together with earthworms, slugs, other soil invertebrates and insects. In spring, males stand in an upright posture with their tails on the ground and start calling from field corners and other vantage points. The usual sequence is two or three slow wing flaps preceding a loud, harsh 'karrk, karrk' which is immediately followed by a rapid flutter of wings that produces a loud whirring. Displaying males parade with puffed feathers in front of females with drooped wings. The nest is a shallow scrape made by the female in the ground within a copse or under a hedge beneath a thick cover of brambles, leaves, grass or bracken. Eight to fifteen eggs are laid in April and incubated by the female for just under a month and the male takes no part in tending and feeding the free living young. They are single brooded.

Two pigeons, the Woodpigeon and Stock Dove, co-exist on lowland farms throughout the British Isles. In south and east England they are joined by a third, the Turtle Dove, for the summer. The first two are resident and similar in appearance and ecology and will be considered together. The Turtle Dove is distinct and is described with other summer migrants occupying marginal woodland habitat. Both Woodpigeon and Stock Dove evolved in woodland where they were dependent for food on the vegetation, fruits and seeds of wild flowers and trees. The limitations of this food source restricted their numbers and distribution and it was not until the great expansion in arable farming in the latter half of the nineteenth century when they were able to rely on crops for their food supply that numbers began to increase. The large acreage of crops such as turnips, kale, brassica and cereals now available throughout the year in most parts of the British Isles accounts for their present large numbers and wide distribution. The Woodpigeon is much the commoner of the two with a current breeding population in the British Isles of about five million pairs compared to about 100,000 pairs of Stock Doves. In winter, Stock Doves remain in pairs or small groups whereas Woodpigeons will gather in huge flocks and it is highly probable that this behaviour enables large numbers of individuals to exploit to the full the available food supply. The wide variety of nest sites used by the Woodpigeon – woodland, copses, hedges and, increasingly, commercial conifer plantations – provides abundant opportunity for breeding, in contrast to the more restricted requirements of the Stock Dove which occupies holes in old trees, old buildings, quarries and cliffs. It is not difficult to see why the Woodpigeon, in particular, is regarded by farmers as a serious pest and the future of both species will largely be determined by any further changes in agricultural practices.

The **Woodpigeon** is the largest (41cm) of our pigeons with a heavy body, short legs, small head and generally light grey coloration. Distinguishing characters are the white patches on the neck and white wing bars. Males and females are alike but juveniles are duller and lack the white on the neck. When disturbed, it will rise with a clatter of rapidly beating wings before settling into a fast, direct flight with steady beats. On the ground it walks with its body held horizontally and head high, bobbing back and forwards with each step. Its call is a simple 'coo, coo, coo, coo'. For its flying display it will rise steeply into the air and then glide slowly down with horizontally held wings. This performance may be repeated several times in succession and not infrequently the wings are clapped sharply together at the top of the climb. Courtship on the ground or in branches takes the form of bowing with spread tail raised.

The nest is a thin flat framework of fine twigs through which the eggs can be seen and while egg laying is at its height in July, the season extends from April to September. Incubation of the two white glossy eggs lasts for seventeen days and is shared, males sitting during the day and females taking over at night. Both parents feed the young on 'pigeons' milk', a secretion produced in the crop, by allowing the nestlings to thrust the bill into the adults' throat. Fledging takes three or four weeks and two or three broods are undertaken.

The **Stock Dove** is smaller (33cm) and has a shorter tail than the Woodpigeon and is darker grey in its general coloration. It lacks white patches, but has two short black wing bars and obvious black tips to the wings and can be separated from the Rock Dove by the absence of the white rump which is so characteristic of the latter. The sexes are alike though juveniles are duller and in flight it is more dashing and swerving than the Woodpigeon. When cooing, it puts the emphasis on the second syllable of a short 'coo, woo'. In an aerial display, two or more birds will fly and glide round in graceful sweeps, sometimes including faint wing claps, and pairs will bow to each other when perched. If old buildings are used for nest sites, several pairs may nest in close proximity and the two dull, creamy eggs will be laid on the floor of the nest hole and incubated by both parents for sixteen to eighteen days. Laying extends from March to July and both parents feed the young for about a month on 'pigeons' milk', rearing two and sometimes three broods.

Two birds of prey are found in this sub-division of the woodland habitat – the Kestrel and Little Owl. These have very different feeding and breeding requirements, the Kestrel hunting for small mammals in daylight by hovering over open ground and nesting in old nests high in trees or on elevated ledges and the Little Owl dropping onto large insects from low perches during dawn and dusk and nesting in holes low down in trees. There is thus little, if any, competition between the two.

The **Kestrel**, a medium sized (34cm) falcon, is the most common, widespread and best known of all our raptors, being seen not only over a wide variety of farmland, but also on motorway verges, on wasteland, in the uplands, along the coast and in the centre of towns and cities. It is found throughout the British Isles except Shetland and the total number of breeding pairs possibly exceeds 100,000 although locally populations may fluctuate in relation to the number of voles. Its method of hunting by habitually hovering with rapidly beating wings and dropped open tail provides easy confirmation of its identity. Normal flight is rapid with shallow beats and the long pointed wings and long tail can be clearly seen. The general coloration is rich chestnut boldly speckled with black and the underparts are paler and streaked dark brown. Adult males have a blue-grey head and tail and juveniles resemble adult females. The usual cry is a trilling 'kee, kee, kee'.

Small mammals, voles, mice, shrews, moles and young rabbits predominate in the diet, but lizards, large insects and worms are also taken, together with numerous species of small birds, the House Sparrow and Starling being particularly important for urban Kestrels. When hunting, a Kestrel will hover over one site for a short period and, if no prey is seen, move forward a short distance before hovering again.

When prey is spotted, it drops a short distance, hovers again and repeats this performance several times before making a final short, steep, headlong dive and grasping the prey with its talons. It will also dive directly onto prey from a vantage point on a tree, post, wire or telegraph pole and prey is usually plucked on the ground.

In spring, displaying males circle and pursue each other over the breeding territory and males will dive at perched females. They do not build a nest, but will use holes in trees, old nests of Carrion Crows and other birds or old squirrels' dreys, cliff ledges or ledges on or in old buildings and occasionally, on moorland, will even lay in a depression in the ground. They also take readily to nest boxes. The four to six dark brown, blotched eggs are laid in April and incubated for a month, mostly by the female. At intervals the male brings food to a perch in the vicinity of the nest and with a soft trill calls the female off and the food is transferred from one to the other. The young take just over a month to fledge and in the initial period are brooded and fed by the female with prey caught by the male but later the female will also hunt. Single brooded, the family remains together for a short period after the young are on the wing and before they disperse. Most Kestrels are resident and pass the winter singly or in pairs not far from the breeding areas, but some winter migrants arrive in autumn.

The **Little Owl** is easy to identify, its small size, compact, short-tailed appearance and unmistakable silhouette making recognition simple. Its plumage is a spotted grey-brown and it can be seen to best

RAH.

Little Owl

advantage perching on exposed boughs, fence posts, telegraph poles and walls. Flight is regular and undulating, close to the ground, and it makes a 'kiew, kiew' alarm note, bobbing and bowing when alarmed. Little Owls are not indigenous in Britain and our present population almost certainly originated from extensive introductions of birds from The Netherlands between 1888 and 1890 in Northamptonshire by Lord Lilford. Some earlier attempts appear to have failed, but later introductions may have supplemented Lord Lilford's successful venture. Favouring farmland with scrub and hedges, orchards and parklands, it has now spread to most lowland areas of England and many in Wales, but occurs only exceptionally in Scotland and is absent from Ireland. Locally its numbers have recently shown some decrease, and the total British breeding population is now thought to lie between 7,000 and 14,000 pairs. A resident, it passes the winter singly or in pairs.

As an alien with a hooked bill the Little Owl was immediately accused of preying heavily on young gamebirds but an extensive study showed this to be incorrect. Worms, slugs and large insects (particularly beetles) form its basic diet, supplemented with mice, voles, rats, shrews, lizards and small birds. When feeding young, it will hunt in full daylight. Three to five white eggs are laid in May in a scrape in holes in trees, in the crowns of pollarded willows, inside old buildings or down rabbit burrows. Incubation for a month is principally undertaken by the female which leaves the eggs for short spells to feed. Initially the male catches the food for the young but later is assisted by the female. Fledging takes just under a month and second broods are only occasionally attempted.

SUMMER VISITORS

These include two warblers – the Whitethroat and Lesser Whitethroat. Both are small (*c.* 14cm), slim, greyish-brown, insectivorous birds, which begin to arrive in the British Isles in late April and lay their eggs in May. They spend the winter in different regions and arrive by different migration routes, the Whitethroat coming primarily from West Africa and the Lesser Whitethroat from East Africa. Their breeding distribution also differs, the Whitethroat occurring throughout the British Isles with the exception of the central Highlands, Orkney and Shetland while most of the Lesser Whitethroat population is concentrated in the southern half of England.

The male **Whitethroat** has a grey head, a white throat, rufous wings and white outer tail feathers. The underparts are light buff with a pinkish tinge to the breast. Females and juveniles have a brown rather than grey head. Active feeders, they move rapidly through bushes, appearing from time to time on the outer twigs as they search for caterpillars, other larvae and adult insects and spiders. When alarmed, they have a habit of raising the crown feathers and make a 'tacc, tacc' alarm note and a scolding 'charr'. Until the late 1960s it was possibly the most numerous of our warblers, but in the 1969 breeding season something like three-quarters of the breeding population failed to arrive and the population has remained at this depressed level ever since. This decrease is attributed to mortality in the wintering areas following severe droughts in the Sahel zone of West Africa. While still widely distributed in the British Isles, densities are low and the total breeding population is now estimated to be between 500,000 and 700,000 pairs.

Thick scrub and low bushes with deep ground cover and isolated trees or tall bushes for song posts are favoured breeding sites. Males quickly take up territories and start singing. The song is a repeated short warble lasting two or three seconds and is made from a high exposed perch or during a song flight in which the bird will rise to a height of a few metres before erecting its head feathers, spreading its tail and descending in an erratic, tumbling flight to the perch. When perched, displaying males with raised crest feathers and shivering wings will make headlong dashes at females. The deeply cupped nest is built by the female in nettles and deep grass close to the ground, sometimes using one of the false nests started by the male. It consists of dead grass and roots, decorated on the outside with down and wool and lined with hair. Both birds incubate the five eggs for just under two weeks and then feed the young in the nest for ten or twelve days by bringing food in the bill. Two broods are usually reared and the adults will chatter boldly and noisily at intruders near the nest.

The plumage of the **Lesser Whitethroat** is less distinctive with greyer and more uniform upper parts and lacks the rufous colour of the wings, but it has a distinctive dark patch on the ear coverts. The underparts are whitish buff. It is more secretive and skulking than the Whitethroat but makes a similar 'tacc, tacc' warning note and a hoarse 'charr' alarm. The British Isles are at the western limit of its world breeding range and this is reflected in its absence from Ireland, exceptional occurrence in Scotland and scarceness in northern and south-west England and Wales. The population did not suffer a decline in the 1960s similar to that of the Whitethroat, so that in parts of its stronghold in south-east England the Lesser Whitethroat may now be the commoner of the two even though its total British breeding population is only about 25,000–50,000 pairs.

Male Lesser Whitethroats begin to arrive in the British Isles during the second half of April, about a week in advance of the females, and breeding activity starts almost immediately. In contrast to the Whitethroat, there is no song flight and the song, a rather repetitive, tuneless rattle 'chikka, chikka, chikka, chikk', is made from cover, often while the bird is moving about. Displaying males pursue females in and out of cover and confront them with erect crown feathers, fluffed breasts, spread tails and fluttering wings. The nest, started by the male

Lesser Whitethroat

and finished by the female, will usually be in a Hawthorn or Blackthorn or similar thick shrub at a height of between one and three metres above the ground. Dry stems and roots, lined with hair and fine grass, are used and the five eggs laid in May. Both birds share incubation for ten or eleven days and together feed the young for a similar period on insects and their larvae. Second broods are occasionally undertaken and pairs may be bold in defence of the nest, either feigning injury or making noisy demonstrations to distract intruders.

The **Tree Pipit** is another African migrant and arrives in Britain in mid-April. It requires trees or tall bushes from which to make its distinctive song flight and open grassy areas for feeding, so prefers parkland and pastures with scattered trees, open broadleaf woodland or scattered pines. Favouring remote, relatively undisturbed areas, it is often numerous along the fringes of upland valley woods and amongst scattered hillside trees. During the last hundred years or so it has extended its breeding range and is now to be found in most parts of Britain except the northern Isles although it is still absent from Ireland. The total breeding population is between 50,000 and 100,000 pairs.

A small (15cm), slim pipit, it has a slender bill and long tail which is spasmodically flicked as it walks or makes quick dashes amongst short vegetation to catch spiders and insects. In appearance it is difficult to distinguish from the Meadow Pipit, as both have the same brown back with dark markings, streaked pale underparts and white outer tail feathers. The Tree Pipit tends to be yellower underneath and its legs are a pinker, flesh colour, but the best means of identification is its territorial behaviour. In marked contrast to the Meadow Pipit, it perches on prominent twigs and the obtrusive song flight, begun soon after their arrival and continued until July, starts from a high perch, the male flying steeply upwards to a height of about thirty metres before gliding back down to the same or another perch with wings inclined upwards and tail spread. The far carrying song, a single repeated note terminating with a loud 'see-er, see-er, see-er' starts at the top of the ascent. A shortened, quieter version of the song is sometimes made from a perch. A simple depression in the ground in rough grass or bank sides forms the basis of the nest, built with moss and dry grass and lined with fine grass and hair. Four to six eggs are laid in May and incubated for a fortnight by the female. Both birds then feed the young in the nest for a fortnight by bringing food in the bill. Second broods are frequently completed before the return migration starts in July.

With its distinctive call and wide distribution, the **Cuckoo** must be the best known of our summer migrants and although it has been included with birds of marginal woodland it occupies a wide range of countryside including open woodland, scrub, fields, downs, reedbeds, sand dunes and open moorland. It is found throughout the British Isles and has a total breeding population numbering about 10,000 pairs. Males make the familiar, far carrying 'cuckoo' song and females have a bubbling trill. When singing, the head is raised and lowered with each note, the throat distended and wings drooped. A medium-sized (33cm) bird with grey back, long, graduated, white-spotted and white-tipped tail and boldy barred breast, in flight it can look hawk-like because of the pointed wings and long tail. The flight is distinctive, however, as the quick beats of the wings barely rise above the horizontal but are depressed far down. It keeps low and makes a long glide before landing and will perch in the open on trees, bushes, walls and posts.

It passes the winter in Africa and returns to breed in April in the British Isles. Females often return to the same area and parasitize the same hosts, which frequently turn out to be the species which was their own foster parent. On the ground it waddles and hops looking for insects, specializing somewhat unusually in hairy caterpillars which are easily picked up in the fine, slightly curved bill. Before mating, males confront females, bobbing their bodies up and down and fanning their tails to display the white markings. From vantage points a female Cuckoo will watch potential hosts building their nests and then, usually before the host has completed its clutch, glide onto the nest, remove one of the eggs and, holding it in the bill, lay one of its own in its place. The stolen egg is then swallowed or destroyed.

Most Cuckoos lay in the afternoon and twelve or more eggs are laid at forty-eight hour intervals during a season. Small insectivorous birds are selected as foster parents and each female specializes on one species and can produce an egg bearing a striking resemblance to that of its host. Common species such as Dunnocks in woodland, Pied Wagtails and Robins on farmland, Reed Warblers in wet areas and Meadow Pipits in the hills are most usually chosen, but a wide variety of species, ranging from the Blackbird to the Wren in size, has been used. Egg laying continues through May and June and then early in July the adults begin to leave.

Incubation takes about twelve days and, shortly after hatching, the young Cuckoo ejects the eggs or other young in the nest by rolling them into a hollow on its back and tipping them over the side. Juvenile Cuckoos are a deep rust-brown, barred black above and have white barred underparts and they make the return migration during August and the first half of September.

The **Turtle Dove**, another African migrant, arrives in the British Isles in late April or early May. A vegetarian, specializing on the seeds of Fumitory, it takes a wide variety of leaves and seeds of common wild flowers. It enjoys warm, dry conditions and most live in open lowland woods, along woodland borders and in orchards. It increased in the nineteenth century with the development of arable farming, but the majority are still concentrated throughout the eastern half of England with much smaller numbers in the West Country and eastern parts of Wales. It only breeds very occasionally in north-west England, Scotland and Ireland. The total breeding population is about 120,000 pairs.

It is a medium-sized (27cm) dove, distinguished by bright chestnut blotched black upperparts and a long dark, graduated tail with broad white tips to all but the central feathers. The breast is tinged pink and it

Turtle Dove

has a black and white patch on the side of the neck but juveniles are browner and lack the neck patches. Flight is fast and twisting with quick flicking beats and while occasionally they will form small flocks, they are most usually to be found singly or in pairs. Small trees, wires and telegraph poles are used as perches and the call is a soothing faint purr 'turr, turr, turr'.

Several pairs may nest in the same vicinity, the location of breeding pairs being indicated by calling and displaying birds. After calling from a high tree perch in the presence of its mate, a bird will rise steeply with rapid beats and spread tail and then glide round in a circle back to the perch. Nests, frail platforms of thin twigs, are built low down, usually under three metres, in hedgerows and scrub, preferably hawthorn, blackthorn, whitethorn and elder. First clutches are laid in May and the two eggs are incubated in turn by the male and female for a fortnight. During the three weeks' fledging period, the parents feed the young regurgitated 'pigeons' milk'. Two and occasionally three broods are fledged before the return migration starts in August.

OPEN COUNTRY

FARMLAND

A small number of birds living naturally on flat, open, featureless plains have adapted to living off farmland. The constant change and diversity of crops ensures an adequate food supply through the year and the strips of rough, uncultivated ground bordering fields provide cover for nesting. For some, for example the Swallow, the farm buildings are a necessary component, providing the only available nest sites in the absence of natural features. As we have seen, farmland retains remnants of woodland or substitutes such as hedges, and is thus also able to support certain woodland species also. The present trend in some parts of the country towards greater uniformity and continuity of crops grown on larger, better drained fields without hedges, has already had a detrimental effect on woodland species. The impact has been less on birds of open fields but if these trends continue they, combined with the continuing reduction in the numbers of wild plants and insects in crops brought about by the use of pesticides, will eventually also have a deleterious effect on the birds of open ground, as already appears to be the case with the Partridge.

The **Skylark**, which has been shown to be the most universally present of all the birds of the British Isles, must also be the best known of the birds of open country because of its attractive and conspicuous song flight. Almost any open ground, whether it be farmland (arable or grass), waste ground, downland, moorland, coastal dunes or salt-marshes, is found suitable. It requires no song posts or woody cover for nesting and its diet of vegetation, seeds, soil invertebrates and insects is

Skylark

readily available on farmland. The total breeding population of the British Isles is between two and four million pairs. Many of our birds remain throughout the winter, often forming into flocks, but there is a southerly movement in autumn and some emigration accompanied by an influx of continental birds.

The Skylark (18cm) is a little larger than most of the finches and buntings occurring on farmland in winter. Nondescript and streaky brown, its only distinctive plumage features are a longish tail with white outer feathers and a small crest. Juveniles have shorter tails and no crest. It crouches when disturbed and then makes a short, low, wavering flight with a fluttering wing action. When flying at height the flight is swifter and more direct, but the wing action still appears slow and fluttering and pauses follow a series of beats. Most of the time is spent on the ground and it walks while feeding, but will perch on fence posts and walls and enjoy a dust bath. It has a rippling 'chirrup' flight call.

Its presence in an area is quickly indicated by singing. Even on gusty days the song, a shrill, continuous warbling and bubbling which lasts for several minutes, is audible over a wide area. Singing starts immediately the male leaves the ground and continues throughout the flight. Initially he rises almost vertically and then hovers and drifts on open wings before finally sinking slowly back to the ground with wings inclined upwards, ending with an abrupt drop with closed wings. On the ground a displaying male will run round a female with raised crest

190

and drooped tail. The nest, built of grass, is placed in a shallow depression in the ground and the three or four speckled eggs laid in April. They are incubated for eleven days by the female and then both birds feed the young for about ten days in the nest, bringing insects in the bill, and for a further ten days after that while the nestlings remain hidden on the ground outside the nest. Two or three broods are raised.

The **Pied Wagtail**, like the Skylark, is common throughout most of the British Isles and occurs in a wide range of habitats extending from the coast to uplands as well as on farms. It favours damp ground, in particular marshy areas adjoining ponds, lakes, rivers and streams, as well as farms and farmyards where cattle or pigs are kept. It will, however, breed away from water in dry, stony conditions. The total breeding population is estimated to number about half a million pairs. Most are resident throughout the year, but there is a general movement onto farmland in winter and outside the breeding season local populations will often gather in the evenings at large communal roosts in reedbeds and other aquatic vegetation which will sometimes contain hundreds of individuals. Primarily insectivorous, it feeds by walking quickly, with sudden dashes in short vegetation or by wading in shallow water to take insects from the surface and by short aerial forays to catch flying insects.

A slim (18cm), black, white and grey bird with strongly undulating flight, it quickly draws attention to itself by its constant activity, continuously bobbing tail and high pitched 'chisick' note. Females are

Pied Wagtail

191

greyer with less black on the crown and breast and juveniles are generally paler. Northern and continental birds migrating through Britain in the autumn belong to a distinct geographical race – the White Wagtail. The birds breeding on Shetland and very occasionally elsewhere in the British Isles are of this race. In spring the lovely warbling song is made while perched on a wall or building or sometimes in flight, but is usually overshadowed by elaborate flight and ground displays. Two or more males will pursue a female in a fast, noisy, aerial chase or approach in a zig-zag run, with spread, depressed tail, fluttering wings and head bobbing and flicking. They will also crouch in front of the females with head raised to display the black breast. Females build a nest, using twigs and dead leaves, and line it with hair, feathers and wool, in holes in walls, banks and buildings. Thatch, pollard willows or even overhanging lumps of earth are sometimes used. Five or six eggs are laid at the end of April and incubated, mainly by the female, for a fortnight and then both birds feed the young in the nest for a further two weeks by bringing food in the bill. Two and occasionally three broods are reared.

A third species present on most farms, but also found throughout the British Isles, is the **Swallow**. It is the commonest species of the Swallow family in the British Isles with a total breeding population of between a half and one million pairs. Exclusively feeding on insects taken in flight, it is found in all open areas where these are plentiful. To obtain sufficient food, in particular when feeding young and preparing for migration, it will spend a great deal of time on the wing and concentrate on areas with high insect populations – over ponds, near farm animals or under large, widely spaced, broadleaf trees. Twisting, turning and diving in its pursuit of insects, it will fly low or skim the gound and frequently takes insects from the surface of water. Buildings, telegraph poles and exposed bare twigs are used as perches and because of its short legs it waddles on the infrequent occasions it lands on the ground, usually to gather nest material.

Evolved primarily for aerial feeding, it has a slender build (length 19cm), long, curved wings and large, forked tail with the outer feathers extended into streamers. Uniform blue above, the forehead and throat are chestnut and the underneath white, tinged with pink. Juveniles are paler and have shorter tail streamers. The flight call is a sharp 'tswit, tswit'.

Winter is spent in southern Africa and most birds arrive in the British Isles during April. Many pairs return year after year to the same breeding site, sometimes using the same nest, and the twittering song used to proclaim their territory is mainly made while on the wing. Both birds co-operate in building or repairing the nest, using grey pellets of mud mixed with saliva and fibrous material. The nests are usually open and cup-shaped with a lining of hair and feathers and placed on ledges or rafters inside barns, outhouses, porches or under bridges. Cliff ledges, which presumably represent the natural site, are only exceptionally used. Four or five eggs are laid and incubated, mainly by the female, for a fortnight after which both birds feed the young in the nest for about three weeks on food carried in the throat. Two broods are often successfully reared and a third is sometimes attempted. Before the autumn migration, they will gather in flocks on telegraph wires and roost gregariously, some roosts holding thousands of individuals, in reedbeds and osier beds. In mid-July a southerly movement begins and most finally leave the British Isles in August.

Gamebirds are represented by two common species, the Partridge and the Red-legged Partridge, and one rarer species, the Quail. The Corncrake, another bird of open country, can be conveniently considered with the gamebirds. The Red-legged Partridge is an introduced species and both the Corncrake and Quail are migratory. All have benefited greatly from the extensive clearing of woodlands in historical times, without which their numbers would be extremely low and confined to large forest clearings and river flood plains.

The **Partridge** is a medium-sized (30cm), short-tailed, rotund bird with brown plumage. Venturing well out onto open ground, its first reaction to danger is to crouch and then run rapidly for cover with back rounded and head withdrawn. When forced to fly it rises with a whirr of wings and flies quickly and directly with a series of quick beats interspersed by glides on downcurved wings. It keeps low above the ground, skimming hedges and walls, and soon lands again. Confusion

Partridge

193

of identification is only likely with the Red-legged Partridge. The Partridge has a yellow bill, orange face and throat, grey neck, chestnut barred flanks and a prominent, dark chestnut, horseshoe-shaped patch on the lower breast (this patch is less developed and occasionally absent in the female.) Its legs are dark. The Red-legged Partridge, by contrast, has a bright red bill and legs, white cheeks and throat bordered with a black band and the flanks are boldly and most beautifully barred with black, white and chestnut. Both species enjoy dust bathing.

The total breeding population of the Partridge in the British Isles is thought to be about half a million pairs and it is still widely distributed, except for the north-west Highlands, northern Isles and Welsh uplands from which it is largely absent. However, a long term decline began in the 1950s with the result that in most regions numbers are much reduced and in Ireland it is now scarce. The causes are complex and have been the subject of extensive study. Included are artificial factors such as the increased use of pesticides which reduces the supply of insects for the young, autumn ploughing, stubble burning and hedge removal combined with natural factors such as cold, wet springs. The highest densities and breeding success are usually associated with a varied mosaic of small fields. Partridge feed mainly in the early morning and at dusk and the leaves, fruits and seeds of a large variety of wild plants and crops are taken, chickweed being particularly important in late spring and early summer.

A resident, they are gregarious from August to January and remain together in flocks (coveys), usually comprising five to fifteen birds which represent one or several families and some non-breeders. Sexual maturity is attained in the first year and territories are established in February following the break-up of the flocks. Occasionally this involves fighting between rival males which strike at each other with bill, feet and wings and the same pairs often re-unite in subsequent years. Females select the nest site in a hedge bottom, amongst rank vegetation on rough land, under a bush or in a young plantation and scrape a shallow depression which is lined with grass. Nine to twenty olive brown eggs are laid in April and incubated on completion of the clutch by the female for twenty-three to twenty-five days. The young hatch within a few hours of each other and soon leave the nest. Initially they are completely dependent on a diet of insects and are able to flutter short distances when only ten days old and fly quite strongly at sixteen days. They are single brooded and the juveniles are duller and spotted and streaked with yellow and lack the orange face and flank markings.

The first successful introduction of the **Red-legged Partridge** was made by bringing eggs from France in 1790 and further introductions continue to the present day. The total breeding population has now reached between 100,000 and 200,000 pairs, with the majority confined to Lincolnshire and East Anglia. They prefer a drier, warmer climate and densities are much lower in the Midlands and southern Yorkshire where they are now also established and over much of their range they overlap with the Partridge. Their diet, nest and nest sites are similar but they differ in breeding behaviour in that not infrequently they lay two clutches of between ten and sixteen eggs, one of which is incubated by the male and one by the female which each raise a brood.

The **Corncrake** is slightly smaller (27cm) than a partridge and because of its secretive nature and nocturnal habits is rarely seen. Its presence is usually indicated by the male's loud, rasping 'crex, crex' call which is delivered from deep cover and can be heard at any time of the day or night. A slim, brown bird, it is best seen in flight if disturbed from the thick cover in which it passes the day, when its dangling legs and chestnut wings attract attention. Although now usually found in sedge meadows and marshy fields, at one time it was common and widespread in hayfields on farmland. A long term decline, attributed primarily to the mechanization of haymaking which started at the end of the 1800s in south-east England, has since affected the whole of the British Isles. The British population is now reduced to less than 650 pairs mainly restricted to western Scotland and, in its remaining stronghold in Ireland where about 4,000 pairs may still remain, it is probably decreasing. It feeds on soil invertebrates, including worms, slugs and snails and, to a lesser extent, foliage and seeds. The nest is a pad of dry grass in deep vegetation and the six to fourteen eggs are laid in May and incubated by the female for a fortnight. They are single brooded and the young fly after a month.

The **Quail** is the smallest European gamebird. It is thought to have been common in Britain until the end of the eighteenth century, but since then has been rare and although numbers fluctuate from year to year, they rarely exceed a few hundred individuals. It is only exceptionally recorded in Ireland. A typical gamebird in appearance, but difficult to see, its diminutive size (18cm), buff-streaked head and black throat markings in the male help with its identification.

The only owl associated with open farmland is the **Barn Owl**. A large (34cm), typical owl with a round, flat, white face and black eyes, its identity is readily confirmed by its generally white appearance produced by a combination of golden-buff upper parts and white underparts (the continental variety has a darker, buff breast). Males, females and juveniles are similar in appearance. It appears to be suffering a long term decline, but is still widely, albeit thinly, distributed in the British Isles, apart from being absent over most of northern Scotland and in the northern Isles. Local decreases have been attributed to pesticides, reduction of permanent, rough grassland, loss of old barns and other breeding sites, road deaths and the deprivations of severe winters. The breeding population in the British Isles now probably lies between 4,500 and 9,000 pairs.

Barn Owl

The Barn Owl normally hunts singly at night, although in severe weather or when feeding young will venture forth in daylight. An active hunter, it quarters backwards and forward over the ground, twisting and turning, briefly hovering and at intervals watching from a post or wall. The buoyant flight, typically a series of slow flaps with alternating glides, is completely silent, enabling it to hear its prey without itself being heard. It concentrates on the thicker vegetation of ditch sides, banks and hedges. A quick drop with outstretched claws secures the prey which is killed by a bite from its bill. Small nocturnal animals, voles, shrews, mice and rats, form the bulk of the prey and small roosting birds may less commonly be taken.

Breeding starts early in the year but is at its height in April and may continue into summer and autumn. The only display noted is wing clapping, presumably by the male. No nest is built, although the owls' pellets often surround the eggs which are laid on the floor in a hollow tree, derelict building, haystack or crevice in a cliff or quarry. They will use nest boxes. Three to seven dull white eggs are incubated for just under five weeks by the female which is fed during this time by the male and these often hatch at intervals so that the young in a nest may differ considerably in size. Both birds feed the young for nine to twelve weeks, bringing food in their claws. If cornered at the nest the female will crouch low, hissing and snapping its bill, with wings held horizontally. When hunting it makes a shrill scream.

HEATHLAND, DOWNLAND AND COMMONS

There are six species now largely restricted to remnants of semi-natural areas created by older, largely discontinued, forms of management. These areas are principally southern heaths, chalk downs and heather and pine commons surviving amongst the wide expanse of lowland farmland. At one time most of the birds associated with these areas were more numerous and more widely distributed and loss of habitat has been a major, although not the only, cause of their decline. With the exception of the Nightjar, of which several thousand pairs remain, their populations are down to hundreds of pairs.

The decrease of the **Nightjar**, the cause of which has not been established, appears to have begun in the early twentieth century and continues to the present day. Although still thinly scattered throughout much of the British Isles, with the exception of northern Scotland where it is largely absent, its numbers in most areas are now small and the total breeding population has been reduced to under 6,000 pairs. Favouring open heather with scattered clumps of birch and pine and also nesting in mature open woodland and young plantations, it does not appear to have benefited greatly from the planting of commercial conifer blocks, although recently it has been shown to go into second generation conifer plantations which might help to halt the decline.

Because of its crepuscular and nocturnal habits, it is hard to find during daytime when it rests on the ground, with half-closed eyes, in deep cover. A medium-sized bird (27cm), its beautifully mottled and streaked grey-brown coloration provides excellent camouflage and adds to the difficulty of locating it. The head is broad and flat, the eyes large and the bill short but extremely wide. When perched, it usually lies horizontally along the branch, the short legs hidden from view. In flight it is rather hawk-like with long, pointed wings and a long tail and males can be distinguished by white tips to the outer tail feathers and three white spots on the wing.

Winters are spent in Africa and most return to the British Isles in mid-May. The diet consists of moths and other large night flying insects which are caught in the Nightjar's mouth as it twists and turns at low level in silent pursuit flight. Breeding territories are proclaimed by calling from high tree perches. The call is a rapid, low pitched 'churr' which may be sustained for several minutes without a break but now and again varies in pitch, probably due to the bird turning its head. Two camouflaged eggs are laid on bare ground in late May or early June and incubated during the day by the female and at night by the male. Incubation lasts eighteen days and then both parents feed the young in the nest for a further eighteen days by bringing insects in the bill. The young are able to fly at this stage, but are not fully independent until a month or five weeks after hatching. Two broods are commonly attempted and they will readily adopt injury feigning to distract attention from the nest and make a 'coo-ic' alarm note. Return migration takes place in August and they remain in pairs or as single birds throughout the summer.

The next species, the **Stone Curlew**, is also a summer visitor to Britain and mainly active in the evening and through the night. In contrast to the previous species it is sociable, being found in flocks at the beginning and end of the season and even gathering in groups when breeding activity is at its peak. During the day it lies concealed on the ground and at night walks in search of large terrestrial invertebrates such as snails, worms, grasshoppers and beetles which it finds on gravel and sand beds, turf, in open stony areas amongst heather and crops.

A big (41cm), long-legged, streaked, pale brown bird it is distinguished from the Curlew by its large round head, yellow eyes and legs and short straight bill – yellow at the base with a black tip. Flight is usually low with slow regular beats of the large rounded wings, displaying a black and double white bar. It trails its legs. The British Isles are at the northern tip of its world breeding range and it prefers open, dry, stony heaths or chalk turf, so it has always been restricted in numbers and distribution. Until the mid-nineteenth century the population contained 1,000–2,000 pairs and its range extended across south-eastern England and up the eastern half of the country to north Yorkshire. Increased cultivation and afforestation has destroyed much of its habitat, although encouragingly in some areas it has survived in forest rides and on cultivated fields. However, it is now restricted to a few inland and coastal sites in East Anglia and some of the central southern counties and the population is probably less than 500 pairs.

Arriving in later March and April, two camouflaged eggs are laid in a scrape on open ground at the end of April or early in May and incubated for just under a month by both parents. The young leave the nest after hatching and are tended by both parents until they fly at six weeks. Local populations gather into large flocks towards the end of August and depart in September or early October.

The third species, the **Red-backed Shrike**, another summer migrant, has shown an even more dramatic decrease than either of the two previous species. Until just over 150 years ago it bred throughout England up to the southern edge of the Yorkshire and Cumbrian borders and throughout Wales. Now there are under fifty pairs restricted to the south of England, almost three-quarters of which are in East Anglia. The principal cause or causes of its decline are unknown, but are thought to be connected with long term climatic changes. The male has a blue-grey head and rump, a prominent black stripe through the eye, a chestnut back and pale underparts. Females are russet brown above and lack the grey head and black eye stripe. Juveniles resemble females but are speckled. The body length is 17cm and, when perched, the long black tail with white at the sides and hooked tip to the bill are distinctive characters.

They arrive early in May, and when feeding perch prominently on posts, wires and bush tops, watching for large insects such as beetles, bees, grasshoppers and dragonflies which are taken by a dive to the ground and in flight. Small and nestling birds and small mammals are sometimes taken and prey may be temporarily stored by being impaled on the spikes of thorn bushes. Nests are built by males within one or two metres of the ground in gorse or other bushes on open heath or breckland. Five to six eggs are laid in late May or early June and the female which is fed on the nest by the male carries out the two weeks' incubation. The young are fed in the nest and second broods rarely attempted before departure in August. They have a sharp 'chack chack' alarm note.

The **Dartford Warbler** is resident and now almost completely confined to living amongst gorse and heather on the Hampshire and Dorset heathlands. The total breeding population is under 500 pairs and is greatly reduced by hard winters, possibly to as few as twelve pairs after the 1962-63 winter. A small (12.5cm), insectivorous bird, characterized by a long tail with white borders which it habitually flicks upwards, it has dark grey-brown upperparts, a red eye and eye ring and dark pinkish underparts. In spring males display with flapping wings and fanned tail and sing from the top of gorse bushes. Nests are built by the female in long heather within a metre of the ground and the three to four eggs laid in April. Incubation is by the female and then both birds feed the young in the nest by bringing insects in the bill.

The **Woodlark** bears a general resemblance to the Skylark, but is smaller (15cm compared to 18cm), has a noticeably shorter tail and buff eye stripe. It remains throughout the year in Britain, favouring

Woodlark

199

dry, chalky, sandy or gravel soils, with open areas of short turf and scattered bushes and trees. At one time it was more widespread, occurring in most parts of England and Wales and even in a few localities in Ireland. Numbers have shown considerable fluctuations, with recent high peaks in the early 1950s and 1960s, so it is difficult to assess the significance of the changes that have occurred. Habitat loss, cold weather and climatic change have all been advanced as possible contributory factors.

The current total British breeding population is thought to lie between 200 and 400 pairs. They are thinly spread across southern England with scattered small populations in East Anglia and in a few localities in South Wales. High song posts are used for singing and both birds combine to build the grass and moss nest, close to or on the ground. Three to four eggs are laid in April and incubated for a fortnight by the female. Both parents feed the young, bringing insects in the bill, and two or three broods are raised.

The last of the six is a falcon, the **Hobby**, which in contrast to all the others has not suffered any significant population changes. The total British breeding population is about a hundred pairs, mostly confined to central southern England with smaller numbers, apparently increasing, in south-west England. Of similar size (30–36cm) to the Kestrel, the female being larger than the male, it has long, thin, curved wings and a short tail. Above it is dark grey, with broad, black moustachial stripes and the underparts are white, streaked black and the thighs and undertail coverts bright red. Females and juveniles are browner and the juveniles lack the red on the thighs. Its call is a sharp 'kew kew kew'.

On their return from Africa in May, pairs occupy breeding territories in open country and prefer scattered trees or heaths with birch and pine. Prey is taken in the air by direct pursuit or stoop, and includes small birds, in particular Swifts, Swallows and Martins, large dragonflies and large moths. Display flights can be most dramatic with both birds rising, circling and diving at incredible speed. Old nests of Carrion Crows and other large birds are used, the three spotted, red-brown eggs being laid in June. Incubation, which is mainly by the female, lasts for twenty-eight days during which time the male brings food to the nest. The male continues to bring food while the young are small and brooded by the female, but later the female helps with the hunting. They are single brooded.

VILLAGE AND TOWN

There are five species so closely associated with villages and towns that they warrant separate consideration. Three of them, the House Sparrow, House Martin and Swift, have largely deserted their natural breeding sites and now nest almost exclusively in or on buildings. The Collared Dove, a recent arrival to the British Isles, has found a niche for itself in gardens, farmyards and warehouses. The Starling population, on the other hand, is still divided between the woodland sites which are its natural environment and urban sites.

The familiar **House Sparrow** remains in the vicinity of buildings throughout the year, feeding in streets, yards, gardens, parks and nearby farmland. It is a ground feeder and with its short, stout bill is able to exploit a varied assortment of wild seeds, cereals, insects, waste food, rubbish and food put out on bird tables. A small (14.5cm), dull brown bird, males have a grey crown, grey-white cheeks, black throat, grey rump and single white wing bar. Females and juveniles lack the grey colouring and the black throat. When on the ground it hops and perches readily on buildings, fences, bushes and trees. It is gregarious, feeding in flocks in winter, nesting in colonies and roosting in groups in trees and is frequently noisy, constantly repeating a sharp, double, monotonous 'chissip' call note. Occurring throughout the British Isles wherever there are buildings, the total breeding population is between three and a half and seven million pairs.

During the spring, squabbling and displaying males are a common sight. When displaying, several males with elevated tails and drooped wings hop round a female simultaneously, chirruping loudly. Both sexes co-operate to build a large, untidy, round nest from straw, scraps and grass. A round entrance hole is left in the side and it is generously lined with feathers. Nest sites can be under eaves, in cracks and crevices, inside buildings on ledges or in ivy on wall faces. Trees and bushes are less commonly used and they will displace Swallows and House Martins and take over their nests. The first clutch of three to five eggs is laid in May, but three or four broods are commonly raised so breeding extends well into August. Most of the incubation, which lasts a fortnight, is undertaken by the female and then both parents feed the young in the nest for a further fortnight, carrying food in the bill.

The **Starling** must be as well known as the House Sparrow, the two often squabbling noisily and greedily for food put out in gardens at the expense of the tits, finches and thrushes. A considerably bigger (21cm) bird than the sparrow, its uniformly black plumage is sheened with purple and green and in winter speckled with white. The bill is black in winter and yellow in summer and the sexes are alike, while juveniles are a uniform dull mouse-brown. Their bill is long and thin, the tail short and they have a jerky, upright walk. Flight is swift and direct with regular, rapid wing beats and they perch readily on buildings, fences, walls, wires, bushes and trees. The alarm note is a bubbling 'tcheess'.

It is of interest to find that this numerous and widespread bird suffered a major unexplained decline during the eighteenth century. About 150 years ago its recovery started and it is now amongst the most widespread of all our birds, found in all regions of the British Isles and

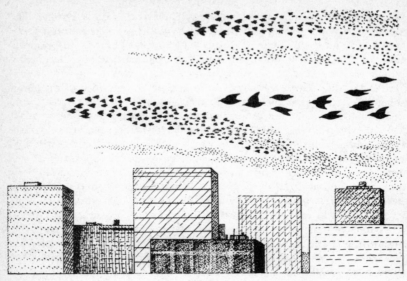

Starling

having a total breeding population of similar size to that of the House Sparrow. Most of our breeding birds are resident throughout the year, but numbers are supplemented by a large influx of continental immigrants. During the breeding season they are more closely associated with woods and buildings where breeding sites are to be found and in winter they form flocks and spend more time on open farmland. In the evening local flocks unite to form huge communal roosts in woods, thickets, reedbeds or on buildings in towns and cities. Prior to settling for the night, they perform mass aerial evolutions with huge numbers rising, falling, twisting and turning with a rush of wings like huge, super-charged plumes of smoke.

The song is an extraordinary cacophony of clucks, throaty chuckles and musical whistling, coupled with mimicry of snatches of the calls and songs of other species. In display aerial chases are common and are continued on the ground with drooped, fluttering wings. Nests in buildings are placed in holes and cracks in walls, under roofs and eaves and in outhouses while natural sites include holes in trees, old nests of woodpeckers, swallows and martins and cracks in cliff faces. They will also use nest boxes. Initially the task of nest building falls to the male which is later joined by the female. Grass, lined with feathers, is used and the five to seven pale blue eggs are laid in April. Both birds share incubation which lasts for just under a fortnight and then for three weeks they feed the young in the nest with food brought in the bill and second broods are not uncommon. The diet is equally divided between vegetable matter, including fruit, cereal, seeds and berries, and a variety of insects and small, ground dwelling invertebrates. In summer they will take advantage of caterpillar plagues in woods or insect swarms in the open where groups of Starlings, sometimes with Black-headed Gulls, can be seen wheeling, hovering and gliding back and forth through clouds of insects, snatching them in their bills.

In contrast with the two previous species, the House Martin and Swift are summer migrants to the British Isles. They feed exclusively on insects taken in full flight at speed and spend much of their time on the wing at high level. This is reflected in their appearance, both having long, thin wings, short tails and short, but very broad bills. Their legs are tiny and primarily adapted to perching or clinging to vertical faces and only exceptionally do they land on the ground. In the case of the Swift, the wings are so long that at times it can have difficulty in becoming airborne from the ground. Their association with buildings is related to their breeding activity and both now rely almost exclusively on artificial structures for nest sites.

The **House Martin** is most likely to be confused with the Swallow and Sand Martin as it is of similar shape and size and often feeds with them. It has blue-black upper parts, a prominent white rump and is white beneath. The blue back separates it immediately from the brown Sand Martin, while the white rump and much shallower fork in the tail and the absence of long streamers distinguishes it from the Swallow. Males and females are alike but juveniles are browner and confusion with the Sand Martin would be easy were it not for the white rump. Telegraph wires and buildings and, less commonly, exposed twigs are used as perches and it makes a hard 'chirrp' flight call. When feeding, it has a swifter, more direct flight than the Swallow and tends to remain at higher levels.

Most arrive between mid-April and mid-May and disperse to their breeding areas which occur throughout the British Isles, although the numbers breeding in north-west Scotland and the northern Isles are less than elsewhere. The total breeding population is between 300,000 and 600,000 pairs and appears to have remained constant at about this level since records were started. A bird will make its thin twittering song from a nearby perch to indicate that a site is occupied and most nests are built on the outside walls of houses under overhanging eaves but colonies also occur under bridges and at cliff sites. Single nests are less usual as most will breed in small colonies with several nests in close proximity, sometimes so close to one another as to be almost touching. Colonies in favourable, rural areas may include up to fifty or more nests but that is exceptional. Nests may face in all directions and it is not clear why a particular side of a house has been selected in the first place.

The nest, an inverted cup with a small entrance at the front where it joins the eaves, is an elaborate structure and its construction involves both birds in considerable time and effort at the start of a breeding season. Soft mud from the margins of puddles and ponds is collected in the bill, mixed with fragments of grass and taken up to the site where it is compacted onto the vertical face and gradually built up to form the outer shell of the nest. This is then generously lined with feathers. The outer coat dries a grey-white colour and forms a substantial structure which may be repaired and re-used for several seasons. The collecting of mud for nest building is almost the only occasion the birds land on the ground and it is then possible to get a good view of the small, white, feathered legs. Four to five eggs are laid in late May or early June and incubated for a fortnight by both birds and then both feed the young by bringing insects to the nest for thirty days. Throughout the season the whole family uses the nest for roosting. Most pairs attempt a second brood and many of these are only just on the wing in late September or early October in time for the return migration.

The **Swift** arrives later and departs earlier than the House Martin, being present in the British Isles for barely four months of the year. Less common than the House Martin, it has a total breeding population estimated at about 100,000 pairs which are widely distributed throughout the British Isles, but numbers over much of Scotland, particularly in the remoter areas, are generally smaller than elsewhere. Flight is fast, direct and vigorous, rapid, shallow beats alternating with glides as it twists and dives in pursuit of insects. Large numbers will gather where insects are abundant and, when feeding, they will range across uplands, along coasts and will hunt at heights of up to 1,000 metres.

Swift

204

It is the largest (16.5cm) of the swallow-like birds and its size, sooty-grey plumage (only relieved by a white throat), long, thin, scimitar-shaped wings and short, slightly forked tail single it out from the others. The sexes are alike, but juveniles have more white on the throat and white borders to the wings. Most of their life is spent on the wing and almost the only time they land is when nesting. During the hours of darkness they rest, drifting in circling flight, and in the first few years of life before they are sexually mature and begin breeding they may remain continuously airborne for three or possibly more years.

The first Swifts appear towards the end of April. Their arrival at breeding sites is soon indicated by the appearance of small groups engaging in noisy aerial chases when birds sweep low over the roof tops uttering long, drawn out, harsh screams. Nests are sited in crevices, in spaces under eaves, in holes in thatch and under roof tiles. Occasionally small colonies are established on cliffs and they will use specially designed nest boxes. The nest itself is slight, consisting of a shallow cup formed from bits of straw, grass and a few feathers held together with saliva. Three eggs are laid towards the end of May or early in June and incubated for eighteen or nineteen days and both birds then feed the young by bringing insects in the bill. The fledging period has been found to vary in relation to the weather and thus the supply of insects available. In poor conditions the young have to make do without food, apparently without harmful effects, for spells sometimes lasting a few days. They are single brooded and the return movement south begins in July with most finally departing in August.

The last of the urban birds, the **Collared Dove**, is a relative newcomer to the British Isles and was only recorded nesting for the first time in 1955. Its arrival in Britain came at the end of a dramatic and successful extension of its breeding range across Europe and it can now be found in all lowland areas of the British Isles from Shetland to the Isles of Scilly. The total breeding population is already about 50,000 pairs and may well continue to rise. Competition with other pigeons appears to have been avoided by its occupation of villages, large suburban gardens, parks and developed coastal areas. It also forms local concentrations around farms, maltings, mills and warehouses where grain is plentiful and only rarely settles on open country away from habitation. In addition to grain and seeds which form the bulk of its diet, it takes vegetation, fruits and berries.

In comparison with the Turtle Dove, the other speices it most closely resembles, it is slightly larger (32cm) and paler. Above it is a dull grey brown and the underparts are pale, tinged with pink. It has a black half-collar, from which its name derives, black wing tips and the bottom half of the underside of the tail is white and shows up clearly in flight which is steady and direct. It has a rather monotonous, constantly repeated, triple 'coo, cooo, cuh' with the emphasis on the middle syllable.

Like all the pigeons, its nest is thin and flimsy, being little more than a flat platform of crossed twigs through which the two eggs can be seen. Generally it will be positioned low in a coniferous tree or thick shrub, but ledges in outhouses may be used. Both birds incubate the eggs for a fortnight and two or more broods are undertaken in quick succession with the juveniles of an earlier brood still being attended after the incubation of the next clutch has started. They are resident, dispersing within the vicinity of the nest.

In a small, densely populated country like the British Isles the pressures on the land are tremendous and constantly changing. Towns expand, new motorways are constructed and farming and forestry techniques change. These changes all have an effect on wild birds, particularly those species discussed in this present chapter where, with the exception of mature woodland, change is a factor of everyday life. Most of these changes are unavoidable but can often be modified with knowledge and understanding so that detrimental effects can be lessened and new opportunities developed. After all, as we have seen, the birds now present on our farms and in our villages have adapted their way of life to artificial conditions created by our ancestors. Not all changes are necessarily bad. The Collared Dove has shown us that nature unaided can bring about unexpected and enriching changes, and simple actions such as putting up nest boxes when combined with larger changes such as the reduction of smoke pollution can benefit such specialized species as the Swift. The birds of this habitat are those with which most of us are in regular contact and as they will also be the ones most subject to future change, we shall watch their progress with interest.

·7·
Birdwatching

It is perfectly possible to get enjoyment from birds without any special preparation or equipment. If one is lucky enough to have even a small garden a surprising variety can be seen by simply keeping one's eyes open and disturbance down. The number and variety can be increased by planting shrubs and trees attractive to birds, by putting out food for them and by erecting nest boxes. By venturing further afield still more species can be found and, as we have seen, by varying the habitat explored very different groups of birds can be located. As the season advances the countryside changes, some species depart while others arrive and a bird missed on one visit may be seen on the next so that repeat visits are rewarding. Wild birds are naturally timid and fly or hide when disturbed. It is usually preferable to remain quietly in an area for a short while and allow the birds to return and resume their normal activity rather than to pursue them and make them even more alarmed and difficult to see.

Two purchases, neither of which need be grossly expensive, can add considerably to the pleasure of watching birds. The first is a good pocket field guide. There are many excellent, fully illustrated versions now readily available and the selection of one rather than another will probably lie with the appeal of the format. Three deserve special mention:

A Field Guide to Birds of Britain and Europe
by Roger Tory Peterson, Guy Mountfort and P.A.D. Hollom,
Collins, London (1974)

The Birds of Britain and Europe
by Hermann Heinzel, Richard Fitter and John Parslow,
Collins, London (1972)

The Hamlyn Guide to the Birds of Britain and Europe
by Bertel Brunn and Arthur Singer,
Hamlyn, London (1978)

All fit easily into the pocket, include a coloured illustration of every species with a brief supporting text and a distribution map. The first has particularly high quality paintings and more text, the other two cover a larger geographical area and have been arranged with the information about a species opposite its picture.

If one has a special interest in nests, eggs and young birds, two books specializing on these topics can be recommended:

A Field Guide to Birds' Nests
by Bruce Campbell and J Ferguson-Lees,
Constable (1972)

A Field Guide to the Nests, Eggs and Nestlings of British and European Birds
by Colin Harrison
Collins, London (1975)

The second worthwhile purchase is a pair of binoculars. Once again a wide variety is available and personal preference must dictate the final choice. There are certain considerations which should be taken into account and can help in selection. Foremost perhaps is the mistaken assumption that it is necessary to spend a large sum to get a good pair. This is not so. Obviously in most cases the more spent the better the quality, but recent advances in optics, design and manufacture mean that there are now many excellent binoculars on the market at prices within the reach of most pockets.

They will be used a great deal and you will want to take them with you on most outings so do not buy ones that are uncomfortably heavy, although if they are to have hard wear you must ensure they are solidly constructed. These days one should have a pair which are prismatic, have bloomed lenses and central focusing. This is now standard for most binoculars. Power is the most important consideration. Usually the greater the magnification the larger and heavier the instrument with correspondingly greater risk of hand-shake. Magnification of 6, 7 or 8 seems to suit most people and certainly provides a good, easily manageable general purpose instrument. Stronger individuals find they can readily manage 10 magnification, but anything above this usually requires the use of a stand. Coupled with magnification is light gathering. This can be calculated by dividing the magnification into the figure given after it. For example, a typical combination is 7 x 40. Seven goes into forty almost six times. Provided the answer comes between four and seven, this is satisfactory. Nowadays many of the keenest birdwatchers combine a small pair of light binoculars for quick spotting and close study with one of the new lightweight telescopes and stands for long distance identification. Most such telescopes provide variable magnification from 15 to 60 and have a simple focusing knob in contrast to the old pull out system. This seems to me to be an admirable solution and avoids the danger of falling between two stools that may arise if one attempts to cover both tasks with a pair of high powered binoculars.

A further modest purchase well worth considering is a simple notebook and pencil. It is surprising how quickly one forgets what has been seen unless it is noted down immediately. Written records allow subsequent checks on identification and observations, comparisons between visits to an area and can guide the planning of future excursions. Any pocket-sized pad will do, but a stiff waterproof cover is an advantage and it is possible to buy one incorporating bird lists to tick species seen. Also, noting where a bird was seen and what it was doing is a way of increasing one's enjoyment and adding to the interest.

As each habitat has been discussed it will have been seen that today most are limited in extent and their future safety is often in doubt. Most people who develop an interest in birds, however casual, soon find that they become concerned about their future wellbeing and the safety of their habitats. The best way to do something positive about this is to join The Royal Society for the Protection of Birds (The Lodge, Sandy Bedfordshire SG19 2DL). This is much the biggest voluntary society in Europe and one of the biggest in the world concerned with the welfare of wild birds. It operates throughout the United Kingdom and has offices in Scotland, Wales, Northern Ireland and in English regions. By January 1982 adult membership was 353,000 and there were over 100,000 members in the Young Ornithologists' Club.

Established in 1889, the RSPB is a registered charity, completely independent and raising its own funds. With a professional staff of over 300 the range of work it undertakes is impressive and includes the management of about 100 nature reserves of national importance, enforcement of the law, advice on legislation, support for international conservation bodies, educational work in schools and through the YOC, providing evidence for planning enquiries, campaigning against such things as avoidable pollution of the seas with oil, research and the production of films and publications. Membership of the Society confers advantages including receipt of *Birds*, the Society's quarterly magazine, free access to the reserves, enrolment in Local Members' Groups which organize filmshows, lectures and conducted outings. The Society's information service provides booklets and advice on such things as what plants will make your garden more attractive to birds, different types of nest boxes and bird tables how to build and where to site them and how to help birds in hard winters.

Should one's interest become more serious it is also well worthwhile becoming a member of the British Trust for Ornithology (Beech Grove, Tring, Hertfordshire HP23 5NR). This is another independent voluntary body concerned with birds. It has a professional staff of ornithologists who undertake a wide range of research and supervise national enquiries involving professionals and amateurs. Each county has a BTO representative providing a local contact. Amongst other things it has responsibility for the national bird ringing scheme, the nest record scheme, the common bird census, national mapping projects and individual species enquiries. Membership provides opportunities to attend conferences, receipt of the Trust's quarterly journal *Bird Study* and more frequently *Bird News* together with the opportunity to participate in national enquiries.

In the Irish Republic the role of the RSPB and BTO is undertaken by the Irish Wildbird Conservancy (Southview, Church Road, Greystones, Co. Wicklow). The Scottish Ornithologists' Club is based at 21 Regent Terrace, Edinburgh EH7 5BT and many counties have local ornithological societies which welcome support. There is an independent national monthly magazine *British Birds* (Fountains, Blunham, Bedford MK44 3NJ) which publishes current notes, reports and reviews and provides an outlet for amateurs to publish their own observations. The British Ornithologists' Union (c/o Zoological Gardens, Regents Park, London NW1) is a learned society which holds meetings and publishes a scientific journal *The Ibis* and international bird protection work is organized by the International Council for Bird Preservation which has its world headquarters at 219c Huntingdon Road, Cambridge CB3 ODL.

Although throughout the book it has been stressed that opportunities to enjoy birds occur widely, there are obviously certain places that are especially rich in birdlife and visits to these are particularly rewarding. Fortunately, many are nature reserves and visits to these can be planned and wasted journeys with access problems avoided. There are other reasons why visits to reserves are to be recommended. Most provide excellent observation hides and nature trails allowing surprisingly large numbers of people to see a wide range of birds, often including shy and rare species, without undue disturbance to the birds or damage to the habitats. Reserves generally incorporate more than one major habitat and are managed in such a way that the different sub-habitats and niches are developed to the full, so that during one visit many different groups of birds can be studied. Bigger reserves have wardening services and interpretative centres to provide information about the history of the reserve and up to the minute reports on the birds present.

Several organizations run nature reserves. The official wildlife agency, the Nature Conservancy Council, has responsibility for 166 National Nature Reserves and a few Local Authorities have declared Local Nature Reserves. Details of these are published in the annual reports of the NCC, published by Her Majesty's Stationery Office and available in local libraries. County Trusts for Nature Conservation, including the Scottish Wildlife Trust, have a total of over 1,000 reserves and information can be obtained from the local Trust's offices (the addresses of these are available from the parent body, The Royal Society for Nature Conservation, The Green, Nettleham, Lincolnshire LN2 2NR). The Wildfowl Trust, which specializes in waterfowl, has several major collections including species from all parts of the world housed in attractive, semi-natural conditions often associated with adjoining nature reserves. Details can be obtained from the Trust's headquarters at Slimbridge, Gloucestershire, GL2 7BT.

For those who want to get away from their fellow human beings and find and explore for themselves undisturbed countryside, the uplands and the coast provide the best opportunities for relatively unrestricted access to large areas, but it is essential to make preliminary enquiries about this before venturing onto any land in case it is private or entry is restricted for some reason, in which case prior permission must always be obtained. Membership of a Society or Trust does *not* confer an automatic right of entry to land and for good reasons permits may even be required to visit some reserves and access to others or parts of them may be forbidden altogether. A helpful guide to good bird areas and vantage points is the book *Where to Watch Birds* by John Gooders, published by Deutsch.

As a finale it is surely right to remind ourselves that birds, which provide so much enjoyment and enrich our lives, were not created by man but form part of his heritage. If a species becomes extinct it is lost forever. Their presence amongst us should be seen as a miraculous inheritance and a privilege to be treasured, never abused or taken for granted and above all preserved for future generations. Mammals, including Man, and birds all evolved from a common ancestor – the reptile. Because birds had to remain light and small to fly, they forfeited the development of the large brain which has enabled Man to dominate all other living things. This divergence of development and fortune surely does not give Man the right to treat birds as he pleases but should rather confer a responsibility to respect and protect his less dominant and more vulnerable fellow creatures.

List of Scientific Names

Family Gaviidae

Gavia arctica	Black-throated Diver
immer	Great Northern Diver
stellata	Red-throated Diver

Family Podicipitidae

Podiceps cristatus	Great Crested Grebe
grisegena	Red-necked Grebe
auritus	Slavonian Grebe
nigricollis	Black-necked Grebe
Tachybaptus ruficollis	Little Grebe

Family Procellariidae

Fulmarus glacialis	Fulmar
Puffinus puffinus	Manx Shearwater

Family Hydrobatidae

Hydrobates pelagicus	Storm Petrel

Family Sulidae

Sula bassana	Gannet

Family Phalacrocoracidae

Phalacrocorax carbo	Cormorant
aristotelis	Shag

Family Ardeidae

Ardea cinerea	Grey Heron
Botaurus stellaris	Bittern

Family Anatidae

Anas platyrhynchos	Mallard
crecca	Teal
querquedula	Garganey
strepera	Gadwall
penelope	Wigeon
acuta	Pintail
clypeata	Shoveller
Aix galericulata	Mandarin Duck
Aythya marila	Scaup
fuligula	Tufted Duck
ferina	Pochard
Bucephala clangula	Goldeneye
Clangula hyemalis	Long-tailed Duck
Melanitta fusca	Velvet Scoter
nigra	Common Scoter
Histrionicus histrionicus	Harlequin Duck
Somateria mollissima	Elder
Oxyura jamaicensis	Ruddy Duck
Mergus serrator	Red-breasted Merganser
merganser	Goosander
albellus	Smew
Tadorna tadorna	Shelduck
Anser anser	Greylag Goose
albifrons	White-fronted Goose
erythropus	Lesser White-fronted Goose
fabalis	Bean Goose
brachyrhynchus	Pink-footed Goose
Branta bernicla	Brent Goose
leucopsis	Barnacle Goose
canadensis	Canada Goose
Cygnus olor	Mute Swan
cygnus	Whooper Swan
bewickii	Bewick's Swan

Family Accipitridae

Aquila chrysaetos	Golden Eagle
Buteo buteo	Buzzard
Accipiter nisus	Sparrowhawk
gentilis	Goshawk
Milvus milvus	Red Kite
migrans	Black Kite
Haliaeetus albicilla	White-tailed Eagle
Circus aeruginosus	Marsh Harrier
cyaneus	Hen Harrier
Circus pygargus	Montagu's Harrier

Family Pandionidae

Pandion haliaetus	Osprey

Family Falconidae

Falco subbuteo	Hobby
peregrinus	Peregrine
rusticolus	Gyrfalcon
columbarius	Merlin
tinnunculus	Kestrel

Family Tetraonidae

Lagopus lagopus	Red Grouse
mutus	Ptarmigan
Lyrurus tetrix	Black Grouse
Tetrao urogallus	Capercaillie

Family Phasianidae

Alectoris rufa	Red-legged Partridge
Perdix perdix	Partridge
Coturnix coturnix	Quail
Phasianus colchicus	Pheasant

Family Rallidae

Rallus aquaticus	Water Rail
Crex crex	Corncrake
Gallinula chloropus	Moorhen
Fulica atra	Coot

Family Haematopodidae

Haematopus ostralegus	Oystercatcher

Family Charadriidae

Vanellus vanellus	Lapwing
Charadrius hiaticula	Ringed Plover
dubius	Little Ringed Plover
Piuvialis squatarola	Grey Plover
apricaria	Golden Plover
Eudromias morinellus	Dotterel
Arenaria interpres	Turnstone

Family Scolopacidae

Micropalama himantopus	Stilt Sandpiper
Gallinago gallinago	Snipe
Scolopax rusticola	Woodcock
Numenius arquata	Curlew
phaeopus	Whimbrel
Limosa limosa	Black-tailed Godwit
lapponica	Bar-tailed Godwit
Tringa hypoleucos	Common Sandpiper
totanus	Redshank
nebularia	Greenshank
Calidris canutus	Knot
maritima	Purple Sandpiper
minuta	Little Stint
Calidris alpina	Dunlin
ferruginea	Curlew Sandpiper
alba	Sanderling

Family Recurvirostridae

Recurvirostra avosetta	Avocet

Family Burhinidae

Burhinus oedicnemus	Stone Curlew

Family Stercorariidae

Stercorarius skua	Great Skua
parasiticus	Arctic Skua

Family Laridae

Larus marinus	Great Black-backed Gull
fuscus	Lesser Black-backed Gull
argentatus	Herring Gull
canus	Common Gull
minutus	Little Gull
ridibundus	Black-headed Gull
Rissa tridactyla	Kittiwake
Sterna hirundo	Common Tern
paradisaea	Arctic Tern
dougallii	Roseate Tern
albifrons	Little Tern
sandvicensis	Sandwich Tern

Family Alcidae

Alca torda	Razorbill
Pinguinus impennis	Great Auk
Plautus alle	Little Auk
Uria aalge	Guillemot
Cepphus grylle	Black Guillemot
Fratercula arctica	Puffin

Family Columbidae

Columba oenas	Stock Dove
livia	Rock Dove
palumbus	Woodpigeon
Streptopelia turtur	Turtle Dove
decaocto	Collared Dove

Family Cuculidae

Cuculus canorus	Cuckoo

Family Tytonidae

Tyto alba	Barn Owl

Family Strigidae

Nyctea scandiaca	Snowy Owl
Athene noctua	Little Owl

216

Strix aluco	Tawny Owl
Asio otus	Long-earned Owl
flammeus	Short-eared Owl

Family Caprimulgidae

Caprimulgus europaeus	Nightjar

Family Apodidae

Apus apus	Swift

Family Alcedinidae

Alcedo atthis	Kingfisher

Family Picidae

Picus viridis	Green Woodpecker
Dendrocopos major	Great Spotted Woodpecker
minor	Lesser Spotted Woodpecker

Family Alaudidae

Lullula arborea	Woodlark
Alauda arvensis	Skylark

Family Hirundinidae

Hirundo rustica	Swallow
Delichon urbica	House Martin
Riparia riparia	Sand Martin

Family Corvidae

Corvus corax	Raven
corone	Carrion/Hooded Crow
frugilegus	Rook
monedula	Jackdaw
Pica pica	Magpie
Garrulus glandarius	Jay
Pyrrhocorax pyrrhocorax	Chough

Family Paridae

Parus major	Great Tit
caeruleus	Blue Tit
ater	Coal Tit
cristatus	Crested Tit
palustris	Marsh Tit
montanus	Willow Tit

Family Aegithalidae

Aegithalos caudatus	Long-tailed Tit

Family Sittidae

Sitta europaea	Nuthatch

Family Certhiidae

Certhia familiaris	Treecreeper

Family Troglodytidae

Troglodytes troglodytes	Wren

Family Cinclidae

Cinclus cinclus	Dipper

Family Timaliidae

Panurus biarmicus	Bearded Tit or Bearded Reedling

Family Turdidae

Turdus viscivorus	Mistle Thrush
pilaris	Fieldfare
philomelos	Song Thrush
iliacus	Redwing
torquatus	Ring Ousel
merula	Blackbird
Oenanthe oenanthe	Wheatear
Saxicola torquata	Stonechat
rubetra	Whinchat

Phoenicurus phoenicurus	Redstart
ochruros	Black Redstart
Luscinia megarhynchos	Nightingale
Erithacus rubecula	Robin

Family Sylviidae

Cettia cetti	Cetti's Warbler
Locustella naevia	Grasshopper Warbler
fluviatilis	River Warbler
luscinioides	Savi's Warbler
Acrocephalus scirpaceus	Reed Warbler
palustris	Marsh Warbler
schoenobaenus	Sedge Warbler
Sylvia atricapilla	Blackcap
borin	Garden Warbler
communis	Whitethroat
curruca	Lesser Whitethroat
undata	Dartford Warbler
Phylloscopus trochilus	Willow Warbler
collybita	Chiffchaff
sibilatrix	Wood Warbler

Family Regulidae

Regulus regulus	Goldcrest

Family Muscicapidae

Muscicapa striata	Spotted Flycatcher
Ficedula hypoleuca	Pied Flycatcher

Family Prunellidae

Prunella modularis	Dunnock or Hedge Sparrow

Family Motacillidae

Anthus pratensis	Meadow Pipit
trivialis	Tree Pipit
spinoletta	Rock Pipit
Motacilla alba	Pied/White Wagtail
cinerea	Grey Wagtail
flava	Yellow/Wagtail

Family Laniidae

Lanius collurio   Red-backed Shrike

Family Sturnidae

Sturnus vulgaris   Starling

Family Fringillidae

Coccothraustes coccothraustes   Hawfinch
Carduelis chloris   Greenfinch
     carduelis   Goldfinch
     spinus   Siskin
Acanthis cannabina   Linnet
     flavirostris   Twite
     flammea   Redpoll
Pyrrhula pyrrhula   Bullfinch
Loxia curvirostra   Crossbill
Fringilla coelebs   Chaffinch
     montifringilla   Brambling

Family Emberizidae

Emberiza calandra   Corn Bunting
     citrinella   Yellowhammer
     schoeniclus   Reed Bunting
Plectrophenax nivalis   Snow Bunting

Family Ploceidae

Passer domesticus   House Sparrow
     montanus   Tree Sparrow

Index

Principal references are indicated by **bold** type